GOBI

2/18

24 ¹²

D1481697

FRAGMENTARY
REPUBLICAN LATIN
II

LCL 537

FRAGMENTARY REPUBLICAN LATIN

ENNIUS

DRAMATIC FRAGMENTS
MINOR WORKS

EDITED AND TRANSLATED BY

SANDER M. GOLDBERG
GESINE MANUWALD

HARVARD UNIVERSITY PRESS
CAMBRIDGE, MASSACHUSETTS
LONDON, ENGLAND
2018

Library of Congress Control Number 2017940159
CIP data available from the Library of Congress

ISBN 978-0-674-99714-1

*Composed in ZephGreek and ZephText by
Technologies 'N Typography, Merrimac, Massachusetts.
Printed on acid-free paper and bound by
Maple Press*

CONTENTS

CONTENTS

DRAMATIC FRAGMENTS

TRAGOEDIAE (F 1–201)

Only fragments explicitly assigned to Ennius by an ancient source or for which Ennian authorship can be securely inferred are included here. These fragments are numbered as in TrRF.

A number of additional fragments preserved without indication of authorship have sometimes been attributed to Ennius' tragedies on the basis of style or content, the names of key figures, or assumptions concerning the plots. Since there is no clear evidence for the attribution in the transmission, these fragments appear among the tragic Incerta *in* FRL. *These include:* Trag. inc. inc. 5–16, 21, 22, 23–24, 26, 27, 28, 29, 30–31, 43, 85–87, 132, 133–37,

ACHILLES (ARISTARCHI) (t 1; F 1–8)

The tragedy with the transmitted titles Achilles *and* Achilles Aristarchi *apparently revolves around the embassy sent to the hero, when he had withdrawn in anger from the fighting before Troy, an incident narrated in Homer's* Iliad 9.

The surviving fragments concern fighting (F 3), possibly including a philosophical or divine assessment (F 7), and perhaps point to a conversation among the envoys sent by Agamemnon (unsuccessfully) to persuade Achilles (F 5).

TRAGEDIES (F 1–201)

156–57, 172–73, 212, 214; Enn. Trag. 114–19, 194–96, 224–25, 226–27, 228–30, 231–32 Ri.²⁻³ = Adesp. 76, 107, 127, 68, 10, 146, 98, 120, 18, 69, 58, 55, 109, 52, 32– 33,136, 132, 5, 124, 34, 71, 73, 25 TrRF. Incerta that have been connected to particular Ennian tragedies are mentioned in the respective introductions.

Bibl.: Mette 1964, 14–16, 55–78; De Rosalia 1989, 95– 119; de Nonno / de Paolis / di Giovine 1991, 232–38; Suerbaum 1994; 2002, 126–28; 2003, 5–21; Manuwald 2001 [2004], 112–58; Goldberg 2007b; see also Rosato 2003b. Lit.: Brooks 1949; Jocelyn 1969b; 1972; Aricò 1997; Huse 1999; Boyle 2006; Gildenhard 2010; Manuwald 2011.

ACHILLES (ARISTARCHI) (t 1; F 1–8)

Achilles and/or the Trojan War appear in other tragedies by Ennius (e.g., Andromacha, Hectoris lytra, Hecuba). Therefore, the following fragments, transmitted without attribution to a particular drama, but belonging to a Trojan War context, might or might not come from this play: Enn. Trag. F 144, 153, 185.

The prologue of Plautus' Poenulus refers to a piece called Achilles Aristarchi (t 1), likely to be an allusion to Ennius' adaptation. The context in Plautus suggests an

3

assembly scene. Yet it is doubtful whether any lines of En-
nius' tragedy can be reconstructed from Plautus' text.

Tragedies of the same title (Achilles) *are known for the*
Greek poets Aristarchus Tegeates (14 F 1a TrGF), Iophon
(22 F 1a TrGF), Astydamas II (60 F 1f TrGF), Carcinus
II (70F 1d TrGF), Cleophon? (77 F 1[3] TrGF), Euaretus
(85 T 1 TrGF) and Diogenes Sinopensis (88 F 1a TrGF) as
well as for the Roman playwrights Livius Andronicus
(Trag. 1 R.$^{2-3}$ *= F 1 TrRF) and Accius (Trag. 1–3 R.*$^{2-3}$*);*
there is also an Achilles Thersitoctonus *by the Greek dra-*
matist Chaeremon (71 F 1a–3 TrGF).

In view of the quotations of the title of Ennius' tragedy,
its model must have been the piece by Aristarchus, a con-

t 1 Plaut. *Poen.* 1–16 [cf. Enn. *Trag.* 13–15 R.$^{2-3}$]

Achillem Aristarchi mihi commentari lubet:
ind' mihi principium capiam, ex ea tragoedia
sileteque et tacete atque animum advortite,
audire iubet vos imperator—histricus,

5   bonoque ut animo sedeant in subselliis
et qui essurientes et qui saturi venerint:
   . . .

11 exsurge, praeco, fac populo audientiam.
   . . .

16 bonum factum † esse † [factumst *Pylades*], edicta ut
    servetis mea.

temporary of Euripides (F 3; T 112). However, it is uncertain whether the two versions of the title attested for Ennius denote one or two tragedies. In the latter case the addition "Aristarchi" would distinguish an Achilles tragedy based on Aristarchus from another one following a different model. In the absence of further evidence, the former alternative is generally assumed. It is also unclear whether Achilles Aristarchi *is Ennius' title or whether later grammarians added the specification.*

Bibl.: *Suerbaum 2003, 218; Manuwald 2001 [2004], 131.* Comm.: *Jocelyn 1967, 161–77; Masiá 2000, 86–153.* Lit.: *Klussmann 1845; Ribbeck 1875, 112–18; Jiráni 1905; Rosner 1970, 32–35; Morelli 1992 [1993].*

t 1 Plautus, *Poenulus*

I want to rehearse the *Achilles* of Aristarchus.[1] From there will I take my opening, from that tragedy: be silent and be quiet and pay attention. You are ordered to listen by the general—of the stage: [5] let them sit on their benches in good spirit, both those who have come hungry and those who have come full. . . . [11] Get up, herald. Make the people attentive. . . . [16] Proper behavior is for you to obey my edicts.[2]

[1] A Greek tragedian contemporary with Euripides (cf. 14 *TrGF*). The reference is presumably to Ennius' adaptation of Aristarchus' tragedy *Achilles* (cf. T 112).   [2] This prologue is generally thought to include phrases and motifs from Ennius' tragedy; lines 3 and 4, 11, and 16 in particular are often assumed to be almost literal quotations (see Jocelyn 1969a).

1

a Cic. *Verr.* 2.1.46

tum subito tempestates coortae sunt maximae, iudices, ut
non modo proficisci cum cuperet Dolabella non posset,
sed vix in oppido consisteret

ia/tr   ita magni fluctus eiciebantur

hic navis illa praedonis istius, onusta signis religiosis, ex-
pulsa atque eiecta fluctu frangitur; in litore signa illa Apol-
linis reperiuntur; iussu Dolabella reponuntur. tempestas
sedatur, Dolabella Delo proficiscitur.

b Schol. Gron. Cic. *Verr.* 2.1.46 (p. 344 Stangl)

"ita magni fluctus eiciebantur": Enniano emistichio usus
est ex ea tragoedia quae Achilles inscribitur.

2 Gell. *NA* 4.17.13–14

congruens igitur est, ut "subices" etiam, quod proinde ut
"obices" compositum est, "u" littera brevi dici oporteat.
[14] Ennius in tragoedia, quae Achilles inscribitur, "sub-
ices" pro aere alto ponit, qui caelo subiectus est, in his
versibus:

tr^7?   per ego deum sublimas subices
tr^7 humidas, unde oritur imber sonitu saevo et spiritu

plerosque omnes tamen legere audias "u" littera producta.

2 spiritu *Fest.*: strepitu *Gell.*

Cf. Fest., p. 394.33–37 L.; Paul. *Fest.*, p. 395.6 L.; Non., p. 169.1–4
M. = 248 L.

6

1

a Cicero, *Verrine Orations*

Then suddenly very severe tempests arose, judges, so that Dolabella not only was unable to set off, as he wished, but could hardly remain in town

> such great floods were being cast ashore

Here that ship of that thief, laden with religious statues, thrust out and cast ashore by the flood, is broken asunder; on the shore those statues of Apollo are found; on Dolabella's orders they are put back. The tempest subsides; Dolabella sets off from Delos.

b Scholia Gronoviana to Cicero, *Verrine Orations*

"such great floods were being cast ashore": He has used an Ennian half-line from the tragedy that is entitled *Achilles*.

2 Gellius, *Attic Nights*

It is therefore fitting that *subices* ["underlying parts": *hapax legomenon*] too, which is formed in the same way as *obices* ["opposing parts"], should be pronounced with a short letter *u*. [14] In the tragedy that is entitled *Achilles* Ennius puts *subices* ["underlying parts"] for high air, which is placed just under the sky, in the following lines:

> I, by the liquid underlayers of the gods high up [i.e., clouds],
> from where the rain comes with fierce sound and uproar, ⟨swear / pray?⟩

still you would hear most people read this with a long letter *u*.

3 Fest., p. 282.9–11 L.

ia/tr prolato aere astitit

Ennius in Achille Aristarchi cum ait, significat clipeo ante se protento.

Cf. Paul. *Fest.*, p. 283.3–4 L.

4 Non., p. 147.17–19 M. = 215 L

OBVARARE, pervertere, depravare: dictum a varis. Ennius Achille:

an[7] nam consiliis ius obvarant, quibus tam concedit hic ordo

consili‹is i›us *Timpanaro*: consilius *codd.*: consiliis *multi edd.*

5 Non., p. 166.20–22 M. = 245 L.

REGREDERE, revocare. Ennius Achille:

ia[6] quo nunc incerta re atque inorata gradum regredere conare?

3 Festus

When Ennius says,

> he took up a position with the bronze held out

in *Achilles Aristarchi*, he means "with a shield held out before him."

4 Nonius

obvarare ["to thwart": *hapax legomenon*], "to corrupt," "to distort": it is derived from *varus* ["bent"]. Ennius in *Achilles*:

> for they thwart what is right with their plans; to them this body[1] still[2] yields

[1] The phrase *hic ordo*, presumably referring to an assembly of the Greek leaders, is a technical term for the Roman Senate (e.g., Cic. *Pis.* 6, 8, 40, 45).   [2] *tam = tamen* (cf. *Trag.* F 188).

5 Nonius

regredere ["to restep": *hapax legomenon* as active infinitive], "to direct backward." Ennius in *Achilles*:

> Where are you [*sing.*] now trying to restep your step, with the matter not decided and not pleaded?

6 Non., p. 277.23–27 M. = 426 L.[1]

DEFENDERE, vindicare, tueri. DEFENDERE, depellere.
Vergilius in Bucolicis [Verg. *Ecl.* 7.47]: "solstitium pecori
defendite." Ennius Achille:

tr^7 serva cives, defende hostes, cum potes defendere

7 Non., p. 472.26–27 M. = 758 L.

PROELIANT. Ennius Achille:

tr   ita mortales inter sese pugnant, proeliant

8 Isid. *Diff.* 1.131(218)

inter famam et gloriam. gloria quippe virtutum est, fama
vero vitiorum. Ennius in Achille:

tr^7?   summam tu tibi
tr^7 pro mala vita famam extolles, {et} pro bona partam
        gloriam.
    male volentes {enim} famam tollunt, bene volentes
        gloriam.

    2 et *del. Ribbeck[1]*   pro bona partam *Ribbeck[1]:* pro
bone / bene parta / pasta / parta(m) / facto *codd.*   3 enim
om. unus cod. (*Codoñer*), *del. Ribbeck[1]*

6 Nonius

defendere ["to ward off"], "to defend," "to protect." *defendere* ["to defend"], "to drive off."[1] Virgil in the *Eclogues* [7.47]: "ward off the midday sun from the flock." Ennius in *Achilles*:

> save the citizens, ward off the enemy, when you can
> ward off[2]

[1] The transmission of this lemma is very corrupt (and has been variously restored); something may have fallen out or got into the wrong order.   [2] The aims of the fighters before Troy are described using Roman terminology (cf. Plaut. *Pers.* 753–54; denarius of 61 BC [Crawford 1974, 443–44, no. 419]; Val. Max. 3.1.1).

7 Nonius

"they engage in battle" [unique active form of the verb in archaic and classical Latin]. Ennius in *Achilles*:

> thus mortals fight among themselves, they engage in
> battle

8 Isidore, *On Differences between Words*

⟨The difference⟩ between "notoriety" and "glory." "Glory" obviously refers to virtues, "notoriety" certainly to vices. Ennius in *Achilles*:

> You will raise the greatest
> notoriety for yourself in response to a bad life, glory
> won in response to a good one.
> Those with bad intentions raise notoriety, those with
> good intentions glory.

11

AIAX (F 9–11)

Ennius' tragedy probably featured Ajax' suicide (F 10) and perhaps the preceding judgment on Achilles' arms, which were given to Ulixes rather than to Ajax (hence Enn. Trag. F 162 has been suggested as possibly belonging to this tragedy).

Tragedies of the same title are known for the Greek poets Sophocles, Astydamas II (60 F 1a TrGF; T 1 [Αἴας μαινόμενος]), Carcinus II (70 F 1a TrGF), and Theodectas (72 F 1 TrGF), and in Rome for Livius Andronicus (Trag. 15–17 R.²⁻³ = F 10–11 TrRF); related material forms the plot of the tragedies Armorum iudicium *by Pacuvius*

9 Varro, *Ling.* 6.6

cum stella prima exorta (. . .), id tempus dictum a Graecis ἑσπέρα, Latine vesper; ut ante solem ortum quod eadem stella vocatur iubar, quod iubata, Pacui dicit pastor [Pac. *Trag.* 347 R.²⁻³]: "exorto iubare, noctis decurso itinere"; Enni{us} Aiax:

?   lumen—iubarne?—in caelo cerno

Cf. Varro, *Ling.* 6.81, 7.76.

AIAX (F 9–11)

*(Trag. 21–42 R.*²⁻³*) and by Accius (Trag. 145–63 R.*²⁻³*). Aspects of Ajax' fate are related in Ovid's* Metamorphoses *(13.1–398) and in Quintus Smyrnaeus (5). Ennius' model is often assumed to be Sophocles' tragedy, although it is uncertain whether Ennius' play covered the same section of the narrative. On performances of* Aiax *in Cicero's time, see T 35.*

Bibl.: Suerbaum 2003, 218; Manuwald 2001 [2004], 131–32. Comm.: Jocelyn 1967, 177–84; Masiá 2000, 154–84. Lit.: Ribbeck 1875, 131–33; Rosner 1970, 35; Masiá González 1992.

9 Varro, *On the Latin Language*

When the first star has come out (. . .), this time ["evening"] is called *hespera* by the Greeks, *vesper* in Latin; just as, because before sunrise the same star is called *iubar* ["the first light of day"], because it has a *iuba* ["crest"], Pacuvius' shepherd says [*Trag.* 347 R.²⁻³]: "when the first light of day has appeared, with the course of night run down" [i.e., in the morning]; Ennius' Ajax:[1]

I see a light—or the first light of day?—in the sky

[1] Varro cites this line several times, and he attributes it to "Ennius' Ajax" on one occasion (if the text is reconstructed correctly), but he does not name the play. Although Ajax seems to have appeared in at least one other Ennian tragedy, the focus on him suggests that this line comes from Ennius' *Aiax*.

10 Fest., p. 482.3–7 L.

‹TULLIOS al›ii dixerunt esse silanos, ali rivos, ali vehementes proiectiones sanguinis arcuatim fluentis, quales sunt Tiburi in Aniene. Ennius in Aiace:

tr⁷? † aiax † misso sanguine tepido tullii efflantes volant

† Aiax † *Mueller*: † a iax † *Jocelyn*: Aiax misso *Lindsay, Vahlen²*: animam misso *Vahlen¹, Ribbeck², Ribbeck³*: ‹. . .› misso *Warmington*: *alii alia*

Cf. Paul. *Fest.*, p. 483.1–4 L.

11 Non., p. 393.7–16 M. = 630 L.

STATIM producta prima syllaba, a stando, perseveranter et aequaliter significat. . . . Ennius Aiace:

ia/tr qui rem cum Achivis gesserunt statim

ALCMEO (F 12–14)

Alcmeo, the son of Amphiaraus and Eriphyla, killed his mother on his father's orders, since it was due to her bribery that Amphiaraus had to participate in the fighting of the Seven against Thebes, where he died. Because of this deed Alcmeo was later pursued by Furies (see, e.g., Apollod. Bibl. *3.7.5 = 3.86–90; Hyg.* Fab. *73).*

Tragedies of the same title are known for the Greek tragedians Sophocles (F 108–10 TrGF), Euripides (F 65–87a TrGF [Ἀλκμέων α' καὶ β']), Achaeus I (20 F 12–15 TrGF [Ἀλκμέων σατυρικός]), Agathon (39 F 2 TrGF),

10 Festus

Some have said that *tullii* ["gushing streams": *hapax lego-menon*] are waterspouts, others that they are rivers, others again that they are forceful discharges of blood flowing in the form of an arc, as there are in the case of the Anio[1] at Tibur.[2] Ennius in *Aiax*:

> Ajax (?); with warm blood released, gushing streams
> fly issuing forth

[1] A river in Italy, a tributary of the Tiber.   [2] Tivoli, known, among other things, for its waterfalls (cf. Plin. *HN* 17.120: *iuxta Tiburtes tullios* [text restored]).

11 Nonius

statim ["suddenly": class. with short first syllable], with long first syllable, from *stare* ["stand"], means "persever-ingly" and "steadfastly." . . . Ennius in *Aiax*:

> they who fought steadfastly with the Achaeans

ALCMEO (F 12–14)

Timotheus (56 F 1 TrGF), Astydamas II (60 F 1b–c TrGF), Theodectas (72 F 1a–2 TrGF), Euaretus (85 T 2 TrGF), and Nicomachus Alexandrinus (Troadis) (127 F 12, T 1 TrGF [Τυνδάρεως ἢ Ἀλκμαίων]) as well as for the Roman playwright Accius (Trag. 58–70 R.[2–3]). It is generally believed that one of Euripides' plays was Ennius' model, but it is uncertain whether it was Alcmeon in Corinth *or* Alcmeon in Psophis, *since details of Ennius' plot cannot be established.*

All fragments preserved from Ennius' tragedy refer to

*Alcmeo considering his deed and reflecting on his situation
and state of mind, as he feels pursued by Furies; this could
occur at different points in the story. What Cicero (Cic.
Rosc. Am. 67; Leg. 1.40; Pis. 46–47) says about the perse-
cution of guilty people by Furies represented on stage and*

12 Cic. *De or.* 3.217–18

aliud enim vocis genus iracundia sibi sumat, acutum, inci-
tatum, crebro incidens: . . . aliud miseratio ac maeror,
flexibile, plenum, interruptum, flebili voce [*Trag.* 231–32
R.$^{2–3}$]: . . . et illa [*Trag.* F 23.10]: . . . et quae sequuntur
[*Trag.* F 23.15–16]: . . . [218] aliud metus, demissum et
haesitans et abiectum:

tr^7 multis sum modis circumventus, morbo, exilio atque
             inopia;
           tum pavor sapientiam omnem mi exanimato
             expectorat.
           † alter † terribilem minatur vitae cruciatum et
             necem;
           quae nemo est tam firmo ingenio et tanta confidentia,
  5   quin refugiat timido sanguen atque exalbescat metu

3 † alter † *Vahlen*^{2} *in app.*: alter *alii codd.*: om. *alii codd.*:
mater *Ribbeck*^{1}, *Warmington*: animus *vel* mens enim *Jocelyn in
comm.*

Cf. Cic. *De or.* 3.154; *Tusc.* 4.18–19; *Fin.* 4.62, 5.31; *Hortensius*
F 102 Grilli, ap. Prisc., *GL* II, p. 250.12–14; Non., pp. 16.1–7,
224.6–25 M. = 23, 331–32 L.

its relationship to real feelings may be inspired by plays such as Ennius' Alcmeo (or Eumenides).

Comm.: *Jocelyn 1967, 184–202; Masiá 2000, 33–85.*
Lit.: *Ribbeck 1875, 197–99; Vahlen 1887/88; Rosner 1970, 36; Paduano 1974, 29–32.*

12 Cicero, *On the Orator*

For anger shall adopt one kind of voice, sharp, excited, frequently breaking off: . . . Lamentation and mourning another one, varying in pitch, sonorous, interrupted, with a tearful voice [*Trag.* 231–32 R.[2–3]]: . . . and this [*Trag.* F 23.10]: . . . and what follows [*Trag.* F 23.15–16]: . . . [218] Fear yet another one, subdued, hesitating and downcast:

> In many ways am I encircled, by illness, exile and
>   want;
> then fear banishes all my wits from my senses, with
>   me paralyzed.
> Someone [my mother? my mind?] threatens my life
>   with terrible torture and death;
> in view of this, nobody is of so firm a spirit and such
>   confidence
> that his blood does not leave him in his anxiety and   5
>   he does not become pale with fear.

13

a Cic. *Acad.* 2.52

quod idem contingit insanis, ut et incipientes furere sen-
tiant et dicant aliquid quod non sit id videri sibi, et cum
relaxentur sentiant atque illa dicant Alcmeonis:

tr⁷?   sed mihi neutiquam cor consentit cum oculorum
                aspectu

b Cic. *Acad.* 2.88–89

dormientium et vinulentorum et furiosorum visa inbecil-
liora esse dicebas quam vigilantium siccorum sanorum.
quo modo? quia cum experrectus esset Ennius non diceret
se vidisse Homerum sed visum esse, Alcmeo autem "sed
mihi neutiquam cor consentit"; similia de vinulentis. . . .
[89] quid loquar de insanis: . . . ; quid ipse Alcmeo tuus,
qui negat "cor sibi cum oculis consentire," nonne ibidem
incitato furore,

?   unde haec flamma oritur?

et illa deinceps:

?   incedunt, incedunt; adsunt; me expetunt

quid cum virginis fidem implorat:

an⁴   fer mi auxilium, pestem abige a me,
5   flammiferam hanc vim, quae me excruciat;

3 incedunt, incedunt *Ribbeck¹*: incede incede *codd.*: † incede
incede † *Jocelyn*

---

¹ The daughter of a king in one of the countries to which Alc-
meo came or a priestess.

18

13

a Cicero, *Prior Academics*

The same thing happens to the insane, so that, when they are beginning to go mad, they feel and say that something that does not exist appears to them, and also when they are recovering, they feel it and say these words of Alcmeo:

> but my heart does not at all agree with the vision of
>   my eyes

b Cicero, *Prior Academics*

You said that the impressions of people sleeping and drunk and insane are weaker than those of people awake, sober and sane. In what way? Because, when he had awakened, Ennius did not say that he had seen Homer, but that he had seemed to [cf. T 27], but Alcmeo says: "but my heart does not agree at all"; similarly with regard to people drunk. . . . [89] What shall I say about the insane: . . . ; well, that Alcmeo of yours himself, who denies that "his heart agrees with the eyes," does he not say in the same context, with madness aroused,

> whence does this flame arise?

and then this:

> they come on, they come on, they are here, they are
>   aiming for me

What then, when he implores the virgin's fidelity:[1]

> bring me help, drive away this plague from me,
> this flame-bearing force, which is torturing me;   5

19

caeruleae incinctae igni incedunt,
circumstant cum ardentibus taedis.

num dubitas quin sibi haec videre videatur? itemque
cetera:

an[4]   intendit crinitus Apollo
arcum auratum luna innixus,
10   Diana facem iacit a laeva

qui magis haec crederet si essent quam credebat quia vi-
debantur? apparet enim iam "cor cum oculis consentire."

6 caeruleae . . . igni *codd.*: caeruleo . . . angui *Ribbeck*[1]: cae-
rula . . . angui *Ribbeck*[2–3]: caeruleae . . . angui *Plasberg*

Cf. Fest., p. 162.14–16 L.

14 Non., p. 127.13–16 M. = 184 L.

IAMDIU pro olim. . . . Ennius Alcmeone:

ia/tr   factum est iam diu

ALEXANDER (F 15–22)

*This tragedy dramatized the story of Priam's son Alexan-
der (= Paris), who, as a young child, was exposed in re-
sponse to a bad omen. Shepherds raised him, and when he
participated with great success in games organized by his
father in Alexander's memory, he was recognized and re-
ceived back into the family, with his sister Cassandra
prophesying events connected with the Trojan War (see,
e.g., Apollod. Bibl. 3.12.5 = 3.148–50; Hyg. Fab. 91,
273.12).*

> they are walking along, dark and girt with fire,
> they are standing around with blazing torches.

Do you doubt that it seems to him that he sees this? And similarly the rest:

> Apollo with long hair bends
> his golden bow, pressing upon the curve [i.e., of the
>   bow],
> Diana throws a brand from the left   10

How would he believe these things more if they were real than he believed them because they seemed to be real? For it is already obvious "that the heart agrees with the eyes."

14 Nonius

iamdiu ["for a long time now, long since now"] instead of *olim* ["a long time ago"], . . . Ennius in *Alcmeo*:

> it was done a long time ago

ALEXANDER (F 15–22)

Tragedies of the same title (Alexandros) are known for the Greek dramatists Sophocles (F 93 TrGF), Euripides (F 41a–64 TrGF), and Nicomachus Alexandrinus (Troadis) (127 F 1; T 1 TrGF). Ennius' model was probably Euripides' play (F 16).

The fragments preserved from Ennius' tragedy cover the celebration of the games (F 15, 20), Alexander as an ordinary person coming to the competition, his victory and recognition (F 16), and comments on elements of the

Trojan War (F 21 22). Moreover, the following unattrib-
uted fragments (including prophecies of Alexander's birth
and the future of Troy) have been suggested as possibly
belonging to this tragedy: Enn. Trag. F 151, 201; Trag. inc.
inc. 5–16, 21, 22 R.$^{2-3}$ = F 76, 107, 127 TrRF.

Bibl.: Suerbaum 2003, 218; Manuwald 2002 [2004],
132–33. Comm.: Jocelyn 1967, 202–34; Masiá 2000, 185–

15 Varro, *Ling.* 6.83

ab auribus verba videntur dicta audio et ausculto; auris ab
aveo, quod his avemus di<s>cere semper, quod Ennius
videtur ἔτυμον ostendere velle in Alexandro cum ait:

ia^6 iam dudum ab ludis animus atque aures avent
avide exspectantes nuntium

16 Varro, *Ling.* 7.82

apud Ennium [*Trag.* F 25]: "Andromachae nomen qui
indidit, recte {ei} indidit." item:

tr^7 quapropter Parim pastores nunc Alexandrum vocant

imitari dum voluit Euripidem et ponere ἔτυμον, est lap-
sus: nam Euripides quod Graeca posuit, ἔτυμα sunt
aperta. ille ait ideo nomen additum Andromach<a>e, quod
ἀνδρὶ μάχεται [*corr. ed. Aldina*]: hoc Ennii quis potest
intellegere in versu{m} significare "Andromach<a>e no-
men qui indidit, recte indidit" aut Alexandrum ab eo

---

[1] This fragment is not explicitly assigned to Ennius' *Alexan-*
der; but it clearly comes from a play on Alexander by Ennius, and
the reference to "herdsmen" alludes to a key element of the as-
sumed plot of *Alexander*.

252. *Lit.: Hartung 1844, 233–50; Ribbeck 1875, 81–94; Snell 1937, 1–68; Biliński 1954; Enk 1957, 285–87; Skutsch 1967, 125–27; Rosner 1970, 36–38; Paduano 1974, 33–36; Reggiani 1986–87 [1990], 39–44; Mactoux / Citti 1988–89 [1991]; Neblung 1997, 114–23; Timpanaro 1996; Jocelyn 1998.*

15 Varro, *On the Latin Language*

From *aures* ["ears"] the words *audio* ["I hear"] and *ausculto* ["I listen"] seem to be derived; *aures* from *aveo* [= *aueo*, "I am eager"], since we are always eager to learn with these, an etymological connection that Ennius seems to wish to show in *Alexander*, when he says:

> for some time now the mind and the ears have been
> eager,
> eagerly awaiting a message [or: messenger] from the
> games

16 Varro, *On the Latin Language*

In Ennius [*Trag.* F 25]: "he who gave Andromache her name, gave it correctly." Likewise:[1]

> that is why the herdsmen now call Paris Alexander

While he [Ennius] wanted to imitate Euripides and put down an etymology, he made a mistake: for since Euripides put it in Greek, the etymologies are obvious. He says that the name was attached to Andromache because she "fights a man" [*andri machetai* in Greek]: who can understand that this is meant in Ennius' verse "he who gave Andromache her name, gave it correctly" or that Alexan-

23

appellatum in Graecia qui Paris fuisset, a quo Herculem quoque cognominatum Alexicacon, ab eo quod defensor esset hominum?

17

a Gell. *NA* 7.5.10

scriptum est autem "purum putum" non in Carthaginiensi solum foedere, sed cum in multis aliis veterum libris, tum in Q. quoque Ennii tragoedia, quae inscribitur Alexander, et in satira M. Varronis, quae inscripta est δὶς παῖδες οἱ γέροντες [Varro, *Sat. Men.* 91 B.].

b Fest., p. 240.9–14 L.

⟨PUTUM⟩ . . . ⟨pro puro dixisse⟩ antiquos . . . ⟨Ennius⟩ in Alexandro:

?   † amidio † purus put⟨us⟩

> † amidio † *Jocelyn* (†—amidio *Ribbeck*[2]): amidio *cod.*
> put⟨us⟩ *suppl. Scaliger*

18 Fest., pp. 416.35–18.3 L.

STOLIDUS: stultus. Ennius [1 *Ann.* F 47] . . . et in Alexandro:

tr[7]   hominem appellat: "quid lascivis, stolide?"—non
             intellegit.

> lascivi⟨s⟩ *Scaliger*: lascivi *cod.*

24

der [Greek, lit., "defender of men"], who had been Paris, was thus called in Greece from the same source from which Hercules too was given the additional name Alexicacos [Greek, lit., "averter of evil"], from the fact that he was a defender of men?[2]

[2] Varro explains Greek names developed from the Greek verb *alexein*. Like the Latin equivalent *defendere*, it can mean "to defend" as well as "to ward off."

17

a Gellius, *Attic Nights*

But *purum putum* ["clean and pure"] is not only written in the treaty with the Carthaginians, but also in many other texts of the ancients [e.g. Plaut. *Pseud.* 989, 1200], especially also in the tragedy by Ennius that is entitled *Alexander* and in the satire by Varro that is entitled *"Dis paides hoi gerontes"* ["*Old men are children twice over*"; *Sat. Men.* 91 B.].

b Festus

. . . that the ancients ‹said "clean" instead of "pure"› . . . ‹Ennius› in *Alexander*:

    . . . (?) clean, pure

18 Festus

stolidus: "mindless." Ennius [1 *Ann.* F 47] . . . and in *Alexander*:

    he addresses the man: "why are you frolicking, you
    mindless man?"—he does not understand

19 Fest., pp. 494.33–96.4 L.

TAENIAS Graecam vocem sic interpretatur Verrius, ut dicat ornamentum esse laneum capitis honorati, ut sit apud
. . . Ennius in Alexandro:

ia^6 volans de caelo cum corona et taeniis

20 Macrob. *Sat.* 6.1.61 (Verg. *Aen.* 5.302 "multi praeterea quos fama obscura recondit")

Ennius in Alexandro:

tr^7 multi alii adventant, paupertas quorum obscurat
         nomina

21 Macrob. *Sat.* 6.2.18 (Verg. *Aen.* 2.281 "o lux Dardaniae, spes o fidissima Teucrum" et reliqua)

Ennius in Alexandro:

an^4 o lux Troiae, germane Hector,
ba^{4c} quid ita cum tuo lacerato corpore
ba^{4c} miser es, aut qui te sic respectantibus
ba^2 tractavere nobis?

     2–4 *dist. Vahlen*   3 ‹es› *suppl. Vahlen*

22 Macrob. *Sat.* 6.2.25 (Verg. *Aen.* 6.515–16 "cum fatalis equus saltu super ardua venit / Pergama et armatum peditem gravis attulit alvo")

Ennius in Alexandro:

ia^8 nam maximo saltu superavit gravidus armatis equus
?   qui suo partu ardua perdat Pergama

     1 gravidus *ed. Ven. 1528*: gravibus *codd.*

19 Festus

Verrius interprets the Greek word *taenia* ["headband"] so
that he says it is a woolen ornament for the head of a re-
spected person, as it is in . . . Ennius in *Alexander*:

> flying from heaven with a garland and headbands

20 Macrobius, *Saturnalia* (on Virgil, "many men besides
whom their fame, obscure, hides away")

Ennius in *Alexander*:

> many others arrive, whose poverty covers their names
>   in darkness

21 Macrobius, *Saturnalia* (on Virgil, "o light of Dardania,
o most trusted hope of the Teucrians" and what follows)

Ennius in *Alexander*:

> O light of Troy, true brother Hector,
> why are you so wretched with your body mutilated,
> or what men have treated you thus
> as we look on?

22 Macrobius, *Saturnalia* (on Virgil, "when the fateful
horse came with a leap over lofty Pergamum and, preg-
nant, brought armed soldiers in its womb")

Ennius in *Alexander*:

> for with a mighty leap the horse, pregnant with
>   armed men, has climbed over,
> which is destroying lofty Pergamum with its offspring

ANDROMACHA (AECHMALOTIS)
(F 23–33)

*This tragedy featured Andromache, Hector's wife, after
the fall of Troy. It shows Andromache lamenting in this
situation (F 23), and it includes the slaying of her son
Astyanax (T 16; F 30) and perhaps that of Priam's daugh-
ter Polyxena (F 24). Enn. Trag. F 179 (referring to Asty-
anax) may belong to this tragedy. Cicero frequently men-
tions a drama* Andromacha, *mostly without a poet's name
(T 16, 24, 26, 34); this must be Ennius' play since no other
Republican tragedy of this title is known. There seems to
have been only one tragedy on Andromache by Ennius; the
epithet "Aechmalotis" ("captive") sometimes added to the
title, a description appearing in Euripides (Eur. Andr. 583,
871, 908, 932, 962, 1059, 1243; Tro. 677–78), looks like an
addition by grammarians to define the setting of the play.
Tragedies of the same title (Andromache) are known for
Euripides and Antiphon (55 F 1 TrGF); related material
is treated in Euripides'* Hecuba *and* Troades *and in Accius'*

23

a Cic. *Tusc.* 1.105

sed plena errorum sunt omnia. trahit Hectorem ad cur-
rum religatum Achilles: lacerari eum et sentire, credo,
putat. ergo hic ulciscitur, ut quidem sibi videtur, at illa
sicut acerbissimam rem maeret:

ia^6 vidi videre quod me passa aegerrume,
         Hectorem curru quadriiugo raptarier

ANDROMACHA (AECHMALOTIS)
(F 23–33)

Astyanax (Trag. 164–88 R.$^{2-3}$). In the view of ancient scholars, Ennius' model was a tragedy by Euripides (F 25; T 24), but none of the known tragedies featuring Andromache displays equivalents of the content of all Ennian fragments preserved for this tragedy.

Skutsch (1967, 125–26) believed that Neptune spoke the prologue (cf. Plaut. Amph. 41–45); since Plautus' Amphitruo alluded to Ennius' tragedy, he concluded that Ennius' play was first performed in ca. 195–191 BC. Auhagen (2000a) connected the play with the war fought by Titus Flamininus in Epirus in ca. 200 BC.

Bibl.: Suerbaum 2003, 219; Manuwald 2001 [2004], 134–35. Comm.: Jocelyn 1967, 234–61; Masiá 2000, 253–306. Lit.: Ribbeck 1875, 135–42; Morel 1937; Schönberger 1956; Grilli 1965, 170–75; Rosner 1970, 38; Skutsch 1987; Auhagen 2000a; 2000b.

23

a Cicero, *Tusculan Disputations*

But everything [concerning burial, body, and soul] is full of misconceptions. Achilles drags Hector fastened to his chariot: he believes, I think, that he [Hector] is being mangled and feels it. Thus he wreaks his vengeance, as it seems to him at least, but she [Andromache] grieves over it as if over a most terrible thing:

I have seen what I have suffered to see with the
    greatest sorrow:
Hector being dragged along by a four-horse chariot

quem Hectorem? aut quam diu ille erit Hector? melius
Accius et aliquando sapiens Achilles [Acc. *Trag.* 667 R.[2-3]]:
"immo enimvero corpus Priamo reddidi, Hectora abstuli."
non igitur Hectora traxisti, sed corpus quod fuerat Hecto-
ris.

b Cic. *Tusc.* 3.44–46

ecce tibi ex altera parte ab eodem poeta

ia⁶   ex opibus summis opis egens, Hector, tuae;

huic subvenire debemus; quaerit enim auxilium:

cr⁴   quid petam praesidi aut exequar? quove nunc
5   auxilio exili aut fugae freta sim?
     arce et urbe orba sum. quo accedam? quo applicem?
tr⁷   cui nec arae patriae domi stant, fractae et disiectae
       iacent,

What Hector? Or for how long will he be Hector? Accius
does better and Achilles, wise at last [Acc. *Trag.* 667 R.[2-3]]:
"indeed, I have returned the body to Priam and taken
away Hector." Thus you have not dragged Hector, but
rather the body that had been Hector's.[1]

[1] This *canticum* by Andromache was apparently famous: Cic-
ero frequently quotes parts of it; it was the object of parody by
Plautus (Plaut. *Bacch.* 933–34; *Cas.* 621–24); and it seems to have
inspired Virgil in the description of the fall of Troy (Verg. *Aen.*
2.241–42 [cf. Serv. ad Verg. *Aen.* 2.241], 2.499–505). The first two
lines are attributed to a woman who laments Hector and declines
the name "Hector" according to Latin conventions, as Ennius did
in contrast to Accius (cf. *Trag.* F 179). The attribution to Ennius'
Andromacha and to the lamenting speech of the title character
therefore is almost certain. In addition, the introduction *vidi* is
picked up later. Euripides' Andromache voices similar laments
(Eur. *Andr.* 8–10, 107–8, 394–405, 523–25).

b Cicero, *Tusculan Disputations*

Look, on the other side you have by the same poet [En-
nius]

> from the greatest resources, now in need of your
> help, Hector;

we ought to support her; for she asks for help:

> What protection shall I seek or pursue? Or what
> help by means of exile or flight can I now trust?   5
> I am bereft of citadel and city. Where shall I turn?
>   Where shall I find support?
> Me, for whom the altars of a fatherland do not stand
>   at home—they lie broken and torn apart—;

fana flamma deflagrata; tosti alti stant parietes,
deformati atque abiete crispa . . .

scitis quae sequantur et illa in primis:

an⁴ 10   o pater, o patria, o Priami domus,
saeptum altisono cardine templum!
vidi ego te adstante ope barbarica
tectis caelatis laqueatis,
auro ebore instructam regifice

[45] o poetam egregium, quamquam ab his cantoribus
Euphorionis contemnitur! sentit omnia repentina et neco-
pinata esse graviora. exaggeratis igitur regiis opibus, quae
videbantur sempiternae fore, quid adiungit?

an⁴ 15   haec omnia vidi inflammari,
Priamo vi vitam evitari,
Iovis aram sanguine turpari

[46] praeclarum carmen! est enim et rebus et verbis et
modis lugubre. eripiamus huic aegritudinem.

8 alti *codd. det., Lambinus*: † alii † *Jocelyn*

Cf. Cic. *Sest.* 120–23; *De or.* 3.102, 3.183, 3.217; *Orat.* 92–93;
Tusc. 1.85, 3.53; Non., p. 181.1–2 M. = 265 L.; Serv. et Serv. Dan.
ad Verg. *Aen.* 1.726, 2.241; Rufin., *RLM*, pp. 577.33–78.13 = *GL*
VI, pp. 568.23–69.15.

24 Varro, *Ling.* 7.6

templum tribus modis dicitur: ab natura, ab auspicando, a
similitudine; ⟨ab⟩ natura in caelo, ab auspiciis in terra, a

sanctuaries are burned down by fire; high walls stand
    scorched,
disfigured and with fir-wood beams charred . . .

You know what follows, and these lines in particular:

O father, o fatherland, o house of Priam,   10
temple guarded by a high-sounding hinge!
I saw you [the building], while barbarian might stood,
with carved and fretted ceilings,
furnished with gold and ivory in kingly fashion.

[45] Oh, excellent poet, however much he is scorned by
these flatterers of Euphorion![1] He recognizes that every-
thing sudden and unexpected is more grievous to bear.
Hence after the royal wealth, which seemed to be eternal,
has been emphasized, what does he add?

I saw all this go up in flames,   15
Priam's life snatched away by force,
the altar of Jupiter defiled by blood.

[46] A wonderful song! For it is mournful in content, lan-
guage, and rhythm. Let us snatch the distress away from
her.

[1] Euphorion of Chalcis, a Greek poet of the 3rd c. BC. Cic-
ero's target is often understood to be the "new poets" in Rome,
including Catullus (see Lyne 1978).

24 Varro, *On the Latin Language*

The word *templum* ["sacred area, temple"] is used in three
ways: with regard to nature, to taking the auspices, to
similarity; <with regard to> nature, in the sky, to taking the

similitudine sub terra. in caelo templum dicitur, ut in
Hecuba [*Trag.* F 72]: . . . in terra, ut in Periboea [Pac. *Trag.*
309–10 R.$^{2-3}$]: . . . sub terra, ut in Andromacha:

ia^6?   Acherusia templa alta Orci salvete infera

25 Varro, *Ling.* 7.82

apud Ennium:

ia^6 Andromachae nomen qui indidit, recte {ei} indidit

item [*Trag.* F 16]: "quapropter Parim pastores nunc Alex-
andrum vocant." imitari dum voluit Euripidem et ponere
ἔτυμον, est lapsus: nam Euripides quod Graeca posuit,
ἔτυμα sunt aperta. ille ait ideo nomen additum Andro-
mach⟨a⟩e, quod ἀνδρὶ μάχεται [*corr. ed. Aldina*]: hoc
Ennii quis potest intellegere in versu{m} significare

ia^6 Andromachae nomen qui indidit, recte indidit

aut Alexandrum . . . ?

ei *del. Victorius*

---

[1] The title of the tragedy is not mentioned with the quotation,
but only a single play by Ennius on Andromache is known (quoted
by Varro elsewhere), so that there is little doubt about the attribu-
tion.   [2] This etymology does not appear in any extant play by
Euripides.

auspices, on the earth, to similarity, beneath the earth. In the sky *templum* is used as in *Hecuba* [*Trag.* F 72]: . . . On the earth, as in *Periboea* [Pac. *Trag.* 309–10 R.[2–3]]: . . . , beneath the earth, as in *Andromacha*:[1]

> Acherusian sacred regions, deep underworld of Orcus, greetings

[1] Although Ennius' name is not mentioned in connection with this quotation, the attribution seems certain, since no other Republican tragedy with the title *Andromacha* is known, and Varro quotes Ennius' tragedy several times. For similar phrasing, see, e.g., Enn. *Trag.* F 85; Cic. *Tusc.* 1.48 [Enn. *Trag.* 70–72 R.[2–3]]; Lucr. 1.120–23.

25 Varro, *On the Latin Language*

In Ennius:[1]

> he who gave Andromache her name, gave it correctly

Likewise [*Trag.* F 16]: "that is why the herdsmen now call Paris Alexander." While he [Ennius] wanted to imitate Euripides and put down an etymology, he made a mistake: for since Euripides put it in Greek, the etymologies are obvious. He says that the name was attached to Andromache because she "fights a man" [*andri machetai* in Greek]:[2] who can understand that this is meant in Ennius' verse

> he who gave Andromache her name, gave it correctly

or that Alexander . . . ?

26 Fest., p. 384.16–23 L.

⟨. . . SUMM⟩USSI dicebantur ⟨murmuratores.⟩ Naevius [*Trag.* 63 R.² = 60 R.³ = 47 *TrRF*]: . . . Ennius in sexto . . . [6 *Ann.* F 5] . . . Enniu⟩s in Andromacha:

?   di . . . on est: nam mussare si . . .

27 Non., p. 76.1–2 M. = 106 L.

AUGIFICAT: auget. Ennius Andromaca:

tr⁷   quid fit? seditio tabetne? an numeros augificat suos?

versum sic dist. Lindsay (alii aliter)   tabetne *Lipsius*: tabesne *codd.*   numeros *ed. princ.*: numerus *codd.*

28 Non., p. 292.7–9 M. = 451 L.

EXANCLARE etiam significat perpeti. Ennius Andromache aechmaloto:

ia⁶   quantis cum aerumnis illum exanclavi diem

⟨aech⟩maloto{r}: quantis *Dübner*: malo torquantis (*vel* torquentis) *codd.*

29 Non., p. 515.12–15 M. = 828 L.

LONGINQUE et LONGITER, pro longe. Ennius [*Columna*: Accius *codd.*] Andromache aechmalo⟨to⟩ [*Quicherat*]:

26 Festus

summussi ["murmurers"] used to be called ‹"people who murmur."› Naevius [*Trag.* 63 R.^{2} = 60 R.^{3} = 47 *TrRF*]: . . . Ennius in his sixth ‹book› [6 *Ann.* F 5] . . . Ennius in *Andromacha*:[1]

. . . (?) it is: for to murmur (?) . . .

[1] This fragment is extremely lacunose and uncertain. Perhaps there is a contrast between "speak" (*di‹cere n›on*) and "murmur" (*mussare*). The repetition of Ennius' name for subsequent quotations from the same author in Festus' list is odd. Therefore, some scholars (Jocelyn 1967, 234 n. 5; Skutsch 1987, 39) have suggested that the fragment may belong to the comic poet Novius.

27 Nonius

augificat ["makes increase": *hapax legomenon*]: "increases." Ennius in *Andromacha*:

What is happening? Is the unrest disappearing? Or does it make its numbers increase?

28 Nonius

exanclare ["to drain, to endure": mainly ante-class.; cf. *Trag.* F 52] also means *perpeti* ["to bear to the end"]. Ennius in *Andromache aechmalotis*:

with what great troubles did I bear that day to the end

29 Nonius

longinque ["far"] and *longiter* ["far"], instead of *longe*: ["far": three different forms of the Latin adverb]. Ennius in *Andromache aechmalotis*:

ia⁶?   annos multos longinque a domo
ia⁶   bellum gerentes summum summa industria

Cf. Non., pp. 401.37–2.5 M. = 645–46 L.

30 Non., p. 504.18–20 M. = 810 L.

LAVERENT etiam inde manavit. Ennius Andromaca:

ia⁶   nam ubi introducta est puerumque, ut laverent,
        locant
in clipeo

2 c‹l›ipeo *edd.*: cypeo *vel* cipeo *codd.*

31 Non., p. 505.12–13 M. = 812 L.

SONUNT etiam inde manavit. Ennius Andromac‹h›e ‹a›ech{e}malotide:

tr⁷   nam neque irati neque blandi quicquam sincere
        sonunt

32 Non., p. 515.24–31 M. = 829 L.

RARENTER. . . . Ennius Andromacha:

ia⁶?   sed quasi aut ferrum aut lapis
        durat rarenter gemitum † conatur trabem †

‹Pomponius› [*add. Lindsay*] Ergastylo [Pomp. *Atell.* 45 R.²⁻³]: . . .

2 † conatur trabem † *Jocelyn*: conatur trabem *codd.*: conatu trahens *Warmington*: conatur trahens *Ribbeck¹*: conatur † trabem *Lindsay*

for many years, far from home,
waging [*plur.*] a glorious war with greatest effort

30 Nonius

lavĕrent ["they wash"; subj.] has also emerged from there
[from *lavĕre*, "to wash," instead of *lavare*]. Ennius in *An-
dromaca*:

for, as soon as she was led in and they put the boy
[Astyanax?] on the shield, so as to wash him

31 Nonius

sonunt ["they utter"] has also emerged from there [from
sonĕre, "to sound, to utter a sound," instead of *sonare*].
Ennius in *Andromache aechmalotis*:

for neither the angry nor the flattering utter anything
in a sincere way

32 Nonius

rarenter ["rarely"]. . . . Ennius in *Andromacha*:

but he / she endures as if a piece of iron or a
rock,
rarely does he / she make an attempt to utter a groan
(?)[1]

⟨Pomponius⟩ in *Ergastylus* [Pomp. *Atell.* 45 R.[2-3]]: . . .

[1] The second half of the second line is corrupt, and the word-
ing cannot be restored with certainty; the translation reflects the
likely meaning.

33

a Serv. ad Verg. *Aen.* 1.224

"velivolum" duas res significat, et quod velis volatur, ut hoc loco, et quod velis volat, ut Ennius: "naves velivolas," qui et proprie dixit.

b Macrob. *Sat.* 6.5.10 (Verg. *Aen.* 1.224 "despiciens mare velivolum")

Ennius in quarto decimo [14 *Ann.* F 4]: . . . idem in Andromache:

an⁴?   rapit ex alto naves velivolas

ANDROMEDA (F 34–41)

Andromeda, the daughter of Cepheus and Cassiope / Cassiepeia, was chained to a rock at the seaside, exposed to a sea monster, after her mother had offended the sea gods; eventually Andromeda was rescued by Perseus (see, e.g., Apollod. Bibl. *2.4.3 = 2.43–44; Hyg.* Fab. *64; Eratosth. 17 [p. 21 Olivieri]; Hyg.* Astr. *2.9, 2.11; Schol. (Bas.) Germ. 184, 192, 201; Ov.* Met. *4.663–764).*

*Tragedies of the same title are known for the Greek poets Sophocles (F 126–36 TrGF), Euripides (F 114–56 TrGF), Lycophron (100 F 1c TrGF), and Phrynichus II (212 F 1v TrGF), and in Rome for Livius Andronicus (*Trag. *18*

33

a Servius, *Commentary on Virgil*

velivolum means two things, both what is being flown through rapidly by means of sails, as in this case [in Virgil], and what flies rapidly with sails, like Ennius: "swift-sailing ships," who in fact used it in its actual sense.[1]

[1] Both meanings and collocations appear in Ovid (Ov. *Pont.* 4.5.42: *velivolas . . . rates*; 4.16.21: *velivolique maris*).

b Macrobius, *Saturnalia* (on Virgil, "looking down on the swift-sailing sea")

Ennius in Book Fourteen [14 *Ann.* F 4]: . . . The same poet in *Andromache*:

it hurries swift-sailing ships from the deep sea

ANDROMEDA (F 34–41)

R.[2–3] = *F 12 TrRF) and Accius (Trag. 100–18 R.*[2–3]*). The model of Ennius' tragedy is generally thought to have been Euripides' play (cf. F 34). That Cicero (Cic. Fin. 2.105) quotes a line from Euripides'* Andromeda *and translates it directly from the Greek is sometimes seen as an indication that this verse was not included in Ennius' tragedy.*

The fragments from Ennius' tragedy feature a comment on Andromeda's predicament (F 41), a description of the sea monster and of Perseus' fight against it (F 36, 37, 38, 39, 40) as well as what seems to be an allusion to the subsequent marriage of Andromeda and Perseus (F 35). Be-

41

*cause of the similarity of content, it has been suggested that
the following unattributed fragments might belong to this
tragedy: Enn.* Trag. *F 187, 192, 195.*

   Bibl.: *Suerbaum 2003, 219; Manuwald 2001 [2004],*

34 Varro, *Ling.* 5.19

omnino ego magis puto a chao cho<um ca>vum [*add.
Goetz / Schoell duce Muellero*] et hinc caelum, quoniam,
ut dixi [Varro, *Ling.* 5.17; Pac. *Trag.* 86–87 R.$^{2-3}$], "hoc
circum supraque quod complexu continet terram," cavum
caelum. itaque dicit Androm<ed>a Nocti [*Scaliger*]:

an⁴/da⁴?	quae cava caeli
an⁴/da⁴	signitenentibus conficis bigis

et Agamemno [*Trag.* F 83.1–2]: . . . ; et Ennius item ad
cavationem [*Trag.* F 149]: . . .

135. Comm.: Jocelyn 1967, 262–67. Lit.: Ribbeck 1875, 162–76; Webster 1965; Cazzaniga 1967; 1971; Rosner 1970, 39; Traina 1974, 155–60; Klimek-Winter 1993, 323–25, 333–49; Resta Barrile 1998.

34 Varro, *On the Latin Language*

On the whole I rather believe that from *chaos* ["shapeless material"] <comes> *choum cavum* ["hollow rounded shape"; cf. Inc. *Ann.* F 96] and hence *caelum* ["sky"], since, as I have said [Varro, *Ling.* 5.17; Pac. *Trag.* 86–87 R.$^{2-3}$], "this around and above that holds the earth in its embrace" is *cavum caelum* ["hollow sky"]. Hence[1] Andromeda[2] says to the Night:

> you who traverse the hollows of the
> sky to the end
> on your star-bearing chariot

and Agamemnon [*Trag.* F 83.1–2]: . . . ; and Ennius likewise with respect to a cavity [*Trag.* F 149]: . . .

---

[1] All quotations in this section seem to come from Ennius. Therefore, this fragment too can be assigned to him, although the poet's name is not mentioned directly with the quotation.

[2] The name of the speaker is most often restored as "Andromeda," though some scholars (e.g., Jocelyn 1967 ad loc.) suggest "Andromacha" and assign the fragment to Ennius' homonymous play. The attribution to Andromeda is supported by a similarity with the address to Night at the opening of Euripides' *Andromeda* (Aristoph. *Thesm.* 1065–69 = Eur. F 114 *TrGF*; Schol. Aristoph. *Thesm.* 1065b).

35 Fest., p. 312.7–14 L.

QUAESO, ut significat idem quod rogo, ita quaesere ponitur ab antiquis pro quaerere, ut est apud Ennium [2 *Ann.* F 12] . . . ; et in C{h}resp‹h›onte [*Trag.* F 44]: . . . ; et in Andromed{o}a:

tr[7] liberum quaesendum causa familiae matrem tuae

  quae sêdm (*i.e.*, secundum) *cod.*

Cf. Paul. *Fest.*, p. 313.3–4 L.

36 Non., p. 169.25–26 M. = 249 L.

SCABRES pro scabra es. Ennius Andromeda:

tr[7] scrupeo investita saxo, atque ostreis squamae
   scabrent

  ‹s›quam‹a›e{x} scaprent *Mercerus*: quam exscabrent *cod. unus*: quam excrabrent *codd. rell.*

Cf. Fest., p. 448.18–24 L.

37 Fest., p. 514.22–27 L.

URVAT [quod dixit *add. codd. nonnulli*] Ennius in Andromeda significat circumdat, ab eo sulco, qui fit in urbe condenda urvo aratri, quae fit forma simillima uncini curvatione buris et dentis, cui praefigitur vomer. ait autem:

---

[1] Festus seems to suggest that Ennius employs *urvare* in the sense of *circumdare,* since the plow's *urvum* is used to circumscribe and mark out an area when founding cities (cf. Pomponius, *Dig.* 50.16.239.6). The shape of the furrow made thereby is de-

35 Festus

As *quaeso* ["I request"] means the same as *rogo* ["I ask"], so *quaesere* ["to request": only used in particular forms and mainly ante-class.] is put by the ancients instead of *quaerere* ["to request"], as it is in Ennius [2 *Ann.* F 12] . . . ; and in *Cresphontes* [*Trag.* F 44]: . . . ; and in *Andromeda*:

> for the sake of begetting children,[1] the mother [*acc.*] of your family

[1] The aim of having children is expressed using Roman technical vocabulary (e.g., Plaut. *Capt.* 889; Gell. *NA* 4.3.2, 17.21.44).

36 Nonius

scabres ["you are rough": main verb] instead of *scabra es* ["you (*fem.*) are rough": adjective + form of "to be"]. Ennius in *Andromeda*:

> clothed [i.e., the monster (*fem.*)] with scraggy stone, and the scales are rough with oysters

37 Festus

With *urvat* ["marks out the boundaries by a furrow"] Ennius in *Andromeda* means *circumdat* ["surrounds"], from that furrow made in founding cities by the beam of the plow; this gives a form very similar to the curvature of the hooked plow beam and the tooth, to which the plowshare is fastened in front.[1] And he says:

termined by the shape of the plow. On the curvature of the plow beam (*buris / urvum*), see Serv. ad Verg. *G.* 1.170; for the parts of the plow, see Varro, *Ling.* 5.135.

circum sese urvat ad pedes
ia/tr   a terra quadringentos, caput

38 Non., p. 20.18–20 M. = 30 L.

CORPORARE est interficere et quasi corpus solum sine anima relinquere. Ennius Andromeda:

tr[7]   corpus contemplatur unde corporaret vulnere

39 Non., pp. 384.32–85.1 M. = 614 L.

RURSUS: retro. . . . Ennius Andromeda:

ia/tr   rursus prorsus reciprocat fluctus feram

Cf. Non., p. 165.8–11 M. = 242 L.

40 Non., p. 183.18–20 M. = 269 L.

VISCERATIM. Ennius Andromeda:

tr[7]?   alia fluctus differt dissupat
tr[7]   visceratim membra; maria salsa spumant sanguine

41 Prisc., *GL* II, pp. 293.5–19

inveniuntur tamen quaedam pauca feminini generis, quae ex masculinis transfigurantur non habentibus neutra, quae

it surrounds itself ‹with . . .›[2]
up to four hundred feet from the ground, the
head . . .[3]

[2] A complement in the ablative seems necessary; it perhaps preceded the quoted excerpt.   [3] The last word appears to be the start of a new phrase.

38 Nonius

corporare ["to strike life out of the body"; from *corpus*, "body"] is "to kill" and to leave just the body behind without life, as it were. Ennius in *Andromeda*:

he [Perseus?] scanned the body whence he might
strike life out of it with a wound

39 Nonius

rursus ["backward" (mainly ante-class.), "again"]; "backward." . . , Ennius in *Andromeda*:

the waves move the monster backward and forward

40 Nonius

visceratim ["piecemeal": *hapax legomenon*]. Ennius in *Andromeda*:

the waves disperse and scatter other
limbs piecemeal; the salty sea foams with blood

41 Priscian

A few words of feminine gender can still be found, which are transferred from masculine ones that do not have neu-

et animalium sunt demonstrativa, naturaliter divisum ge-
nus habentia, quae differentiae causa ablativo singulari
"bus" assumentia faciunt dativum et ablativum pluralem,
quod nulla alia habet declinatio in "bus" terminans supra
dictos casus, ut "a" longam in eis paenultimam habeat, ut
"his natabus," "filiabus," "deabus," . . . et "filiis" tamen in
eodem genere dictum est. Ennius in Andromeda:

tr[7]?   filiis propter te obiecta innocens sum Nerei

{id est Nereidibus}. Plautus in Sticho [*Stich.* 567]: "ego ibo
intro et gratulabor vestrum adventum filiis," pro "filiabus."

innocens sum *Vossius*: sum innocens *codd.*

ATHAMAS (F 42)

*There are several versions of the myth of Athamas' event-
ful life. Since the only surviving fragment of Ennius' drama
describes Bacchic revels, this may refer to the Bacchic
celebrations on Parnassus, during which Ino, Athamas'
second wife, is said to have been rediscovered. Since Atha-
mas had believed Ino to have died, he married Themisto.
When, however, Ino returned to Athamas, Themisto be-
came envious and tried to kill Ino's sons, but, deceived by*

ter forms, which denote living beings and have a naturally divided gender; for the sake of difference, they form the dative and ablative plural by adding -*bus* to the ablative singular, since no other declension ending in -*bus* has the cases mentioned above, so that it has a long *a* in those as the penultimate syllable, like *his natabus* ["these female children"], *filiabus* ["daughters"], *deabus* ["goddesses"], . . . And *filiis* ["daughters" / "sons"] is still used in the same [fem.] gender. Ennius in *Andromeda*:

> because of you I [*fem.*], being innocent, have been
> exposed to the daughters of Nereus[1]

{this is the Nereids}.[2] Plautus in *Stichus* [*Stich.* 567]: "I will go inside and congratulate my daughters [*filiis*] on your arrival," instead of "daughters" [*filiabus*].

[1] The most straightforward interpretation of this line is to connect *filiis . . . Nerei* with *obiecta*; otherwise one would have to assume a word like *ferae* in the adjacent lines.   [2] This phrase, transmitted in a variety of formats, is generally regarded as a gloss that should be deleted.

ATHAMAS (F 42)

Ino, killed her own sons and then herself (see, e.g., Apollod. Bibl. 3.4.3 = 3.27–29; Hyg. Fab. 4, 5).

The meter of these lines is unusual because of the Greek-style trimeters. Therefore, some scholars have doubted Ennian authorship. But this is not a sufficient reason to question the transmission, since such a metrical structure is not impossible in early Latin poetry.

Tragedies of the same title are known for the Greek poets

*Aeschylus (F 1–4a TrGF), Sophocles (F 1–10 TrGF
['Aθάμας α' καὶ β']), and Astydamas II (60 F 1, T 5 TrGF)
as well as for Accius (Trag. 189–95 R.$^{2-3}$) in Rome. Parts of
the myths are also treated in* Ino *by Euripides (F 398–423
TrGF) and* Ino *(?) by Livius Andronicus (pp. 4 R.^{2} = 4–5
R.^{3} = F 15 TrRF).*

42 Charis., *GL* I, p. 241.3–11 = p. 314 B.

EUHOE . . . Ennius in Athamante:

ia^6 his erat in ore Bromius, his Bacchus pater,
       illis Lyaeus vitis inventor sacrae.
       tum pariter † euhan euhium †
       ignotus iuvenum coetus alterna vice
5   inibat alacris Bacchico insultans modo.

1 ‹h›is erat *Fabricius*: is erat *cod.*   3 † euhan euhium †
Jocelyn: euhan euhium *cod.*: euhan ‹euhoe euhoe› euhium *Fa-
bricius*   5 insulta‹n›s *ed. princ.*: insultas *cod.*

CRESPHONTES (F 43–48)

*This drama may be about Cresphontes the Elder or
Cresphontes the Younger. Cresphontes the Elder and his
brothers conquered the Peloponnese and then divided it
up; Cresphontes gained Messenia by deceit when the lots
were cast. Later, the usurper Polyphontes killed Cresphon-
tes and two of his sons, took charge of the kingdom, and
married Cresphontes' wife, Merope. A surviving son, also*

Bibl.: Suerbaum 2003, 219; Manuwald 2001 [2004], 135–36. Comm.: Jocelyn 1967, 267–70. Lit.: Ribbeck 1875, 204–5; Rosner 1970, 39–40; D'Antò 1971; Mariotti 1979; Soubiran 1984.

42 Charisius

"euhoe" [a cry of Bacchantes] . . . Ennius in *Athamas*:

On their lips was Bromius, on theirs Father Bacchus,
on others' Lyaeus,[1] the inventor of the sacred vine.
Then shouting *"euhoe"* (?)[2] in the same manner,
in alternation, an unknown group of young men
entered briskly, dancing in Bacchic manner.[3]   5

[1] Bromius, Bacchus, and Lyaeus are different appellations of the Greek god Dionysus.   [2] The reading is uncertain, but this must be a rendering of a Bacchic cry.   [3] The fragment seems to describe how an unrecognized and unfamiliar group of young men disturb Bacchic celebrations carried out by women, somewhat similar to the behavior of Pentheus in Euripides' *Bacchae.*

CRESPHONTES (F 43–48)

called Cresphontes (in Euripides, differently in other versions), avenging his father's death, killed Polyphontes and recovered the kingdom (see, e.g., Paus. 4.3.3–6; Hyg. Fab. 137).

Ennius' tragedy includes mention of the division of territory by lot, likely to refer to the generation of Cresphontes the Elder (F 47), a comment on someone marrying

Merope (F 44), and complaints by a female speaker about not being given the chance to attend to dead bodies (F 48). The unattributed fragments Enn. Trag. 114–19 R.[2–3] (Rhet. Her. 2.38–39) = Adesp. 5 TrRF and Enn. Trag. F 143 have been suggested as possibly belonging to this tragedy.

For Euripides a tragedy of the same title is known (F 448a–59 TrGF), which dealt with the fate of Cresphontes the Younger. If the plot of Ennius' tragedy presented the same phase of the story, this tragedy by Euripides may have been Ennius' model. Since both Lucilius and Cicero refer directly to lines from Euripides' Cres-

43 Gell. *NA* 7.16.8–10

sed neque solus Catullus ita isto verbo [i.e., "deprecor"] usus est. pleni sunt adeo libri similis in hoc verbo significationis, ex quibus unum et alterum, quae subpetierant, apposui. [9] Q. Ennius in Erectheo [*Trag.* F 49] non longe secus dixit quam Catullus [Catull. 92.3]: . . . ; signat "abigo" et "amolior" vel prece adhibita vel quo alio modo. [10] item Ennius in Cresphonte:

tr[7]   ego meae cum vitae parcam, letum inimico deprecer

meae cum *transp. Bothe*: cum meae *cod.*

44 Fest., p. 312.7–13 L.

QUAESO, ut significat idem quod rogo, ita quaesere ponitur ab antiquis pro quaerere, ut est apud Ennium [2 *Ann.* F 12] . . . ; et in C{h}resp<h>onte:

phontes, *some scholars believe that Ennius did not trans-fer these passages into his play or did not follow Euripides' model (Gell. NA 6.3.28–29 [Lucil. 1169 M. = 1260 W.]: cf. Eur. F 451 TrGF; Cic. Tusc. 1.115: cf. Eur. F 449.3–6 TrGF). Comments by Roman authors on Merope in the context of dramas may refer to Ennius' tragedy (Quint. Inst. 11.3.73; Amm. Marc. 28.4.27).*

Bibl.: Suerbaum 2003, 219; Manuwald 2001 [2004], 136–37. Comm.: Jocelyn 1967, 270–81. Lit.: Ribbeck 1875, 186–91; Wecklein 1880; Rosner 1970, 39–41; Frassinetti 1981.

43 Gellius, *Attic Nights*

But Catullus was not the only one to use this word [*deprecor*, "I try to avert by prayer"] in this sense. Books are full of ‹instances of› similar meaning for this word, out of which I have set down one or two that were at hand. [9] Ennius in *Erecthous* [*Trag*. F 49] said, not much different from Catullus [Catull. 92.3]: . . . ; it signifies "I drive away" and "I remove," either by using a prayer or by any other means. [10] Likewise Ennius in *Cresphontes*:

while I spare my own life, should I try to avert death from the enemy?

44 Festus

As *quaeso* ["I request"] means the same as *rogo* ["I ask"], so *quaesere* ["to request": only particular forms and mainly ante-class.] is used by the ancients in place of *quaerere* ["to request"], as it is in Ennius [2 *Ann*. F 12] . . . ; and in *Cresphontes*:

ia^8 ducit me uxorem liberorum sibi quaesendum gratia

et in Andromed{o}a [*Trag.* F 35] . . .

Cf. Paul. *Fest.*, p. 313.3–4 L.

45 Fest., p. 334.8–16 L.

REDHOSTIRE: referre gratiam. . . . nam et hostire pro ae-
quare posuerunt. Ennius in C{h}resp‹h›onte:

ia^6 audi atque auditis hostimentum adiungito

et in Hectoris ly‹t›ris [*Trag.* F 56] . . .

audi{s} *Scaliger*: audis *cod.*

46 Non., p. 144.12–14 M. = 210 L.

NITIDANT: abluunt. dictum a nitore. Ennius Cresp‹h›onte:

?   † opie †
tr^7 eam secum advocant, eunt ad fontem, nitidant
              corpora

1 † o pie *Ribbeck*[2]: opie *codd.*: o pie‹tas› *Vahlen*[2]: "opie cor-
rupt. ex Meropen quasi gloss. seclud." *Warmington in app.*

47 Non., p. 471.2–5 M. = 755 L.

SORTIRENT, pro sortirentur. . . . {SORTIUNT} [*del. et* sor-
tiunt . . . agros *transp. Quicherat*] Ennius Cresphonte:

ia/tr   an inter se sortiunt urbem atque agros

he leads me home as his wife for the sake of
    begetting children for him

and in *Andromeda* [*Trag.* F 35] . . .

45 Festus

redhostire ["to make a repayment": rare and ante-class.]:
"to return thanks." . . . For they also put *hostire* ["to
recompense": rare and ante-class.] for "to make equal."
Ennius in *Cresphontes*:

listen and to what you have heard add a requital

and in *Hectoris lytra* [*Trag.* F 56] . . .

46 Nonius

nitidant ["they make bright": rare word]: "they wash
clean." It is derived from "brightness." Ennius in
Cresphontes:

. . . (?)
they call her <to come> with them, they go to the
    spring, they make their bodies bright

47 Nonius

sortirent ["they assign by lot": active form], instead of *sor-
tirentur* [standard deponent form]. Ennius in *Cresphon-
tes*:

do they share the town and its territory among
    themselves by lot?

48 Macrob. *Sat.* 6.2.21 (Verg. *Aen.* 9.486–87 "nec te tua funera mater / produxi pressive oculos aut vulnera lavi")

Ennius in Cres{i}phonte:

ia^8 neque terram inicere neque cruenta convestire
              corpora
         mihi licuit, neque miserae lavere lacrimae salsum
              sanguinem

1–2 corpora / mihi *transp. Bothe*: mihi corpora *codd.*

ERECTHEUS (F 49–51)

When besieged by an army led by the Thracian Eumolpus, a son of Neptune, Erectheus, king of Athens, sought an oracle in Delphi and was told to sacrifice one of his daughters. Erectheus sacrificed his daughter Chthonia, and according to some versions, his other daughters then killed themselves. Additionally, in other versions, Neptune demanded the sacrifice of a daughter as recompense after Erectheus' victory (see, e.g., [Demosth.] Epitaph. 60.27; Lycurg. Orat. in Leocratem 24.98–100 [pp. 67.13–68.3 Conomis]; Apollod. Bibl. 3.15.4 = 3.201–4; Hyg. Fab. 46, 238.2).

A tragedy with the same title is known for Euripides

49 Gell. *NA* 7.16.8–10

sed neque solus Catullus ita isto verbo [i.e., "deprecor"] usus est. pleni sunt adeo libri similis in hoc verbo significationis, ex quibus unum et alterum, quae subpetierant,

48 Macrobius, *Saturnalia* (on Virgil, "nor did I, your mourning mother, lead your procession or close your eyes or wash your wounds")

Ennius in *Cresphontes*:

> I was not allowed either to throw earth upon them or
>   shroud the bloody bodies,
> nor have miserable tears washed the salty blood

ERECTHEUS (F 49–51)

(F 349–70 TrGF) and is generally thought to have been Ennius' model.

The fragments of Ennius' tragedy feature a comment on the effect of self-sacrifice (F 49) and a description of fighting (F 51). Scholars have suggested that the unattributed fragments Enn. Trag. F 183, 186, 198 and Trag. inc. inc. *43 R.$^{2-3}$ = F 69 TrRF may also belong to Ennius' Erectheus.*

Bibl.: Manuwald 2001 [2004], 137. Comm.: Jocelyn 1967, 281–83. Lit.: Hartung 1843, 465–76; Ribbeck 1875, 181–86; Rosner 1970, 41; Traina 1974, 160–61; Zimmermann 2000; Stockert 2004, 274–76.

49 Gellius, *Attic Nights*

But Catullus was not the only one to use this word [*deprecor*, "I try to avert by prayer"] in this sense. Books are full of ‹instances of› similar meaning for this word, out of which I have set down one or two that were at hand.

apposui. [9] Q. Ennius in Erectheo non longe secus dixit quam Catullus [Catull. 92.3]:

> quibus nunc

inquit,

ia^6
> aerumna mea libertatem paro,
> quibus servitutem mea miseria deprecor

signat "abigo" et "amolior" vel prece adhibita vel quo alio modo. [10] item Ennius in Cresphonte [*Trag.* F 43] . . .

1 qui<bus> (= quibu') *Bentinus*: qui *Gell.*: cui *Non.*   libertatem paro *Gell.*: libertate para *Non.*

Cf. Non., p. 290.15–19 M. = 448 L.

50 Fest., p. 158.10–14 L.

NEMINIS <genitivo casu Cato usus est>: . . . <Enni>us Erectheo:

tr^7 lapideo sunt corde multi, quos non miseret neminis

Cf. Paul. *Fest.*, p. 159.4–5 L.

51 Macrob. *Sat.* 6.4.6 (Verg. *Aen.* 11.601–2 "tum . . . ferreus hastis / horret ager")

"horret" mire se habet; sed et Ennius in quarto decimo [14 *Ann.* F 7]: . . . , et in Erectheo:

ia arma arrigunt, horrescunt tela

et in Scipione [F 6] . . .

[9] Ennius in *Erectheus* said, not much differently from Catullus [Catull. 92.3]:

> those

he says,

> for whom I now obtain liberty by my suffering,
> for whom I try to avert servitude by my misery[1]

It signifies "I drive away" and "I remove," either by using a prayer or by any other means. [10] Likewise Ennius in *Cresphontes* [*Trag.* F 43] . . .

[1] For a similar notion, cf. Eur. F 360.38–41, 50–52 *TrGF*.

50 Festus

neminis ["of nobody": rare and ante-class. form of geni-tive]: ⟨this form of the genitive case was used by Cato⟩: . . . Ennius in *Erectheus*:

> many there are with heart of stone, who would not pity anyone

51 Macrobius, *Saturnalia* (on Virgil, "then . . . the field, full of iron, bristles with spears")

"bristles" is a remarkable usage, but so too Ennius in Book Fourteen [14 *Ann.* F 7]: . . . , and in *Erectheus*:

> they raise the weapons, the spears bristle

and in *Scipio* [F 6] . . .

EUMENIDES (F 52–55)

A tragedy of the same title is known for Aeschylus, presumably the model for Ennius' play. This drama features the persecution of Orestes by Furies, after he killed his mother, Clytaemnestra, to avenge the murder of his father, Agamemnon; the trial on the Areopagus, in which he is cleared of guilt by Athena's intervention; and the transformation of the Erinyes ("persecutors") into Eumenides ("well-meaning ghosts").

The fragments of Ennius' tragedy include Orestes' talking about taking revenge for his father (F 52) and elements of the trial (F 53, 55). Because of their content, the following unattributed fragments have been thought to

52 Non., p. 292.18–19 M. = 452 L.

EXANCLARE: effundere. Ennius Eumenidibus:

tr⁷   nisi patrem materno sanguine exanclando ulciscerem

53 Non., p. 306.32–33 M. = 477 L.

FACESSERE significat recedere. Ennius Eumenidibus:

tr⁷?   dico vicisse Orestem; vos ab hoc facessite

    Orestem *ed. princ.*: oresten *codd.*

EUMENIDES (F 52–55)

belong to this tragedy: Enn. Trag. *F 146, 172;* Trag. inc. inc. *132, 133–37 R.²⁻³ = F 109, 52 TrRF. What Cicero (*Rosc. Am. 67; Leg. *1.40;* Pis. *46–47) says about the persecution of guilty people by Furies on stage and its relationship to real feelings may be inspired by plays such as Ennius'* Eumenides *(or Alcmeo).*

Bibl.: Suerbaum 2003, 219; Manuwald 2001 [2004], 137–38. Comm.: Jocelyn 1967, 283–89. Lit.: Ribbeck 1875, 146–49; Fleckenstein 1953, 65–66; Rosner 1970, 41–42; Paduano 1974, 36–38; Traina 1974, 115–24; Zimmermann 2000.

52 Nonius

exanclare ["to drain, to endure": mainly ante-class.; cf. *Trag.* F 28]: "to pour out." Ennius in *Eumenides*:

> if I [Orestes?] did not take revenge for my father by pouring out my mother's blood

53 Nonius

facessere ["to carry out, to go away": mainly ante- and post-class.] means "to withdraw." Ennius in *Eumenides*:

> I say that Orestes has won; you, withdraw from him[1]

[1] For Athena proclaiming Orestes the winner, cf. Aesch. *Eum.* 752–53.

54 Non., pp. 474.35–75.5 M. = 761 L.

OPINO, pro opinor. . . . Ennius Eumenidibus:

ia[6]   tacere opino esse optumum et pro viribus
       sapere, atque fabulari tute noveris

55 Non., p. 505.16–24 M. = 812 L.

EXPEDIBO, pro expediam. . . . Ennius Eumenidibus:

tr[7]   id ego aecum ac iustum fecisse expedibo atque
       eloquar

       ac{c} ius‹tum› fecisse *Jocelyn*: accius fecisse *codd.*

HECTORIS LYTRA (F 56–71)

Hectoris lytra ("Hector's ransom"; *the Greek words in the
title often corrupted in the transmission) denotes Priam's
visit to Achilles toward the end of the fighting before Troy
to reclaim the body of his dead son Hector. However, it is
uncertain when exactly the plot of this tragedy begins, i.e.,
how much of the action preceding Priam's visit is included*

54 Nonius

opino ["I believe": rare and ante-class. active form], instead of *opinor* [standard deponent form]. . . . Ennius in *Eumenides*:

> I believe that it is best to be silent and to show good
> sense in relation to one's strengths,
> and then you should know to speak without risk[1]

[1] For a reflection by Orestes on when to speak or be silent, cf. Aesch. *Eum.* 276–79.

55 Nonius

expedibo ["I will explain": rare and ante-class. form], instead of *expediam* [standard form of future]. . . . Ennius in *Eumenides*:

> I will explain and declare that I[1] have done this as
> something fair and just[2]

[1] The fragment lacks a subject accusative for the infinitive construction, probably because the subject is the same as that of the main verb.   [2] For discussion of whether Orestes' deed was just, cf. Aesch. *Eum.* 462–69, 609–21.

HECTORIS LYTRA (F 56–71)

(on the story see Hom. Il. 22, 24; Aesch. Myrmidones *[F 131–42 TrGF],* Nereidae *[F 150–54 TrGF],* Phrygae vel Hectoris lytra *[F 263–72 TrGF]; Hyg. Fab. 106).*
   Greek tragedies of the same title are known for Aeschylus (F 263–72 TrGF [Φρύγες ἢ Ἕκτορος λύτρα]; *perhaps the last play of a trilogy on Achilles [TRI B III TrGF]),*

Dionysius (76 F 2a TrGF), and Timesitheus (214 T 1 TrGF); similar material might have been presented in Hector by Astydamas II (60 TrGF 1[h]). Most scholars believe that the latter books of Homer's Iliad and a tragedy or tragedies by Aeschylus were the sources of Ennius' play.

The fragments of Ennius' tragedy seem to refer to the provision of arms for Achilles upon his return to the fighting (F 65), the combat between Achilles and Hector

56 Fest., p. 334.8–17 L.

REDHOSTIRE: referre gratiam. . . . nam et hosti⟨r⟩{a}e pro aequare posuerunt. Ennius in C{h}resp⟨h⟩onte [*Trag.* F 45]: . . . et in *H*ectoris ly⟨t⟩ris:

tr⁷?   quae mea comminus machaera atque hasta † hospius
         manu †

    † hospius manu † *Jocelyn*: hospius manu *cod.*: hostibit e manu *Vahlen*[1]: hostibitis manu *Vahlen*[2]

57 Diom., *GL* I, p. 345.3–4

similiter halare et halitare: Ennius in Lu{s}tris:

?   sublime iter ut quadrupedantes flammam halitantes

(F 56, 61, 64, 69, 70, 71), and Priam visiting Achilles to obtain Hector's body (F 66). The following unattributed fragments have been thought to belong to this tragedy: Enn. Trag. F 153, 169, 177, 185.

Bibl.: Suerbaum 2003, 219. Comm.: Jocelyn 1967, 290–303; Masiá 2000, 307–75. Lit.: Schöll 1839, 472–98; Ribbeck 1875, 118–30; Riposati 1960; Rosner 1970, 42.

56 Festus

redhostire ["to make a requital": rare and ante-class.]: "to return thanks." . . . For they also put *hostire* ["to recompense": rare and ante-class.] for "to make equal." Ennius in *Cresphontes* [*Trag.* F 45]: . . . and in *Hectoris lytra*:

> with respect to this my sword and spear will return
> thanks (?) at close quarters[1]

[1] The final part of the line is corrupt, but it must hide a form of *hostire* and include the idea of "requital" or "recompense."

57 Diomedes

Similarly [i.e., a simple and an intensive verb ending in *-tare* from the same stem] *halare* ["to emit"] and *halitare* ["to breathe out": *hapax legomenon*]: Ennius in *Lytra*:

> as the four-footed animals breathing out flame
> <make> their way on high

58 Diom., *GL* I, pp. 387.21–88.2

est tertium his [i.e., "odi" et "memini"] simile, ut quidam
putant (nec enim defuerunt qui hoc verbum praesentis
temporis esse dicerent), novi novisti novit; et id simile est
instanti et perfecto, ut memini. . . . alii similiter declinant
utrumque tempus, quasi nosse, ut meminisse. apud ve-
teres pluraliter huius verbi instans colligitur, cum nomus
dicunt pro eo quod est novimus, ita ut Ennius in Lu{s}tris:

tr　　nos quiescere aequum est; nomus ambo Ulixem

59 Non., p. 111.7–20 M. = 159 L.

FUAM: sim vel fiam. . . . Ennius H{a}ectoris lytris:

tr[8]?　　　　　　　　　　　　　at ego, omnipotens,
tr[7]　　ted exposco ut hoc consilium Achivis auxilio fuat

　　2 te⟨d⟩ *Bothe*: te *codd.*　　　auxilio *Vossius*: auxilii *codd.*

60 Non., p. 222.25–28 M. = 329 L.

SPECUS genere masculino . . . Ennius Lytris:

ia/tr　　inferum vastos specus

58 Diomedes

There is a third one similar to these [the verbs "I hate" and "I remember"], as some believe (for people were not lacking who said that this verb was of the present tense): "I have learned = know," "you have learned = know," "he / she / it has learned = knows"; and this is similar with respect to present and perfect, like "I remember." . . . Others conjugate both tenses similarly, as if "to know" <was> like "to remember." Among the ancients the present of this verb is found in the plural, as they say *nomus* ["we know": unusual contracted form in first person plural with present meaning] for this that is *novimus* ["we have learned = know"], as Ennius in *Lytra*:

it is right for us to be quiet; we both know Ulixes

59 Nonius

fuam ["I might be"]: "I may be" or "I may become" [present subjunctive of *sum* or *fio*]. . . . Ennius in *Hectoris Lytra*:

but you, almighty one,
I ask that this plan be of benefit to the Achaeans

60 Nonius

specus ["cave"], of masculine gender . . . Ennius in *Lytra*:

the vast caves [*acc.*] of those below

61 Non., p. 355.3–19 M. = 562–63 L.

OCCUPARE est proprie praevenire. . . . Ennius H{a}ectoris ly{s}tris:

ia⁶   Hector vi summa armatos educit {in} foras
castrisque castra ultro iam conferre occupat

    1 H{a}ector vi *Delrius*: haectorei (-ii) *codd.*   {in} *del.*
Iunius   2 ‹con›ferre *Vossius*: ferre *codd.*

62 Non., p. 399.8–10 M. = 641 L.

SPERNERE rursum segregare. Ennius H{a}ectoris lytris:

tr⁷   melius est virtute ius: nam saepe virtutem mali
nanciscuntur; ius atque aecum se a malis spernit pro-
cul

    1 {e}ius *Scaliger*: eius *codd.*

63 Non., p. 407.24–26 M. = 655 L.

TENACIA est perseverantia et duritia. Ennius H{a}ectoris lytris:

?   † ducet quadrupedum iugo invitam doma infrena
et iuge valida quorum tenacia infrenari minis †

61 Nonius

occupare ["to seize, to be the first with an action"] is strictly speaking "to arrive first, to forestall." . . . Ennius in *Hectoris lytra*:

> Hector leads armed men outside with full force,
> and on his own initiative he is now the first to pitch
>   camp against camp

62 Nonius

spernere ["to spurn"; "to dissociate": rare and ante-class.] also ‹means› "to dissociate." Ennius in *Hectoris lytra*:

> better than manliness is the law: for often bad people
> acquire manliness; the law and what is right
>   dissociate themselves far from the bad

63 Nonius

tenacia ["tenacity": otherwise only attested in late Latin] is "steadfastness" and "endurance" [i.e., in a positive sense, not "stubbornness"]. Ennius in *Hectoris lytra*:

> he will lead . . . (?)[1]

[1] The fragment describes someone leading yoked horses by the bridle against their will, perhaps in a simile, but the status of the text is too corrupt to attempt a translation.

64 Non., p. 467.23–40 M. = 749 L.

VAGAS, pro vagaris. . . . Ennius Hectoris lytris:

tr^7 constitit, credo, Scamander; arbores vento vacant

vacant *Columna*: vagant *codd.*

65 Non., p. 469.25–31 M. = 753 L.

CUNCTANT, pro cunctantur. . . . Ennius [*Praet.* F 3] . . .
idem Hectoris lytris:

? qui cupiant dare arma Achilli † ut ipse † cunctent

† ut ipse † *Jocelyn*: ut ipse *codd.*

66 Non., p. 472.21–25 M. = 758 L.

CONMISERESCIMUS. . . . Ennius Hectoris ly{s}tris:

tr^8?   per vos et vostrum
tr^7 imperium et fidem, Myrmidonum vigiles,
            conmiserescite

1 per vos *Delrius, Palmerius ap. Gruterum*: servos *codd.*

70

64 Nonius

vagas ["you (*sing.*) roam": rare and ante-class. active form], instead of *vagaris* [standard deponent form]. . . . Ennius in *Hectoris lytra*:

> the Scamander, I believe, has come to a standstill; the trees are free[1] from wind

[1] Since the line does not make sense with a form of *vago*, it is generally believed that Nonius mistook *vacant* for *vagant* and explained it as a nondeponent form of the verb *vagor*.

65 Nonius

cunctant ["they hesitate": rare and ante-class. active form], instead of *cunctantur* [standard deponent form]. . . . Ennius [*Praet.* F 3] . . . the same poet in *Hectoris lytra*:

> they who may wish to give arms to Achilles . . . they may hesitate (?)[1]

[1] The text in the line's second half is corrupt, and the precise sense cannot be restored.

66 Nonius

conmiserescimus ["we have pity": ante-class.]. . . . Ennius in *Hectoris lytra*:

> you, by both your
> power and loyalty, watchmen of the Myrmidons, have
>   pity

67 Non., p. 489.29–30 M. = 786 L.

TUMULTI. Ennius H{a}ectoris lytris:

*ia*⁸   quid hoc hic clamoris, quid tumulti est? nomen qui
         usurpat meum?

68 Non., p. 490.6–7 M. = 787 L.

STREPITI, pro strepitus. Ennius Hectoris lytris:

ia/tr   quid in castris strepiti est?

69 Non., p. 504.30–36 M. = 811 L.

SONIT, pro sonat. . . . Ennius H{a}ectoris lytris:

*tr*⁷   ‹a›es sonit, franguntur hastae, terra sudat sanguine

         ‹a›es *Faber*: et *codd.*

67 Nonius

tumulti ["of tumult": rare and ante-class. form of genitive, instead of *tumultūs*]. Ennius in *Hectoris lytra*:

> what is this shouting here, what this tumult? who
> makes use of my name?[1]

1 Sometimes connected with Enn. *Trag.* F 68.

68 Nonius

strepiti ["of noise": rare and ante-class. form of genitive], instead of *strepitūs* [regular form of genitive]. Ennius in *Hectoris lytra*:

> what noise is there in the camp?[1]

1 Sometimes connected with Enn. *Trag.* F 67. The structure of Nonius' dictionary suggests that these two pieces followed closely upon one another.

69 Nonius

sonit ["sounds": third-conjugation form ante-class.], instead of *sonat* [first conjugation]. . . . Ennius in *Hectoris lytra*:

> bronze arms sound, spears are broken, the ground
> sweats with blood

70 Non., pp. 510.32–11.11 M. = 821–22 L.

SAEVITER, pro saeve. . . . Ennius Phoenice [*Trag.* F 114]:
. . . Ennius Hectoris ly{s}tris:

tr^7 saeviter fortuna ferro cernunt de victoria

71 Non., p. 518.3–26 M. = 833–34 L.

DEREPENTE: . . . Ennius Phoenice [*Trag.* F 116]: . . . Ennius Hectoris ly{s}tris:

tr^7 ecce autem caligo oborta est, omnem prospectum
             abstulit
         derepente; contulit sese in pedes

HECUBA (F 72–81)

This tragedy deals with the fate of queen Hecuba, Priam's wife, after the fall of Troy. Tragedies of the same title are known for Euripides and Accius (Trag. 481 R.²⁻³). The model of Ennius' tragedy is probably Euripides' Hecuba (F 73) as well as parts of Euripides' Troades.

The fragments of Ennius' tragedy apparently display Hecuba lamenting (F 74, 78, 80), a dialogue between her and Ulixes (F 73), statements about Hecuba's children (F 74, 79), and an utterance by the herald Talthybius (F 81). The following unattributed fragments have been mentioned as possibly belonging to this tragedy: Enn. Trag. F 155, 166, 170, 200.

70 Nonius

saeviter ["ferociously": ante-class. form of adverb], instead of *saeve* [standard form]. . . . Ennius in *Phoenix* [*Trag.* F 114]: . . . Ennius in *Hectoris lytra*:

> ferociously, with luck and steel, do they decide
>   victory by fighting

71 Nonius

derepente ["suddenly": mainly ante- and post-class.]: . . . Ennius in *Phoenix* [*Trag.* F 116]: . . . Ennius in *Hectoris lytra*:

> but see, darkness arose: it took away the entire view
>   suddenly; he took to his heels

HECUBA (F 72–81)

Della Casa (1962, 73) suggested that the play was first performed in about 188 BC; Fleckenstein (1953, 66–69) tentatively proposed a date of about 200 BC. Osann (1816, 126–49) and Fleckenstein (1953, 59–61) compare the tragedies by Ennius and Euripides.

Bibl.: Suerbaum 2003, 219; Manuwald 2001 [2004], 138. Comm.: Jocelyn 1967, 303–18; Masiá 2000, 376–418. Lit.: Osann 1816, 126–49; Ribbeck 1849, 5–6; 1875, 142–46; Fleckenstein 1953, 59–61; Della Casa 1962; Rosner 1970, 42; Paduano 1974, 38–39; Traina 1974, 125–44; Masiá 1999; Broccia 2000; Rosato 2003a; Stockert 2004, 278; Scafoglio 2007.

72 Varro, *Ling.* 7.6

templum tribus modis dicitur: ab natura, ab auspicando, a similitudine; ⟨ab⟩ natura in caelo, ab auspiciis in terra, a similitudine sub terra. in caelo templum dicitur, ut in Hecuba:

ia[8]   o magna templa caelitum, commixta stellis splendidis

in terra, ut in Periboea [Pac. *Trag.* 309–10 R.[2–3]]: . . . . sub terra, ut in Andromacha [Enn. *Trag.* F 24]: . . .

73 Gell. *NA* 11.4

Euripidis versus sunt in Hecuba verbis, sententia, brevitate insignes inlustresque; [2] Hecuba est ad Ulixen dicens [Eur. *Hec.* 293–95]:

> τὸ δ᾽ ἀξίωμα, κἂν κακῶς λέγῃ⟨ς⟩ [*Muretus; cf.* dices in *Enn.*], τὸ σὸν
> νικᾷ [πείσει *vel* πείθει *codd. Eur.*]· λόγος γὰρ ἔκ τ᾽ ἀδοξούντων ἰὼν
> κἀκ τῶν δοκούντων αὐτὸς [αὐτὸς *plur. codd. Eur.*] οὐ ταὐτὸν σθένει.

[3] hos versus Q. Ennius, cum eam tragoediam verteret, non sane incommode aemulatus est. versus totidem Enniani hi sunt:

72 Varro, *On the Latin Language*

The word *templum* ["sacred area, temple"] is used in three ways: with regard to nature, to taking the auspices, to similarity; ‹with regard to› nature, in the sky; to taking the auspices, on the earth; to similarity, beneath the earth. In the sky *templum* is used as in *Hecuba*:[1]

> you mighty sacred areas of those dwelling in heaven,
>   combined with shining stars

On the earth, as in *Periboea* [Pac. *Trag.* 309–10 R.[2–3]]: . . . , beneath the earth, as in *Andromacha* [Enn. *Trag.* F 24]: . . .

[1] This line is assigned to a tragedy entitled *Hecuba*, but not explicitly attributed to Ennius. So it could also come from Accius' *Hecuba*, but Varro quotes Accius rarely and his *Hecuba* never. Moreover, this verse is comparable to lines in Euripides' *Hecuba*, presumably Ennius' model (Eur. *Hec.* 68–70).

73 Gellius, *Attic Nights*

There are verses by Euripides in his *Hecuba*, outstanding and brilliant in their diction, thought and conciseness; [2] Hecuba is saying to Ulixes [Eur. *Hec.* 293–95]:

> But your reputation, even if you speak falsely,
> prevails; for a speech coming from those without
>   reputation
> and the same coming from those enjoying reputation
>   do not have the same force.

[3] When Ennius adapted this tragedy, he emulated these verses, certainly not unbecomingly. The Ennian verses, the same in number, are the following:

tr^7 haec tu etsi perverse dices, facile Achivos flexeris;
     nam cum opulenti locuntur pariter atque ignobiles,
     eadem dicta eademque oratio aequa non aeque valet.

[4] bene, sicuti dixi, Ennius; sed "ignobiles" tamen et
"opulenti" ἀντὶ ἀδοξούντων καὶ δοκούντων satisfacere
sententiae non videntur; nam neque omnes ignobiles
ἀδοξοῦσι, ‹neque omnes opulenti εὐδοξοῦσιν› [add.
codd. rec.].

2 nam cum opulenti *Columna*: opulenti nam *codd.*

74 Non., pp. 115.28–16.1 M. = 166 L.

GUTTATIM: . . . Ennius Hecuba:

ia^6 vide hunc meae in quem lacrumae guttatim cadunt

hunc *Mercerus*: hinc *codd.*: hanc *Delrius*   in quem *Mer-
cerus*: inquam *codd.*: in quam *Delrius*

75 Non., p. 116.31–32 M. = 167 L.

GRATULARI: gratias agere. Ennius Hecuba:

tr^7 Iuppiter tibi summe tandem male re gesta gratulor

Even if you say this mistakenly, you will easily move
    the Achaeans;
for when wealthy people and those of low birth speak
    in the same way,
the same words and the same speech, though equal,
    do not have value equally.

[4] Ennius, as I said, did well; but "of low birth" and
"wealthy," in place of "those without reputation" and
"those enjoying reputation" do not seem to render the
meaning satisfactorily; for neither are all people of low
birth without reputation, ‹nor do all wealthy people enjoy
reputation›.

74 Nonius

guttatim ["drop by drop": rare and ante- and post-class.]:
. . . Ennius in *Hecuba*:

look at him, on whom my tears fall drop by drop[1]

[1] Cf. Eur. *Hec.* 760.

75 Nonius

gratulari ["to congratulate"]: "to give thanks" [ante-class.
meaning]. Ennius in *Hecuba*:

highest Jupiter, I give thanks to you indeed, the deed
    having been done badly

76 Non., p. 153.22–32 M. = 225 L.

PERBITERE: perire. . . . Ennius Hecuba:

*ia*⁶   set numquam scripstis qui parentem aut hospitem
      necasset quo quis cruciatu perbiteret

> 1 scrip{si}stis *Vossius*: scripsistis *codd.*   qui{s} *Iunius*: quis *codd.*   2 necasset *ed. princ.*: necassat *codd.*   quo quis *cod. unus*: quos quis *codd. rel.*   cruciatu *cod. unus*: cruciatur *codd. rel.*

77 Non., p. 223.24–26 M. = 330 L.

SALUM neutri generis est vulgari consuetudine. masculini. Ennius Hecuba:

ia/tr   undantem salum

78 Non., p. 224.6–11 M. = 331 L.

SANGUIS masculino genere in consuetudine habetur. . . . neutro Ennius Hecuba:

*tr*⁷   heu me miseram! interii. pergunt lavere sanguen
          sanguine.

Cf. Non., pp. 466.18–2, 503.38–4.7 M. = 746–47, 809–10 L.

79 Non., p. 342.23–32 M. = 541 L.

MODICUM in consuetudine pausillum volumus significare; modicum veteres moderatum et cum modo dici volunt. . . . Ennius Hecuba:

*tr*⁷   quae tibi in concubio verecunde et modice morem
          gerit

76 Nonius

perbitere ["to perish": ante-class.]: *perire* ["to perish"]. . . .
Ennius in *Hecuba*:

> but you [*plur.*] have never written down by what
> torture someone should perish who killed a parent
> or guest

77 Nonius

salum ["sea"] is of neuter gender in general usage. ‹It also
exists in› masculine gender [*hapax legomenon*]. Ennius in
Hecuba:

> the surging sea [*acc.*]

78 Nonius

sanguis ["blood"] is treated as being of masculine gender
in common usage. . . . Ennius in *Hecuba* ‹uses it as a›
neuter [*sanguen*]:

> Alas, wretched me [*fem.*]! I am undone. They go on
> to bathe blood in blood.[1]

1 Cf. Eur. *Hec.* 154–58, 180, 231–33, 438–40.

79 Nonius

modicum ["modest"] we intend to mean "a little" in com-
mon usage; *modicum* the ancients intended to be used as
"moderate" and "with moderation." . . . Ennius in *Hecuba*:

> a woman who in bed grants your wish decently and
> with restraint

80 Non., p. 474.32–34 M. = 761 L.

MISERETE. Ennius ‹H›ecuba:

an	miserete anuis;
an⁴	date ferrum qui me anima privem

1 {m}anu‹i›s *Scaliger*: manus *codd.*

81 Non., p. 507.19–21 M. = 816 L.

EVENAT, pro eveniat. Ennius Hecuba:

ia⁶	senex sum: utinam mortem obpetam prius quam
	evenat
	quod in pauperie mea senex graviter gemam!

Cf. Non., p. 494.3–5 M. = 792 L.

IPHIGENIA (F 82–88)

*Tragedies of the same title are known for the Greek dra-
matists Aeschylus (F 94 TrGF), Sophocles (F 305–12
TrGF), Euripides* (Iphigenia Taurica *and* Iphigenia Auli-
densis) *and Polyidus (?) (78 F 1–2 TrGF [*’Ιφιγενεία ἡ ἐν
Ταύροις?*]) as well as for the Roman poet Naevius (Trag.
19 R.² = 16 R.³ = F 16 TrRF [fort. Taurica]). The model for
Ennius' tragedy is probably Euripides'* Iphigenia in Aulis,
*which revolves around the sacrifice of Agamemnon's
daughter Iphigenia at Aulis to enable the Greeks to sail to*

82

TRAGEDIES: IPHIGENIA

80 Nonius

miserete ["have pity": deponent forms more common for personal verb]. Ennius in *Hecuba*:

> have pity on an old woman;
> give ⟨me⟩ a sword by which I can deprive myself of
> life[1]

[1] Cf. Eur. *Hec.* 419.

81 Nonius

evenat ["may happen": rare and ante-class. form of subjunctive], instead of *eveniat* [standard form]. Ennius in *Hecuba*:

> I [Talthybius?] am an old man: if I could meet death
> before something happens
> that I, as an old man in poverty, would deeply
> lament![1]

[1] Cf. Eur. *Hec.* 497–98.

IPHIGENIA (F 82–88)

Troy (see, e.g., Aesch. Ag. 104–247; Lucr. 1.84–101; Prokl. Cypria [p. 32.55–63 Davies]; Apollod. Epit. 3.21–22; Hyg. Fab. 98; Dict. 1.20–23). Yet in Ennius there is a chorus of soldiers rather than of maidens.

In addition to a song of this chorus (F 84), the fragments of Ennius' tragedy seem to include a conversation between Agamemnon and his servant (F 83, 86), an argument concerning Agamemnon and Menelaus (F 87), Achilles criticizing observers of heavenly bodies (F 82), and pre-

83

sumably the sacrifice of Iphigeneia (F 85). The following unattributed fragments have been suggested as possibly belonging to this tragedy: Enn. Trag. *F 194;* Trag. inc. inc. *23–24, 26;* Enn. Trag. *194–96 R.*[2–3] *= Adesp. F 68, 10, 124 TrRF.*

On the relationship between the Greek and the Roman versions, see Bergk 1844, 229–30; Lo-Cascio 1892, 117–18; Skutsch 1905, 2595–96; Lenchantin de Gubernatis 1913, 416/28; Fleckenstein 1953, 61–65.

82 Cic. *Rep.* 1.30

cuique [i.e., Aelio Sexto] contra Galli studia disputanti in ore semper erat ille [ille *fort. cod. corr.*: illa *cod.*] de Iphigenia Achilles:

tr^8 astrologorum signa in caelo quid sit observationis,
        cum Capra aut Nepa aut exoritur nomen aliquod
           beluarum:
tr^7 quod est ante pedes nemo spectat, caeli scrutantur
           plagas.

Cf. Cic. *Div.* 2.30; Sen. *Apocol.* 8.2–3; Donat. ad Ter. *Ad.* 386; Non., p. 145.12–17 M. = 211 L.

83 Varro, *Ling.* 7.73

an^4 quid noctis videtur?—in altisono
     caeli clipeo temo superat

     1–4 *sic dist. Kent*: alii alia

Bibl.: Suerbaum 2003, 219; Manuwald 2001 [2004], 139–40. Comm.: Jocelyn 1967, 318–42; Masiá 2000, 419–72. Lit.: Ribbeck 1875, 94–104; Vahlen 1878; Skutsch 1906; Fleckenstein 1953, 61–65; Skutsch 1953; Ziegler 1957; Rychlewska 1957/58; Selem 1967; Courcelle 1970; Rosner 1970, 42–44; Büchner 1973; Paduano 1974, 39–42; Traina 1974, 144–55; Pelosi 1988; Baker 1989; Aretz 1999, 231–88; Faller 2000; Stockert 2004, 276–77; Caldini Montanari 2007.

82 Cicero, *On the Republic*

And when he [Sextus Aelius] was arguing against Gallus' [C. Sulpicius Gallus'] pursuits, there constantly was on his lips the famous Achilles from *Iphigenia*:

> as regards the star-readers' signs in the sky, what observation there is,
> when Capella or Scorpio or some other constellation named after beasts appears:
> what is before one's feet nobody watches, they scrutinize the expanses of the sky.

83 Varro, *On the Latin Language*

> What time of night does it seem to be?—In the high-sounding
> shield of the sky the Wain surmounts

      stellas sublimen agens etiam
an   atque etiam noctis iter.

hic multam noctem ostendere volt a temonis motu; . . .

   3 sublime‹n› *Buecheler*: sublime *cod.*

Cf. Varro, *Ling.* 5.19; Apul. *De deo Soc.* 2 (121); Fest., pp. 454.36–
56.6 L.

84 Gell. *NA* 19.10.11–13

atque ibi Iulius Celsinus admonuit in tragoedia quoque
Enni, quae Iphigenia inscripta est, id ipsum, de quo quae-
rebatur [i.e., "praeterpropter"], scriptum esse et a gram-
maticis contaminari magis solitum quam enarrari. [12]
quocirca statim proferri Iphigeniam Q. Enni iubet. in eius
tragoediae choro inscriptos esse hos versus legimus:

tr   otio qui nescit uti,
tr⁷   plus negoti habet quam cum est negotium in negotio.
       nam cui, quod agat, institutum est, non ullo negotio

   2 negoti{i} *Carrio*: negotii *codd.*   3 ‹n›on ullo *Hermann*:
in illo *codd. pler.*

---

   [1] An educated Numidian, a friend of Gellius, a member of the
circle of grammarians and rhetoricians in Fronto's house.
   [2] There is no chorus of soldiers in Euripides' *Iphigenia in
Aulis*; therefore, it is uncertain whether Ennius added an element
from another Greek tragedy and/or to what extent he changed the
Greek model. Play with the same word in different forms and

the stars, making its journey
of night high up more and more.[1]

He intends to indicate late night from the movement of
the Wain [the constellation also called the Wagon or the
Great Bear, Ursa Major]; . . .

[1] These lines are not explicitly attributed to Ennius' *Iphige-
neia*, but various pieces are assigned to Ennius or to Agamemnon
by the quoting authors, and they are similar to verses in Euripi-
des' *Iphigeneia in Aulis*, where Agamemnon inquires about the
stars (Eur. *Iph. A.* 6–10).

84 Gellius, *Attic Nights*

And here Iulius Celsinus[1] called attention to the fact that
also in Ennius' tragedy that is entitled *Iphigeneia* this very
word that was being investigated [*praeterpropter*, "more
or less"] had been written and was normally spoiled rather
than explained by grammarians. [12] Therefore he or-
dered Ennius' *Iphigeneia* to be brought forward immedi-
ately. We read the following verses written in a chorus of
this tragedy:[2]

> He who does not know how to use *otium*
>   ["leisure"]
> has more *negotium* ["work"] than in *negotium* ["when
>   occupied"] when there is *negotium* ["work"].
> For he, for whom what he should do is arranged,
>   does this, he devotes himself to this with no
>   *negotium* ["difficulty"] at all,

senses occurs elsewhere in Ennius (e.g., Enn. *Trag.* F 111; *Inc.*
F 1; *Sat.* F 11).

id agit, id studet, ibi mentem atque animum delectat
suum;

tr 5 otioso in otio animus nescit quid velit.

tr[7] hoc idem est; em neque domi nunc nos nec militiae
sumus:

imus huc, hinc illuc; cum illuc ventum est, ire illinc
lubet.

incerte errat animus, praeterpropter vitam vivitur.

[13] hoc ubi lectum est, tum deinde Fronto ad grammati-
cum iam labentem "audistine," inquit "magister optime
Ennium tuum dixisse 'praeterpropter' et cum sententia
quidem tali, quali severissimae philosophorum esse obiur-
gationes solent? petimus igitur, dicas, quoniam de En-
niano iam verbo quaeritur, qui sit remotus huiusce versus
sensus: 'incerte errat animus, praeterpropter vitam vivi-
tur.'"

4 <id> *suppl. Ribbeck*[1]   5 in otio *Stephanus*: initio *codd.*

85 Fest., p. 218.21–25 L.

OB praepositione antiquos usos esse pro "ad" testis est
Ennius, cum ait lib. XIIII [14 *Ann.* F 9] . . . et in Iphigenia:

ia[6] Acherontem obibo, ubi Mortis thesauri obiacent

obibo *ed. princ.*: ad(h)ibo *codd.*

therein he delights his intellect and mind;
in *otiosum otium* ["leisurely leisure"] the mind does   5
    not know what it wants.
This is the same: look, we are now neither at home
    nor on campaign:
we go here, then there; when one has gone there, it
    pleases to move from there.
The mind wanders doubtfully; one lives a life more or
    less.

[13] As soon as this was read, Fronto[3] then said to the grammarian, who was already wavering: "Did you hear, greatest master, that your Ennius used *praeterpropter* ["more or less"] and indeed with the kind of meaning for which the criticisms of philosophers tend to be most serious? We are therefore seeking—do tell us—since an Ennian word is now being investigated, what the deep sense of this line is: 'the mind wanders doubtfully; one lives a life more or less.'"

[3] Marcus Cornelius Fronto, the rhetor and tutor of Marcus Aurelius.

85 Festus

That the ancients used the preposition *ob* for *ad* ["toward"] has Ennius as a witness, since he says in Book 14 [14 *Ann.* F 9] . . . and in *Iphigenia*:[1]

I will go toward Acheron, where the treasures of
    Death lie nearby

[1] This fragment is sometimes connected with a quotation in Cic. *Tusc.* 1.116. Yet, while both extracts concern Iphigeneia, there is no clear evidence that they belong together or that the piece Cicero quotes is by Ennius.

86 Fest., p. 292.7–16 L.

PEDUM est quidem baculum incurvum, quo pastores utun-
tur ad conprehendendas oves, aut capras, a pedibus. cuius
meminit etiam Vergilius in Bucolicis, cum ait [Verg. *Ecl.*
5.88]: "at tu sume pedum." sed in eo versu, qui est in
Iphigenia{e} Enni:

an⁴ procede, gradum proferre pedum,
an⁴ᶜ/ nitere, ccssas, o fide
paroem

id ipsum baculum significari cum ait Verrius, mirari satis
non possum, cum sit ordo talis, et per eum significatio
aperta: "gradum proferre pedum cessas nitere."

o fide *Schol. Veron., om. Fest.*

Cf. Schol. Veron. ad Verg. *Ecl.* 5.88.

87 Iul. Ruf., *RLM*, p. 41.28–30

ἀγανάκτησις: indignatio, quae fit maxime pronuntiati-
one. Ennius in Iphigenia:

tr⁷ Menelaus me obiurgat; id meis rebus regimen restitat

rest<it>at *Bentley*: restat "*cod.*"

86 Festus

pedum ["shepherd's crook"] is in fact a curved staff that shepherds use to catch hold of ewes or she-goats, ⟨derived⟩ from *pedes* ["feet"]. Virgil too mentions it in the *Eclogues*, when he says [Verg. *Ecl.* 5.88]: "but you take the *pedum*." But in this line, which is in Ennius' *Iphigenia*:

> move forward, you hesitate to advance the step of
>   your feet,
> make an effort, O trusty one[1]

when Verrius says that this very word denotes a staff, I cannot wonder enough, since the order is as follows, and thereby the meaning is obvious: "you hesitate to advance the step of your feet, make an effort."[2]

[1] Cf. Eur. *Iph. A.* 1–3, 138–39.   [2] Since *pedum* ("shepherd's crook": nom. or acc. sing. neut.) and *pedum* ("feet": gen. plur. masc.) look the same and the word order of this fragment (with *nitere* on its own inserted into the construction) is intricate, there was uncertainty even in antiquity about its punctuation and construction.

87 Iulius Rufinianus

"vexation" [in Greek]: "indignation" [in Latin], which mainly comes about by the way of speaking. Ennius in *Iphigenia*:

> Menelaus upbraids me; his exercise of control keeps
>   offering resistance to my affairs[1]

[1] Cf. Eur. *Iph. A.* 327, 329, 331.

88 Serv. Dan. ad Verg. *Aen.* 1.52

sane "vasto" pro desolato veteres ponebant. Ennius Iphigenia:

tr⁷?   quae nunc abs te viduae et vastae virgines sunt

MEDEA (EXUL) (F 89–100)

Tragedies with the title "Medea" were written by Euripides, Neophron (15 F 1–3 TrGF), Euripides II (17 T 1 TrGF), Melanthius I (23 F? TrGF), Morsimus (29 F 1? TrGF), Dicaeogenes (52 F 1a TrGF), Carcinus II (70 F 1e TrGF), Theodorides (78A T 1 TrGF), Diogenes Sinopensis (88 F 1e TrGF), Biotus? (205 F 1 TrGF) in Greek, and by Ovid (p. 230 R.² = p. 267 R.³ = Vol. I, pp. 156–57 TrRF) and Seneca in Latin. Sections of the Medea myth were dramatized in Pacuvius' Medus (Trag. 218–43 R.²⁻³) and Accius' Medea sive Argonautae (Trag. 391–423 R.²⁻³). The part of the myth presented in Ennius (as can be inferred from the fragments) is what happens in Corinth (Medea's revenge on Jason, who is leaving her for another wife), as in Euripides' Medea and Seneca's Medea.

The model for Ennius' tragedy is probably Euripides' Medea (T 28; F 89): many fragments can be compared to similar lines in Euripides (even if altered by Ennius). Since the plots of the two tragedies seem similar, the order of the Ennian fragments according to the plot is likely to be as follows: F 89, 96, 91, 90, 93, 92, 99, 97, 94; the position of the remaining fragments is uncertain. Because of their content, the following unattributed fragments have been suggested as belonging to this tragedy: Enn. Trag. 224–25, 226–27, 228–30, 231–32; Trag. inc. inc. 156/57,

88 Servius Danielis, *Commentary on Virgil*

Indeed the ancients used to put *vastus* ["deserted": commonly used of places] instead of *desolatus* ["left alone"]. Ennius in *Iphigenia*:

> maidens who are now deprived of you and left alone

MEDEA (EXUL) (F 89–100)

172–73 R.[2–3] = Adesp. *34, 71, 73, 25, 32–33, 136* TrRF. *On the order of fragments in the prologue and its setting, see Fraenkel 1932; Maas 1932; Monaco 1950; Nosarti 1999, 55; Rosato 2005, 48–49.*

   Both Medea *(F 89, 94, 97, 98, 99, 100) and* Medea exul *(F 93, 95, 96) have been transmitted as titles for dramas by Ennius. Whether there was one tragedy by Ennius on* Medea *(with two titles denoting the same piece) or whether there were two, a* Medea exul *following Euripides'* Medea *and another* Medea *(set in Athens) after another Greek tragedy (perhaps Euripides'* Aegeus*: F 1–13 TrGF), is therefore debated. It is also uncertain whether the title* Medea exul *is to be attributed to Ennius or to later grammarians. All fragments except F 94 can be fitted into a version of the plot of Euripides'* Medea. *Comparisons between the tragedies by Ennius and Euripides can be found in, e.g., Skutsch 1905, 2596; Röser 1939, 4–31; Fleckenstein 1953, 50–58; Dondoni 1958, 85–95; Kutáková 1969; Lennartz 2001.*

   Arcellaschi (1976; 1990, 38–44) argues that the play was first performed at the Ludi Ceriales *in about 204 BC. Lefèvre (2001, 48–49) suggests 194 BC as the date for the first performance (see also Vogt-Spira 2000). Fleckenstein (1953, 66–69) tentatively proposed about 200 BC.*

Bibl.: Suerbaum 2003, 220; Manuwald 2001 [2004], 141–44. Comm.: Drabkin 1937; Jocelyn 1967, 342–82; Galasso / Montana 2004, 263–75. Lit.: Ribbeck 1875, 149–59; Vahlen 1877; Fraenkel 1932; Maas 1932; Röser 1939, 4–31; Monaco 1950; Fleckenstein 1953, 50–58; Dondoni

89 *Rhet. Her.* 2.34

item vitiosa expositio est quae nimium longe repetitur, hoc modo: . . . hic id quod extremum dictum est, satis fuit exponere, ne Ennium et ceteros poetas imitemur, quibus hoc modo loqui concessum est:

ia[6]   utinam ne in nemore Pelio securibus
            caesa accidisset abiegna ad terram trabes,
            neve inde navis inchoandi exordium
            coepisset, quae nunc nominatur nomine
5   Argo, quia Argivi in ea delecti viri
            vecti petebant pellem inauratam arietis
            Colchis imperio regis Peliae per dolum:
            nam numquam era errans mea domo efferret pedem
            Medea, animo aegro, amore saevo saucia.

nam hic satis erat dicere, si id modo quod satis esset curarent poetae: "utinam ne era errans mea domo efferret pedem / Medea, animo aegro, amore saevo saucia."

9 medea egro amore saucia *add. unus cod. i. m.: ultimum versum non habent codd. pler.*

Cf. Cic. *Inv. rhet.* 1.91; *Cael.* 18; *Fin.* 1.5; *Tusc.* 1.45; *Nat. D.* 3.75; *Fat.* 34–35; *Top.* 61; Varro, *Ling.* 7.33; Quint. *Inst.* 5.10.84; Donat. ad Ter. *Phorm.* 157(4); Iul. Vict., *RLM*, p. 415.23–34; Hieron. *Ep.* 127.5.2; Oros. *Hist.* 1.12.10; Prisc., *GL* II, p. 320.15–18; *GL* III, pp. 423.35–24.8; Lactant. ad Stat. *Theb.* 5.335–37.

1958; Contin Cassata 1967; Williams 1968, 359–63; Ku-táková 1969; Rosner 1970, 44–46; Paduano 1974, 42–43; Arcellaschi 1976; 1990; Zilliacus 1978; Bruno 1980; Arkins 1982; Fantuzzi 1989; Classen 1992, 124–32; Nosarti 1999; Vogt-Spira 2000; Lefèvre 2001; Lennartz 2001; Rosato 2005, 41–154; Boyle 2006, 71–78.

89 *Rhetorica ad Herennium*

Likewise faulty is exposition that is traced back too long, in this way: . . . Here, what was said last would have been sufficient to set forth, so that we do not imitate Ennius and other poets, for whom it is permissible to speak in this way:

> If only the firwood timber had not fallen
> to the ground in the Pelian grove, hewn by axes,
> and if only the ship had not taken from there the first
>   steps to a beginning
> —the ship that is now known by the name of
> Argo, since selected Argive men traveling in her   5
> sought the Golden Fleece of the ram
> from the Colchians, at the behest of king Pelias, by
>   trickery.
> For never would my mistress, Medea, going astray,
>   set her foot outside the house,
> sick in her mind, wounded by savage love.[1]

For here it would be sufficient to say, if the poets were concerned only with what was sufficient: "If only my mistress, Medea, going astray, would not set her foot outside the house, sick in her mind, wounded by savage love."

[1] This speech by Medea's nurse was apparently famous in antiquity and is cited with minor variations a number of times. It is similar to the beginning of Euripides' *Medea* (Eur. *Med.* 1–8).

90 Cic. *Fam.* 7.6.1–2

tu [i.e., Trebatius] modo ineptias istas et desideria urbis et urbanitatis depone et, quo consilio profectus es, id adsiduitate et virtute consequere. hoc tibi tam ignoscemus nos amici quam ignoverunt Medeae

tr[8]   quae Corinthum arcem altam habetis matronae opulentae optumates,

quibus illa manibus gypsatissimis persuasit ne sibi vitio illae verterent quod abesset a patria. nam

tr[7]   multi suam rem bene gessere et publicam patria procul;

tr[8]   multi qui domi aetatem agerent propterea sunt improbati

quo in numero tu certe fuisses nisi te extrusissemus. [2] sed plura scribemus alias. tu, qui ceteris cavere didicisti, in Britannia ne ab essedariis decipiaris caveto et (quoniam Medeam coepi agere) illud semper memento:

tr[7]   qui ipse sibi sapiens prodesse non quit, nequiquam sapit

1 habetis *Politianus apud Gruterum*: habebant [*or. obl.*] *codd.*

Cf. Cic. *Off.* 3.62.

96

90 Cicero, *Letters to Friends*

You [Trebatius] just set aside these follies and longing for
the city and a city lifestyle and accomplish with persever-
ance and energy the plan with which you set off. We, your
friends, will pardon you for this as they pardoned Medea,
the

> rich and noble ladies who have Corinth, the high
> citadel,

whom she persuaded, her hands very white with plaster,
not to count it as a fault of hers that she was away from her
fatherland.[1] For

> many have managed their own and public business
> well, being far away from their fatherland;
> many who spent their lives at home have therefore
> met with disapproval

Among this group you would certainly have been if we had
not thrust you out. [2] But we will write more on another
occasion. You, who have taught others to beware, beware
of being tricked by fighters from war chariots in Britain
and (since I have started to play Medea) always think of
this:

> who, though wise himself, cannot help himself is wise
> in vain[2]

[1] Cicero quotes verses from Ennius as part of his argument
and also seems to paraphrase some of Ennius' wording around
the literal quotations. Only the above lines, however, can be re-
stored as Ennian verses with some degree of certainty.

[2] Cf. Eur. *Med.* 214–24, 252–58; F 905 *TrGF*; Neophron, *Me-
dea*, Pap. Brit. Mus. 186, Milne, Catal. 77.3, p. 56.

91 Cic. *Tusc.* 3.63

sunt autem alii quos in luctu cum ipsa solitudine loqui saepe delectat, ut illa apud Ennium nutrix:

ia[6]   cupido cepit miseram nunc me proloqui
caelo atque terrae Medeai miserias.

    2 Medeai *Turnebus*: medeae *codd.*

92 Cic. *Tusc.* 4.69

quid ait ex tragoedia princeps ille Argonautarum?

tr[7]   tu me amoris magis quam honoris servavisti gratia

quid ergo? hic amor Medeae quanta miseriarum excitavit incendia!

    serva<vi>sti *ed. Ald. / Crat.*: servasti *codd.*

93 Varro, *Ling.* 6.81

cerno idem valet: itaque pro video ait Ennius [*Trag.* F 9]:
. . . . ab eodem est quod ait Medea:

98

91 Cicero, *Tusculan Disputations*

There are others whom it frequently delights in their grief to talk to solitude itself, like the well-known nurse in Ennius:[1]

> Desire has now seized me, poor wretch, to declare Medea's miseries to heaven and earth.[2]

[1] Though not explicitly attributed to Ennius' *Medea*, the attribution to Ennius of an utterance by a nurse talking about Medea makes the fragment's assignation to Ennius' *Medea* virtually certain.   [2] Cf. Eur. *Med.* 56–58.

92 Cicero, *Tusculan Disputations*

What does the famous leader of the Argonauts say in a tragedy?[1]

> you have saved me for the sake of love rather than for the sake of honor[2]

What then? This love of Medea, what conflagrations of misery did it kindle!

[1] These are words by the tragic character Jason about Medea's love following after the events in Colchis. The only Republican tragedy known with an appropriate plot is Ennius' *Medea*, frequently cited by Cicero. Hence, the attribution seems virtually certain, even though the title of the tragedy is not mentioned.

[2] Cf. Eur. *Med.* 526–31.

93 Varro, *On the Latin Language*

cerno ["I see"] means the same [as *video*]: therefore Ennius [*Trag.* F 9] uses it instead of *video* ["I see"]: ... From the same ‹source› is what Medea says:

ia^6 nam ter sub armis malim vitam cernere
quam semel modo parere.

quod, ut decernunt de vita eo tempore, multorum videtur
vitae finis.

1 nam *Non., p. 261.22, om. Varro, Non, p. 261.9*   vita(m)
Non.: multa *Varro*

Cf. Non., pp. 261.7–10, 261.18–22 M. = 398, 398–99 L.

94

a Varro, *Ling.* 7.9

in hoc templo faciundo arbores constitui fines apparet et
intra eas regiones qua oculi conspiciant, id est tueamur, a
quo templum dictum, et contemplare, ut apud Ennium in
Medea: "contempla et templum Cereris ad laevam as-
pice." contempla et conspicare idem esse apparet, . . .

b Non., pp. 469.34–70.6 M. = 753 L.

CONTEMPLA. . . . Ennius Medea: "asta atque Athenas,
anticum opulentum oppidum, / contempla."

ia^6 asta atque Athenas anticum opulentum oppidum
contempla et templum Cereris ad laevam aspice

1 anticum *Roth*: anti eum *codd.*

for I would rather fight for my life under arms three
times
than give birth just once[1]

since, as they decide by fighting over life at this point, the
end of life of many people is seen.[2]

[1] Cf. Eur. *Med.* 248–51.　　[2] Varro explains the meaning
and use of *decernere* (a compound of *cernere*) also with reference
to "to see."

94

a Varro, *On the Latin Language*

In creating this *templum* ["sacred area"] it is evident that
trees are set as boundaries and inside those areas where
the eyes are to see, that is, we are to watch, whence *tem-
plum* ‹is› developed and *contemplare* ["to look at"], as in
Ennius in *Medea*: "look at and behold the temple of Ceres
to the left." That *contempla* ["look at!"] and *conspicare*
["see!"] are the same is evident, . . .

b Nonius

contempla ["look at!"]. . . . Ennius in *Medea*: "stand and
look at Athens, an ancient and wealthy city."

stand and look at Athens, an ancient and wealthy city,
and behold the temple of Ceres to the left[1]

[1] The two separate quotations share one word and the general
tone; the two parts were first connected to form a single fragment
by Scaliger. This piece may come from a different Ennian play on
Medea; at any rate, it goes beyond the plot of Euripides' *Medea*.

95 Prob. ad Verg. *Ecl.* 6.31 (vol. 3.2, pp. 337.29–38.10 Th.-H.)

sed et Homerum ipso hoc loco [Hom. *Il.* 18.483] possumus probare quattuor elementorum mentionem fecisse. . . . similiter et Ennius in Medea exule in his versibus:

tr^7	Iuppiter tuque adeo summe Sol qui omnis res inspicis
?	quique lumine tuo mare terram caelum contines
tr^7	inspice hoc facinus, prius quam fiat, prohibessis scelus.

iam et hic Iuppiter et Sol pro igni, qui mare et terram et caelum continet, ⟨ut⟩ [*Keil*] non dubie caelum pro aere dixerit, . . .

1 omnis res *transp. Keil*: res omnis *codd.*   2 lumine tuo *transp. Porson*: tuo lumine *codd.*   3 fi⟨a⟩t *Keil*: fit *vel* sit *codd.*   prohibessis *Bothe*: prohibesse *vel* prohibe êê *vel* prohibe prohibe esse *codd.*

96 Non., pp. 38.29–39.4 M. = 56 L.

ELIMINARE: extra limen eicere. . . . Ennius Medea exule:

ia^6	antiqua erilis fida custos corporis,
	quid sic te extra aedis exanimatam eliminat?

2 sic *Pius*: sit *codd.*   ⟨te⟩ *Mercerus*   exanimata⟨m⟩ *Jocelyn*: examinata *vel* examinata *codd.*   eliminat *Non., p. 292*: elimina *Non., p. 38*

Cf. Non., p. 292.20–22 M. = 452 L.

95 Probus

But we can prove that Homer too in this very line [*Il.* 18.483] made mention of the four elements. . . . In a similar way [like Virgil and Homer] Ennius too ⟨says⟩ in *Medea exul* in these lines:

> Jupiter and indeed you, greatest Sun, who see all
>   things
> and who surround sea, earth and sky with your light,
> look at this deed before it happens: you may prevent
>   a crime.[1]

Now here too both Jupiter and the Sun instead of fire, who covers sea and earth and sky, so that he doubtlessly said "sky" instead of air, . . .

[1] Cf. Eur. *Med.* 1251–60.

96 Nonius

eliminare ["to turn out of doors": active]: "to throw outside the threshold." . . . Ennius in *Medea exul*:

> Aged loyal guardian of our mistress' person,
> what is turning you, being so out of your mind, out of
>   the house?[1]

[1] The sense of the remark is clear (cf. Eur. *Med.* 49–51). But since Nonius uses the same example to illustrate *eliminare* and *eliminari*, and a few words are corrupt or transmitted in different forms, the precise restoration of the text is not certain (see Jocelyn 1967, ad loc.).

97 Non., pp. 84.31–85.3 M. = 120 L.

CETTE significat dicite vel date, ab eo quod cedo. . . . Ennius in Medea:

?   salvete, optima corpora,
     cette manus vestras measque accipite

98 Non., p. 170.8–9 M. = 250 L.

SUBLIMARE: extollere. Ennius Medea:

ia^6 sol qui candentem in caelo sublimat facem

99 Non., p. 297.16–25 M. = 461 L.

EFFERRE significat proferre. . . . Ennius Medea:

tr^8 utinam ne umquam, Medea Colchis, cupido corde
       pedem extulisses

     Mede<a> Colchis *Lipsius*: Mede cordis *codd.*

100 Non., p. 467.7–14 M. = 748 L.

AUCUPAVI: activum positum pro passivo. . . . Ennius Medea:

ia/tr   fructus verborum aures aucupant

104

97 Nonius

cette ["give me, tell me": plural] means "say" or "give," ‹derived› from that what ‹is› *cedo* [same word in sing., more frequent]. . . . Ennius in *Medea*:

goodbye, you best of loved ones,
give me your hands and take mine[1]

[1] Cf. Eur. *Med.* 1069–72.

98 Nonius

sublimare ["to raise": mainly ante- and post-class.]: "to raise" [more widely used word]. Ennius in *Medea*:

the Sun, who raises a gleaming brand in the sky[1]

[1] Cf. Eur. *Med.* 746–47, 752–53, 764; Acc. *Trag.* 581–82 R.[2–3].

99 Nonius

efferre ["to bring out"] means "to bring forth" [*proferre pedem*: "to step forth, advance"]. . . . Ennius in *Medea*:

if only you, Medea of Colchis, had never stepped
    forth with passionate heart[1]

[1] Cf. Eur. *Med.* 6–8, 431–33.

100 Nonius

aucupavi ["I have caught"]: an active form used instead of the passive one. . . . Ennius in *Medea*:

the ears are catching a harvest of words

MELANIPPA (F 101–6)

*Melanippa, the daughter of Aeolus, was raped by Neptune
and produced two sons (Aeolus and Boeotus). When her
father learned this, he blinded her and put her into prison.
The infants were cast out, but raised first by a cow and
then by herdsmen. When Theano, the wife of Metapontus,
king of Icaria, was pressed for offspring, she sent to herds-
men, who brought her the two boys. Later, Theano bore
two sons of her own and wanted the other ones to be re-
moved. In a fight instigated by Theano, however, Nep-
tune's sons killed the others; thereupon, Theano killed her-
self. Then Neptune appeared to the other pair and informed
them about their parentage. This prompted them to free
their mother and bring her to Metapontus, who then mar-
ried her and adopted her sons. Neptune gave Melanippa
back her sight (see, e.g., hypothesis to Euripides' Μελα-
νίππη ἡ Σοφή [TrGF V.1, pp. 525–26]; Dion. Hal. Rhet.*

101 Gell. *NA* 5.11.10–14

"est autem" inquit "tertium quoque inter duo ista, quae
diiunguntur, cuius rationem prospectumque Bias non
habuit. [11] inter enim pulcherrimam feminam et defor-
missimam media forma quaedam est, quae et a nimiae
pulcritudinis periculo et a summae deformitatis odio va-
cat; [12] qualis a Q. Ennio in Melanippa perquam eleganti
vocabulo

?   stata

MELANIPPA (F 101–6)

8.10 (300–302) [pp. 308–9 Usener / Radermacher]; 8.11 (354–56) [pp. 345–46 Usener / Radermacher]; Hyg. Fab. 186; Hyg. Astr. 2.18; Greg. Cor. [vol. VII, p. 1313 Walz]).

Tragedies of the same title are known for Euripides (F 480–514 TrGF [Μελανίππη ἡ Σοφή et Μελανίππη ἡ Δεσμῶτις]). The model of Ennius' tragedy is believed to be Euripides' Μελανίππη ἡ Σοφή, and it is thought that all preserved fragments belong to a single tragedy.

The fragments of Ennius' tragedy seem to allude to the order to burn the boys (F 104). The unattributed fragment Enn. Trag. F 159 may also belong to this play. On performing Melanippa, *presumably referring to the Ennian tragedy, see T 35.*

Bibl.: Suerbaum 2003, 220. Comm.: Jocelyn 1967, 382–87. Lit.: Hartung 1843, 113–24; Ribbeck 1875, 176–81; Rosner 1970, 46–47.

101 Gellius, *Attic Nights*

"But there is," he[1] said, "also a third thing between those two that are being distinguished, which Bias[2] did not take into account or regard. [11] For between a very beautiful woman and a very ugly one there is one of middling looks, who is free of both the danger of too much beauty and the repulsion of extreme ugliness; [12] such a woman is called

well-balanced

---

[1] Favorinus, a rhetor and philosopher, one of Gellius' interlocutors.   [2] One of the Seven Sages.

dicitur, quae neque κοινή futura sit neque ποινή." [13] quam formam modicam et modestam Favorinus non mi hercule inscite appellabat "uxoriam." [14] Ennius autem in ista, quam dixit, tragoedia eas fere feminas ait incolumi pudicitia esse, quae stata forma forent.

102 Prisc., *GL* II, pp. 516.15–17.11

vetustissimi tamen etiam "scicidi" proferebant, quod solum quoque in usu esse putat Asmonius in arte, quam ad Constantium imperatorem scribit, sed errat. nam . . . Ennius in Melanippa:

ia/tr   cum saxum sciciderit

Cf. Gell. *NA* 6.9.15–17.

with an extremely elegant word by Ennius in *Melanippa*, a woman who will be neither 'common property' [*koinē*] nor 'punishment' [*poinē*]."[3] [13] Indeed, Favorinus called these moderate and modest looks "wifely," not unskillfully. [14] But Ennius in this tragedy, which he mentioned, says that those women who are of well-balanced looks are usually of unblemished chastity.[4]

[3] The pun alludes to a *sententia* attributed to Pittacus, another of the Seven Sages: he did not want to marry, to avoid both women who are "common property" and those who are "punishment" (Stobaeus, *Flor.* 67.17 = 4.22a.17 [IV, p. 497] Hense / Wachsmuth).

[4] The word *"stata"* ("well-balanced") is a quotation from the Ennian tragedy, and the thought reproduced in the last sentence of the extract presumably reflects its context in the tragedy.

102 Priscian

The very ancients, however, also used to give voice to *scicidi* ["I have split": early form of perfect tense, in addition to *scidi*], which [the first person singular] Asmonius,[1] in the art that he writes to the emperor Constantius, believes to be the only one in use, but he errs. For . . . [examples for *scidit, scicidistis, sciciderat, scicidimus*] . . . Ennius in *Melanippa*:

when he / she has split the rock

[1] A grammarian and metrician in the 4th c. AD, author of *Ars ad Constantium imperatorem.*

103 Non., p. 170.10–11 M. = 250 L.

SUPERSTITENT: salvent. Ennius Melanippa:

ia[6]   regnumque nostrum ut sospitent superstitentque

hyperm./
r[v]   Cf. Non., p. 176.2–3 M. = 258 L.

104 Non., p. 246.9–12 M. = 370 L.

AUSCULTARE est obsequi. . . . Ennius Melanippa [mena-
lippa *codd.*]:

cr[4]   mi ausculta, nate: pueros cremari iube

mi{hi} *Fruterius / Vossius*: mihi *codd.*

105 Non., p. 469.3–9 M. = 752 L.

AUGURO. . . . Ennius Melanippa:

ia[6]   certatio hic est nulla quin monstrum siet:
hoc ego tibi dico et coniectura auguro

1 cert<ati>o *Passerat*: certo *codd.*

106 Macrob. *Sat.* 6.4.7 (Verg. *Aen.* 7.9 "splendet tremulo
sub lumine pontus")

"tremulum lumen" de imagine rei ipsius expressum est.
sed prior Ennius in Melanippe:

da[6]   lumine sic tremulo terra et cava caerula candent

103 Nonius

superstitent ["they may keep alive"]: "they may save." Ennius in *Melanippa*:

and so that they may preserve and keep alive our
kingdom

104 Nonius

auscultare ["to listen to"] is "to oblige." . . . Ennius in *Melanippa*:

oblige me, my son: order the boys to be burned

105 Nonius

auguro ["I foretell by augury, I predict"]. . . . Ennius in *Melanippa*:

there is no dispute that there is a portent:
I tell you this and predict it from inference

106 Macrobius, *Saturnalia* (on Virgil, "the sea gleams under the quavering light")

"quavering light" is an expression derived from the appearance of the phenomenon itself. But earlier Ennius ‹used it› in *Melanippe*:

the earth and the blue hollows ‹of the sky› shine thus
with quavering light

NEMEA (F 107–8)

A tragedy of the same title is known for Aeschylus (F *149a TrGF); and there is also a Greek comedy by Theopompus (F 33 K.-A.). The plot of Ennius' tragedy is uncertain: it may have been similar to Euripides' tragedy Hypsipyle *(F 752–69 TrGF), about the Lemnian woman who, as a slave in Nemea, was given charge of the king's son and temporarily neglected him, so that he was killed by a*

107 Non., p. 183.14–15 M. = 269 L.

VENOR: circumvenior. Ennius Nemea:

an⁴?   teneor consaepta, undique venor

108 Prisc., *GL* II, p. 171.4–7

"hic" et "haec" et "hoc pecus"—Ennius in Nemea:

?   pecudi dare vivam marito

potest tamen figurate hoc esse prolatum, ut si dicam "aquila maritus" vel "rex avium" . . .

NEMEA (F 107–8)

snake, which provoked the king's anger; or it may have been about Nemea as the mother of the boy Archemorus (see, e.g., Aesch. F *149a TrGF; Paus. 2.15.2–3; Stat. Theb. 4.646–6.946).

Bibl.: Suerbaum 2003, 220; Manuwald 2001 [2004], 144. Comm.: Jocelyn 1967, 387–88. Lit.: Ribbeck 1875, 159–62; Przychocki 1909; Rosner 1970, 47; Faoro 1989.

107 Nonius

venor ["I am hunted": passive sense]: "I am surrounded." Ennius in *Nemea*:

> I [*fem.*] am held fenced in, I am hunted on all sides

108 Priscian

pecus ["animal"], masculine, feminine and neuter—Ennius in *Nemea*:

> to give her alive to an animal as husband

Yet it can be put forward metaphorically, as if I were to say "an eagle as husband" or "the king of the birds"[1] . . .

[1] In the fragment *pecus* is linked with a masculine noun (*maritus*) and is therefore interpreted as masculine; in the subsequent examples the words retain their grammatical gender, but may still refer to male figures.

PHOENIX (F 109–16)

On the advice of his mother, Phoenix formed a liaison with a courtesan to turn her away from his father, Amyntor. The latter responded with a curse that his son should never have children. This provoked in Phoenix the desire to kill his father, but he did not realize this plan, due to the intervention of the gods and/or his friends and relatives. Instead, Phoenix fled to Phthia, where he was well received by Peleus. He then became Achilles' tutor and later accompanied him to Troy (see, e.g., Hom. Il. *9.447–84; Schol. ad Hom.* Il. *9.453; Apollod.* Bibl. *3.13.8 = 3.175; Suda α 1842 Adler).*

Greek tragedies of the same title are known for Sophocles (F 718–20 TrGF), Euripides (F 803a–18 TrGF), Ion (19 F 36–43 TrGF [Φοῖνιξ ἢ Καινεύς (vel Οἰνεύς?) et Φοῖνιξ β']), Astydamas II (60 F 5d TrGF), and]ẹnodorus

109 Gell. *NA* 6.17.1–11

percontabar Romae quempiam grammaticum . . . , sed discendi magis studio et cupidine, quid significaret "obnoxius" quaeque eius vocabuli origo ac ratio esset. . . . [6] . . . "mittamus" inquam "sicuti vis, . . . [10] iam vero illud etiam Q. Enni quo pacto congruere tecum potest, quod scribit in Pho⟨e⟩nice in hisce versibus?

tr[7] sed virum vera virtute vivere animatum addecet
fortiterque innoxium astare adversum adversarios.

1 addecet *Carrio*: adiecit *codd.*
2 {v}astare *Mueller*: vocare *codd.*

PHOENIX (F 109–16)

(154 F 1 TrGF). The plot of Ennius' tragedy may have used material from Homer's Iliad 9 and/or from Euripides' play.

Ennius' tragedy appears to have dramatized the first stages of the story, focusing on the conflict between Phoenix and Amyntor. It seems to have featured a consultation of Phoenix with friends (F 115), and there are reflections of a confrontation, perhaps between Phoenix and Amyntor (F 110, 112, 114). The following unattributed fragments have been suggested as belonging to this tragedy: Enn. Trag. F 152 and Trag. inc. inc. 214 R.$^{2-3}$ = F 132 TrRF.

Bibl.: Suerbaum 2003, 220; Manuwald 2001 [2004], 144. Comm.: Jocelyn 1967, 389–94; Masiá 2000, 473–94. Lit.: Ribbeck 1875, 191–96; Caviglia 1970, 470–73; Rosner 1970, 47–48.

109 Gellius, *Attic Nights*

In Rome I was questioning a certain grammarian . . . , but rather more out of eagerness and desire to learn what *obnoxius* ["indebted, servile, vulnerable"] meant and what the origin and nature of this word were. . . . [6] . . . "Let's disregard this," I said, "as you wish, . . . [10] but now in what way can this utterance of Ennius, which he writes in the following verses in *Phoenix*, agree with you [your view that *obnoxius* means 'exposed to harm']?

> But it is proper for a man to live animated with real
> virtue
> and, innocent, to stand courageously against
> opponents

115

ea libertas est: qui pectus purum et firmum gestitat;
aliae res obnoxiosae nocte in obscura latent.

[11] at ille oscitans et alucinanti similis: "nunc" inquit
"mihi operae non est. cum otium erit, revises ad me atque
disces, quid in verbo isto et Vergilius et Sallustius et
Plautus et Ennius senserint."

110 Charis., *GL* I, p. 197.22–27 = p. 257 B.

DURITER: Terentius in Adelphis [*Ad.* 45–46] "ruri agere
vitam, semper parce ac duriter / {se}se habere"; ubi Acron
"secundum antiquorum" inquit "consuetudinem." nam et
Ennius in P‹h›oenice

tr⁷   quam tibi ex ore orationem duriter dictis dedit

Cf. Non., p. 512.1–10 M. = 823 L.

111 Non., p. 91.4–8 M. = 129–30 L.

CUPIENTER: cupidissime. . . . Ennius Phoenice:

?   stultus est qui † cupida † cupiens cupienter cupit

cupida *codd.*: † stultus est qui cupida † *Jocelyn*: ‹non›
cupi‹en›da *Ribbeck*

This is liberty: who wears a pure and firm heart;
   other things [i.e., other types of conduct], servile
     ones, are in hiding in shadowy darkness.

[11] But he, gaping and like someone with wandering mind, said: "Now I cannot spare the effort. When there is leisure, you may return to me and you will learn what Virgil, Sallust, Plautus, and Ennius meant by that word."

110 Charisius

duriter ["austerely," "uncouthly"]: Terence in *Adelphoe* [*Ad.* 45–46] "to spend his life in the countryside, always keeping himself thriftily and austerely"; where Acro says "according to the conventions of the ancients." For Ennius too in *Phoenix* ‹says›:

what a speech he gave to you from his mouth with
   words uncouthly spoken

111 Nonius

cupienter ["eagerly": ante-class. adverb]: "most desirously." . . . Ennius in *Phoenix*:

he is stupid who . . . (?), desiring, desires most
   desirously[1]

[1] Part of the fragment is corrupt, but the general sense and the wordplay are clear. To complete the clause an object seems to be required, perhaps denoting something that one should not wish for.

112 Non., p. 245.30–32 M. = 369 L.

ARGUTARI dicitur loquacius proloqui. Ennius Phoenice:

?   † tum tu isti credere † atque exerce linguam ut
        argutarier possis

> † tum tu isti credere † *Jocelyn*: tum tu isti crede *vel* credere
> *codd.*

113 Non., p. 507.22–23 M. = 816 L.

FAXIM: fecerim. Ennius Phoenice:

tr[7]   plus miser sim si scelestum faxim quod dicam fore

> sim *Delrius*: sum *codd.*   scelestum *ed. princ.*: scelestim
> *vel* scelestem *codd.*

114 Non., pp. 510.32–11.10 M. = 821–22 L.

SAEVITER, pro saeve. . . . Ennius Phoenice:

tr[7]   saeviter suspicionem ferre falsam futtilum est

> . . . Ennius Hectoris ly{s}tris [*Trag.* F 70]: . . .

115 Non., p. 514.11–13 M. = 827 L.

FUTTILE: futtiliter. Ennius Phoenice:

tr[7]   ut quod factum est futtile, amici, vos feratis fortiter

> f{u}eratis *ed. princ.*: fueratis *codd.*

112 Nonius

argutari ["to chatter": ante-class. verb] is used for "to talk rather loquaciously." Ennius in *Phoenix*:

> . . . (?) and train your tongue so that you can talk rather loquaciously[1]

[1] The first part of the fragment is too corrupt to be translated, and the meaning is unclear.

113 Nonius

faxim ["I might do": ante-class. form of perfect subjunctive]: *fecerim* [standard form]. Ennius in *Phoenix*:

> I would be more wretched were I to do what I may say will be criminal

114 Nonius

saeviter ["fiercely": ante-class. form of adverb], instead of *saeve* [standard form]. . . . Ennius in *Phoenix*:

> it is a sign of useless people to bear a false suspicion fiercely

. . . Ennius in *Hectoris lytra* [*Trag.* F 70]: . . .

115 Nonius

futtile ["in vain": ante-class. form of adverb]: *futtiliter* [standard form]. Ennius in *Phoenix*:

> so that you, my friends, may bear bravely what has been done in vain

116 Non., p. 518.3–24 M. = 833–34 L.

DEREPENTE. . . . Ennius Phoenice:

tr[7] ibi tum derepente ex alto in altum despexit mare

. . . Ennius Hectoris ly{s}tris [*Trag.* F 71]: . . .

TELAMO (F 117–24)

*Telamon, king of Salamis, had two sons, Teucer and Ajax.
Teucer, his illegitimate son by Hesione, was a strong war-
rior in the Trojan War, often fighting together with his
half-brother Ajax. After the Trojan War and the assign-
ment of Achilles' arms to Ulixes rather than to Ajax, the
latter killed himself while Teucer was away in Mysia. Upon
his return Teucer challenged Agamemnon's decision not to
give Ajax a proper burial. When Teucer eventually came
back to Salamis, his father refused to receive him, since he
regarded him as responsible for the death of his half-
brother or expected him to have avenged it.*

*No tragedies of the same title are known. On the story
see, e.g., Aeschylus'* Salaminiae *(F 216–20 TrGF), Sopho-
cles'* Aiax *and* Teucer *(F 576–79b TrGF), Livius Andro-
nicus'* Teucer *(Trag. inc. inc. 12 R.[2–3] = T 2 TrRF), Pacu-
vius'* Teucer *(Trag. 313–46 R.[2–3]), Schol. ad Pind. N. 4.76,
Vell. Pat. 1.1.1.*

116 Nonius

derepente ["suddenly": mainly ante- and post-class.]. . . .
Ennius in *Phoenix*:

> there then he suddenly looked down to the high sea
>   from on high

. . . Ennius in *Hectoris lytra* [*Trag.* F 71]: . . .

TELAMO (F 117–24)

Ennius' tragedy seems to have focused on the con-
flict between the father Telamon and his son Teucer. The
fragments include a dispute between Telamon and Teucer
(F 118, 120, 123, 124), thoughts by Telamon on the care of
the gods (F 117), and the description of the grief of a
woman (F 122). The following unattributed fragments
may belong to this tragedy: Enn. Trag. F 160 and Trag. inc.
inc. 85–87 R.$^{2-3}$ = F 58 TrRF. On the plot and the order of
fragments, cf. Hermann 1838, 378–82; Ladewig 1848, 24.
*   Bibl.: Suerbaum 2003, 220; Manuwald 2001 [2004],*
145. Comm.: Jocelyn 1967, 394–404; Masiá 2000, 495–
532. Lit.: Schöll 1839, 636–38; Ribbeck 1875, 133–35; Sa-
lem 1938; Caviglia 1970; Rosner 1970, 49; Paduano 1974,
44–46; Grilli 1996.

117

a Cic. *Nat. D.* 3.79

ac nos quidem nimis multa de re apertissuma; Telamo autem uno versu totum locum conficit cur di homines neglegant:

tr⁷   nam si curent, bene bonis sit, male malis; quod nunc
abest

debebant illi quidem omnis bonos efficere, si quidem hominum generi consulebant; sin id minus, bonis quidem certe consulere debebant.

b Cic. *Div.* 1.132

nunc illa testabor non me sortilegos neque eos qui quaestus causa hariolentur, ne psychomantia quidem quibus Appius, amicus tuus, uti solebat, agnoscere; non habeo denique nauci Marsum augurem, non vicanos haruspices, non de circo astrologos, non Isiacos coniectores, non interpretes somniorum; non enim sunt hi aut scientia aut arte divini sed superstitiosi vates inpudentesque harioli

---

[1] The Marsi are a people of central Italy, known as magicians and snake charmers.

[2] Where Cicero's comments or paraphrase surrounding lines 2–5 begin and end is controversial. Here, only the section that clearly has a metrical structure and sounds like an addition to Cicero's argument is assigned to Ennius.

117

a Cicero, *On the Nature of the Gods*

And we ⟨are saying⟩ indeed far too much on a very obvious matter; but Telamon finishes the entire issue, why gods ignore humans, in a single verse:[1]

> for if they cared, good people would fare well, bad
> people badly; this is not the case now

In fact, they should have made all people good, if they really cared for the human race; if not, they should certainly have cared for the good people.

[1] The title of the tragedy is not mentioned in connection with any of the quotations, but lines assigned to Telamon and to Ennius can only appear in the Ennian tragedy named after Telamon. Cicero's comments imply that the order of lines in the tragedy was 6–7, 2–5, 1, and that these lines were not too far away from each other, though they apparently did not follow upon one another directly.

b Cicero, *On Divination*

Now I [Quintus Cicero, the author's brother] will declare that I do not recognize ⟨the value of⟩ fortune-tellers nor those who prophesy for the sake of gain, not even places where the dead are conjured up, whom Appius [Appius Claudius], your friend, was accustomed to employ; hence I regard as nothing a Marsian[1] augur, as nothing diviners in villages, as nothing astrologers from the circus, as nothing soothsayers, worshippers of Isis, as nothing interpreters of dreams; for they are not diviners by either knowledge or skill, but superstitious seers and shameless prophets[2]

tr[7]   aut inertes aut insani aut quibus egestas imperat,
           qui sibi semitam non sapiunt, alteri monstrant viam;
           quibus divitias pollicentur, ab iis drachumam ipsi
               petunt.
5   de his divitiis sibi deducant drachumam, reddant
               cetera.

atque haec quidem Ennius, qui paucis ante versibus esse
deos censet, "sed eos non curare" opinatur, "quid agat
humanum genus." ego autem, qui et curare arbitror et
monere etiam ac multa praedicere, levitate, vanitate, ma-
litia exclusa divinationem probo.

4 ab iis *Lambinus*: ab his *codd.*

c Cic. *Div.* 2.104

primum enim hoc sumitis: "si sunt di, benefici in homines
sunt." quis hoc vobis dabit? Epicurusne? qui negat quic-
quam deos nec alieni curare nec sui; an noster Ennius? qui
magno plausu loquitur adsentiente populo:

tr[7]   ego deum genus esse semper dixi et dicam caelitum,
           sed eos non curare opinor, quid agat humanum genus

et quidem, cur sic opinetur, rationem subicit; sed nihil est
necesse dicere quae sequuntur; tantum sat est intellegi, id
sumere istos pro certo quod dubium controversumque sit.

---

[1] Criticism of seers and comments on their plight as well as
remarks on the lack of interest on the part of the gods also appear
in other ancient dramas and Epicurean texts: e.g., Soph. *Ant.*
1033–47; Eur. *Bacch.* 255–57; *El.* 399–400; *Hec.* 488–91; *Phoen.*
954–59; F 286.1–12 *TrGF*; *Adesp.* F 465 *TrGF*; Men. *Epitr.* 1084–
86; Enn. *Trag.* F 160; Plaut. *Mil.* 692–94; Acc. *Trag.* 142–43,
169–70 R.[2–3]; Lucr. 2.1093–94, 5.82 = 6.58; Hor. *Sat.* 1.5.101–3.

or unskilled or insane or people whom poverty
    governs,
who do not know the path for themselves, ⟨but⟩
    show the way to another;
from those to whom they promise riches, they
    themselves demand a drachma.
From these riches let them deduct a drachma for
    themselves and hand over the rest.

And this Ennius ⟨says⟩, who a few lines earlier voices the
opinion that there are gods, "but" believes that "they do
not care what the human race does." But I, who believe
that they care and also admonish and predict many things,
approve of divination when unreliability, vanity, and wick-
edness have been excluded.

c Cicero, *On Divination*

For first you [Stoics] embrace this: "if there are gods, they
are beneficial toward humans." Who will grant you this?
Epicurus? He who denies that the gods care for any mat-
ter of someone else or their own; or our Ennius? He who
says to great applause, with the agreement of the people:

I have always said and will say that there is a race of
    gods and heaven dwellers,
but I believe that they do not care what the human
    race does.[1]

And indeed he adds a reason why he thinks so; but there
is no need to quote what follows; this much is sufficient to
have it understood, that they embrace as certain what is
doubtful and controversial.

118 Fest., p. 218.2–5 L.

OBSIDIONEM potius dicendum esse, quam obsidium, ad-
iuvat nos testimonio suo Ennius [Pacuvius *unus cod.*] in
Telamone cum ait:

tr^7 scibas natum ingenuum Aiacem, cui tu obsidionem
             paras

item alio loco [*Trag.* F 185]: . . .

   ingenuum *ed. princ.*: ingenium *codd.*

119 Diom., *GL* I, p. 382.10–14

cui enim in dubium cadit quin abnuo abnuis dicamus?
verum apud veteres et abnueo dictum annotamus, ut En-
nius octavo annalium [8 *Ann.* F 6] . . . ; idem in Telamone
ex eo futurum

?   abnuebunt

120 Non., p. 85.20–25 M. = 121 L.

CLARET: clara est vel clareat. . . . Ennius Telamone:

tr^7 nam ita mihi Telamonis patris atque Aeaci et proavi
             Iovis
tr^7?   gratia † ea est † atque hoc lumen candidum claret
             mihi

   1 <Ae>{f}aci et *Vahlen (sec. Bergk)*: faciet *codd.*   2 † ea
est *Lindsay*: ea est *codd.*: ecstat *Traglia*

118 Festus

In that one should say *obsidio* ["blockade"] rather than *obsidium* ["blockade": less common form, mainly ante- and post-class.] Ennius supports us by his testimony in *Telamo*, when he says:

> you knew that Aiax was born in wedlock, to whom
> you present a blockade [i.e., trouble]

Likewise elsewhere [*Trag.* F 185]: . . .

119 Diomedes

For, for whom is this an issue of doubt that we may say *abnuo* ["I refuse"], *abnuis* ["you refuse"]? But we note that among the ancients *abnueo* ["I refuse": old form of verb, apparently only attested here] was also said, as Ennius in the eighth ‹book› of the *Annals* [8 *Ann.* F 6] . . .; the same ‹poet uses› the future from this ‹verb› in *Telamo*:

> they will refuse

120 Nonius

claret ["shines brightly"]: "she is bright" or "it may shine brightly." . . . Ennius in *Telamo*:

> for thus the gratitude to my father Telamon and
> Aeacus [i.e., his grandfather] and my great-
> grandfather Jupiter
> . . . (?), and this radiant light shines brightly for me[1]

[1] For these partly corrupt verses, many conjectures have been proposed; the wording is difficult to restore. The lines seem to include a solemn assertion by Teucer on the loyalty to his paternal family.

121 Non., pp. 159.38–60.6 M. = 235–36 L.

PORCET significat prohibet. . . . Ennius Telamone:

*tr*⁷   deum me sentit facere pietas, civium porcet pudor

122 Non., p. 172.19–20 M. = 253 L.

SQUALAM, pro squalidam. Ennius Telamone:

*tr*⁷   strata terrae lavere lacrimis vestem squalam et
         sordidam

Cf. Non., pp. 503.38–4.6 M. = 809–10 L.

123 Non., p. 475.20–29 M. = 762–63 L.

PARTIRET, pro partiretur. . . . Ennius Telamone:

*tr*⁷   eandem me in suspicionem sceleris partivit pater

124 Non., pp. 505.35–6.1 M. = 813 L.

AUDIBO, pro audiam. Ennius Telamone:

*tr*⁷   more antiquo audibo atque auris tibi contra utendas
         dabo

121 Nonius

porcet ["prevents"] means "keeps off." . . . Ennius in *Telamo*:

> reverence for the gods advises that I do ⟨this⟩, regard
> for the citizens keeps me off

122 Nonius

squalus ["unkempt": *hapax legomenon*], instead of *squalidus* ["filthy"]. Ennius in *Telamo*:

> she stretched out on the ground, to bathe with tears
> her filthy and squalid garment

123 Nonius

partiret ["he would apportion"], instead of *partiretur* [deponent form, more common in class. Latin]. . . . Ennius in *Telamo*:

> my father has apportioned to me a share in the same
> suspicion of the crime[1]

[1] The construction of this line is unusual. It seems to mean that Teucer assumes that his father suspects him as well as the Atridae of being responsible for the death of Ajax and/or the plan not to give him a proper burial.

124 Nonius

audibo ["I will hear"], instead of *audiam* [class. form of future tense]. Ennius in *Telamo*:

> according to ancient custom I will hear and will give
> my ears for you to use in turn

TELEPHUS (F 125–31)

Telephus, the son of Hercules and Auge, was wounded by Achilles' spear when the Greeks stopped in Mysia on their way to Troy. Having received an oracle saying that what wounded him would also heal him, Telephus, clothed in a beggar's rags, traveled to Mycenae, where the Greek leaders were assembled. He was indeed healed, by being touched with Achilles' spear, and he then led the Greeks to Troy, but, as a son-in-law of Priam, did not participate in the fighting (see, e.g., Hor. Ars P. 95–107; Hyg. Fab. 101; Lib. Decl. 5.8–9 [pp. 5.308–9 Foerster]; Apollod. Epit. 3.17–20).

Tragedies of the same title are known for Aeschylus (F 238–40 TrGF), Sophocles (F 580 TrGF), Euripides (F 696–727c TrGF; cf. Ar. Ach. 326–490; Thesm. 689–758), Iophon (22 F 2c TrGF), Agathon (39 F 4 TrGF), Cleophon? (77 F 1 TrGF), and Moschion (97 F 2 TrGF) in

125 Fest., p. 128.24–25 L.

MUTTIRE: loqui. Ennius in Telepho:

ia^6 palam muttire plebeio piaculum est

Cf. Phaedr. 3, *Epil.* 33–35; Paul. *Fest.*, p. 129.13–14 L.

126 Non., p. 537.23–27 M. = 862 L.

STOLAM veteres non honestam vestem solum, sed etiam omnem quae corpus tegeret. Ennius Telepho:

?   † cedo et caveo cum vestitus † squalida saeptus stola

TELEPHUS (F 125–31)

Greek, as well as for Accius (Trag. 609–33 R.$^{2-3}$) in Latin.
Ennius' model is probably Euripides' tragedy.

The fragments of Ennius' tragedy allude to Telephus'
feigning to be a beggar (F 126). Because of their content,
some unattributed fragments may belong to this tragedy:
e.g., Enn. Trag. F 145; Trag. inc. inc. 27, 28, 29, 30–31 R.$^{2-3}$
= F 146, 98, 120, 18 TrRF.

Bibl.: Suerbaum 2003, 220; Manuwald 2001 [2004],
145–46. Comm.: Jocelyn 1967, 404–12; Masiá 2000, 533–
64. Lit.: Geel 1830; Welcker 1839, 477–92; Jahn 1841;
Hartung 1843, 196–216; Ribbeck 1875, 104–12; Hand-
ley / Rea 1957; Rosner 1970, 49–50; Reggiani 1986–87
[1990], 44–46; Masiá González 1997; Petaccia 1999.

125 Festus

muttire ["to mutter": rare, mainly ante-class.]: "to speak."
Ennius in *Telephus*: . . .

to speak in public is a sin for an ordinary person

126 Nonius

The ancients <called> *stola* ["a long upper garment"] not
only a respectable dress [worn by married women], but
also anything that could cover the body. Ennius in *Tele-*
phus:

. . . (?) wrapped in a filthy garment[1]

[1] The first part of this line is too corrupt to be restored and
translated securely.

idem in eadem:

ia[6]   regnum reliqui saeptus mendici stola

> 1 † cedo et caveo cum vestitus † *Mueller*: cedo et caveo cum vestitus *codd.*   2 me‹n›dici *Iunius*: medici *codd.*

Cf. Fest., pp. 440.34–42.3 L.

127 Non., pp. 15.3–10 M. = 21–22 L.

ENODA significat explana; et quae sit proprietas, manifestum est, hoc est, nodis exsolve. . . . Ennius Telepho:

tr[7]?   verum quorum liberi leto dati
tr[7]   sunt in bello, non lubenter haec enodari audiunt

128 Non., p. 232.17–23 M. = 345 L.

ADVORSUM rursum apud significat. . . . Ennius Telepho:

ia[6]   te ipsum hoc oportet profiteri et proloqui
ia[6]?   advorsum illam mihi

129 Non., pp. 342.6–20 M. = 540–41 L.

MACTARE malo adficere significat. . . . {et} Ennius Telepho:

ia[6]   qui illum di deaeque magno mactassint malo

> di{i} *edd.*: dii *codd.*

The same ⟨poet⟩ in the same ⟨play⟩:

> I have left the kingdom, wrapped in a beggar's
>   garment[2]

[2] Characters in rags also appear in Euripides and Accius (see Lucilius' criticism: Lucil. 597–98, 599–600 M. = 729–30, 727–28 W.).

127 Nonius

enoda ["unravel!"] means "explain!"; and what the proper significance is, is obvious, i.e., "release from knots [*nodus*]." . . . Ennius in *Telephus*:

> but they whose children have been
>   exposed to death
> in war do not hear cheerfully these things being
>   unraveled

128 Nonius

ulvorsum ["opposite of"] on the other hand means "in front of." . . . Ennius in *Telephus*:

> it is necessary that you yourself state and declare this
>   openly
> for me in front of her

129 Nonius

mactare ["to afflict"] means "to affect with misfortune" [*malo adficere*]. . . . Ennius in *Telephus*:

> would that the gods and goddesses affect that man
>   with great misfortune

133

130 Non., p. 429.1–5 M. = 692 L.

inter URBEM et CIVITATEM hoc interest: URBS est aedificia, CIVITAS incolae. . . . Ennius Telepho:

ia^6 set civitatem video Argivum incendere

telefus et *vel* telefo et *codd.*

131 Non., p. 490.10–11 M. = 787 L.

ITINER, pro iter. Ennius Telepho:

tr^7 deumque de consilio hoc itiner credo conatum modo

THYESTES (F 132–41)

*In the confrontation between the two Mycenaean brothers
Atreus and Thyestes (who had an affair with Atreus' wife),
Atreus killed Thyestes' sons and served them to him for
dinner. When Thyestes had realized the terrible crime, he
fled to king Thesprotus in Epirus, where he, in line with
an oracle, raped his own daughter Pelopia, and Aegisthus,
the future avenger of his father, was conceived (see, e.g.,
Aesch. Ag. 1583–602; Schol. ad Eur. Or. 812 [vol. II,
pp. 210–11 Dindorf]; Accius' Atreus [Trag. 196–234²
R.²⁻³], Pelopidae [Trag. 512–19 R.²⁻³]; Hyg. Fab. 86, 87, 88).*
*Tragedies of the same title are known for the Greek poets
Sophocles (F 247–69 TrGF), Euripides (F 391–97b TrGF),*

130 Nonius

Between *urbs* ["city"] and *civitas* ["community"] is the following difference: a city is buildings, a community inhabitants. . . . Ennius in *Telephus*:

> but I see ‹someone› setting the community of the
> Achaeans on fire[1]

[1] A second accusative in the infinitive construction is required; it is more likely that *civitatem* is the object and the subject accusative followed in the next line (distinct from the speaker).

131 Nonius

itiner ["way, journey": rare and mainly ante-class.], instead of *iter* [standard form]. Ennius in *Telephus*:

> and I believe that by counsel of the gods ‹he / you›
> just attempted this journey

THYESTES (F 132–41)

Agathon (39 F 3 TrGF), Diogenes Athen. (45 T 1 TrGF), Apollodorus (64 T 1 TrGF), Carcinus II (70 F 1 TrGF), Chaeremon (71 F 8 TrGF), Cleophon? (77 F 1 TrGF), and Diogenes Sinopensis (88 F 1d TrGF), as well as for the Roman poets Varius Rufus (Did. in Cod. Paris. 7530 et Casin. 1086 [p. 309 Klotz]), Gracchus (Trag. 3 R.$^{2-3}$ = F 3 TrRF [cf. Prisc., GL II, p. 269.8–10]), and Seneca; the material is also treated in Accius' Atreus (Trag. 196–234^2 R.$^{2-3}$). A play "Thyestes" is attributed to Pacuvius in Fulgentius presumably by error (cf. Fulgentius, Serm. ant. 57; see Schierl 2006, 9). Euripides' tragedy was probably Ennius' model.

Many scholars regard Thyestes' dinner as the subject of the tragedy; Jocelyn (1967, ad loc.) suggests that Ennius' tragedy covered events at the court of King Thesprotus in Epirus slightly later. At any rate, the surviving fragments include Thyestes lamenting about his fate (F 135, 140), cursing Atreus (F 132), and referring to Apollo's authority (F 136). Because of their content, the following unattributed fragments have been suggested as belonging

132 Cic. *Tusc.* 1.107

exsecratur luculentis sane versibus apud Ennium Thyestes primum ut naufragio pereat Atreus. durum hoc sane; talis enim interitus non est sine gravi sensu. illa inania:

tr[8]   ipse summis saxis fixus asperis, evisceratus,
       latere pendens, saxa spargens tabo, sanie et sanguine
          atro

non ipsa saxa magis sensu omni vacabunt quam ille "latere pendens," cui se hic cruciatum censet optare. quam essent dura, si sentiret! nulla ‹autem› [*Giusta*] sine sensu. illud vero perquam inane:

tr[7]   neque sepulchrum quo recipiat habeat, portum
          corporis,
       ubi remissa humana vita corpus requiescat malis

---

[1] The title of the tragedy is not mentioned with the quotations, but these are clearly utterances of Thyestes in Ennius and hence can come only from the tragedy named for Thyestes. Some scholars have tried to extract further Ennian fragments from the Ciceronian context, but how closely Cicero's wording echoes Ennius' drama is uncertain.

to this tragedy. Enn. Trag. *F 143, 150, 157, 163, 165;* Trag. inc. inc. *108–9 R.*[2–3] *= F 55 TrRF.*

Thyestes *was the last tragedy Ennius produced (T 19).*

Bibl.: Suerbaum 2003, 221; Manuwald 2001 [2004], 146–47. Comm.: Jocelyn 1967, 412–26. Lit.: Ribbeck 1875, 199–204; Rosner 1970, 50; Paduano 1974, 47–48; Garelli-François 1998; Boyle 2006, 78–83.

132 Cicero, *Tusculan Disputations*

Thyestes curses with really splendid verses in Ennius,[1] first that Atreus perish in a shipwreck. This is indeed harsh; for such a death is not without serious feeling. This is nonsense:

> he himself fixed to the top of rough rocks,
>   disemboweled,
> hanging by his side, sprinkling the rocks with gore,
>   filth, and black blood

The rocks themselves will not be freer of any feeling than the man "hanging by his side," for whom he [Thyestes] thinks that he intends torment. How hard would they be if he [Atreus] had sensation! But <they are> nothing without sensation. This, however, is complete nonsense:

> and he shall not have a tomb where he can withdraw,
>   a haven for the body,
> where, once human life has been dismissed, the body
>   can rest from troubles

vides quanto haec in errore versentur: portum esse corpo-
ris et requiescere in sepulcro putat mortuum; magna culpa
Pelopis, qui non erudierit filium nec docuerit quatenus
esset quidque curandum.

Cf. Cic. *Pis.* 43; Non., p. 405.2–3 M. = 651 L.

133 Cic. *Orat.* 183–84

sed in versibus res est apertior, quanquam etiam a modis
quibusdam cantu remoto soluta esse videtur oratio, ...
[184] quorum similia sunt quaedam etiam apud nostros,
velut illa in Thyeste:

ba⁴
hyperm. quemnam te esse dicam, qui tarda in senectute

et quae secuntur; quae, nisi cum tibicen accessit, orationis
sunt solutae simillima.

134 Cic. *Nat. D.* 2.4

quid enim potest esse tam apertum tamque perspicuum,
cum caelum suspeximus caelestiaque contemplati sumus,
quam esse aliquod numen praestantissimae mentis quo
haec regantur? quod ni ita esset, qui potuisset adsensu
omnium dicere Ennius

You see in how great an error they live: he believes there is a haven for the body and the dead person rests in a tomb; a great fault of Pelops [Thyestes' father], who has not educated his son and has not taught him to what degree each thing should be worried about.

133 Cicero, *Orator*

But in poetry the matter [the presence of rhythm] is more obvious, even though, when song is removed from certain meters, the speech seems to be prose, ... [184] Similar to these there are also some ‹instances› among our ‹poets›, like this in *Thyestes*:[1]

who shall I say you are, who in slow old age

and what follows; this, unless the piper has stepped up, is very similar to prose speech.

[1] Since the only known tragedy from the Republican period entitled *Thyestes* is the one by Ennius, well known to Cicero, the attribution of the line to this tragedy is almost certain.

134 Cicero, *On the Nature of the Gods*

For what can be so open and so clear, when we have looked up at the sky and have watched the celestial bodies, as that there is some divinity with an outstanding mind by whom these things are directed? If this were not so, how could Ennius have said,[1] with everyone's approval,

[1] In *Thyestes* according to Festus.

tr^7 aspice hoc sublime candens, quem vocant omnes
         Iovem

illum vero et Iovem et dominatorem rerum et omnia motu
regentem et, ut idem Ennius [Inc. *Ann.* F 124], "patrem
divumque hominumque" et praesentem ac praepotentem
deum?

> vocant *Prob., Fest.*: invocant *Cic., Apul.*

Cf. Cic. *Nat. D.* 2.64–65 (cf. Enn. *Trag.* F 159), 3.10, 3.40; Fest.,
p. 400.17–20 L.; Prob. ad Verg. *Ecl.* 6.31, pp. 332.27–33.5 Th.-H;
Apul. *Mund.* 33 (363).

135   Non., p. 90.13–15 M. = 128 L.

CONGLOMERARE: involvere, superaddere. Ennius Thy-
est{h}e:

tr^7 eheu mea fortuna ut omnia in me conglomeras mala

> <e>heu *Lachmann*: heu *codd.*

136   Non., p. 97.29–30 M. = 139 L.

DELECTARE: inlicere, adtrahere. Ennius Thyeste:

$cr^2 + tr^{4c}$ set me Apollo ipse delectat, ductat Delphicus

> thyestes et *vel* theestes et *codd.*

137   Non., p. 110.11–18 M. = 157 L.

FLACCET: languet, deficit. . . . Ennius Thyeste:

tr^7 sin flaccebunt condiciones, repudiato et reddito

> <s>in *Gulielmius ap. Gruterum*: in *codd.*

look at this thing shining on high, whom all call
  Jupiter[2]

him indeed, Jupiter and lord of the world and governing
everything by his movements and, as the same Ennius
<says> [Inc. *Ann.* F 124], "father of gods and men" and a
present and very powerful god?

  [2] The identification of the highest god with elements also oc-
curs in Euripides (e.g., Eur. *Tro.* 884–86; F 877, 941 *TrGF*).

135 Nonius

conglomerare ["to heap": rare word]: "to roll upon," "to
add on." Ennius in *Thyestes*:

  alas, my fate, how you heap all evils upon me

136 Nonius

delectare ["to delight": ante-class. also "to lure"]: "to en-
tice," "to draw." Ennius in *Thyestes*:

  but the Delphian Apollo himself lures, draws me

137 Nonius

flaccet ["flags": rare word]: "is enfeebled," "becomes
weak." . . . Ennius in *Thyestes*:

  but if conditions become weak, reject and return

138 Non., p. 255.25–26 M. = 387 L.

CREPARE: ferire. Ennius in Thyeste:

ia^6 sed sonitus auris meas pedum pulsu increpat

139 Non., p. 261.13–17 M. = 398 L.

CERNERE: iudicare. . . . Ennius Thy‹e›ste:

?   impetrem facile ab animo ut cernat vitalem
      † babium †

140 Non., p. 268.9–12 M. = 410 L.

CONTINGERE: evenire. . . . Ennius T‹h›yeste:

$cr^2 + tr^{4c}$ quam mihi maxime hic hodie contigerit malum

141 Non., p. 369.29–32 M. = 588 L.

PUTARE: animo disputare. . . . Ennius Thyeste:

ia^6 ibi quid agat, secum cogitat, parat, putat

138 Nonius

crepare ["to clatter"]: "to strike" [a second, rare meaning of *increpare*].[1] Ennius in *Thyestes*:

> but a sound strikes my ears from the stamping of feet

[1] Nonius uses phrases with both the simple verb and the compound to illustrate meanings of *crepare*.

139 Nonius

cernere ["to distinguish, decide, discern"]: "to judge." . . . Ennius in *Thyestes*:

> I may easily obtain from ‹his / her?› mind that
> he / she judges vital . . . (?)[1]

[1] The last word is too corrupt to be restored with certainty. Therefore, the meaning of the rest of the fragment is unclear.

140 Nonius

contingere ["to fall to one's lot"]: "to fall by lot." . . . Ennius in *Thyestes*:

> how misfortune here today has to the greatest extent
> fallen to my lot

141 Nonius

putare ["to think"]: "to discuss in the mind" [rare meaning]. . . . Ennius in *Thyestes*:

> then he considers with himself what he should do,
> plans, thinks over

INCERTA (F 142–201)

Ancient authors frequently quote pieces from Ennius without mentioning a particular work or genre. Some of these may come from tragedies (and have been attributed to tragedies by some scholars). Because of style, meter and/or content, the fragments in this section are likely to

142 Donat. ad Ter. *Eun.* 590

"qui templa caeli summa sonitu concutit": ab auctoritate personae, ut fit in exemplis:

? sonitu concutit

parodia de Ennio. "templa caeli summa": tragice, sed de industria, non errore.

143 *Rhet. Her.* 2.39

item vitiosum est quom id pro certo sumitur quod inter omnes constat, quod etiam nunc in controversia est, hoc modo:

tr^7 eho tu: dii, quibus est potestas motus superum atque
    inferum,
pacem inter sese conciliant, conferunt concordiam

144

INCERTA (F 142–201)

come from tragedies. Where particular tragedies have been suggested, this is indicated in the notes and the introductions to the respective plays.

Bibl.: Suerbaum 2003, 221; Manuwald 2001 [2004], 147–48.

142 Donatus, *Commentary on Terence*

"he who shakes the highest precincts of heaven with thunder":[1] taken from the authority of the character, as it is the case with examples:

he shakes with thunder

a parody of Ennius. "the highest precincts of heaven": in tragic manner, but on purpose, not by mistake.

[1] How much of Terence's line is a direct quotation from Ennius' tragedies is uncertain. Donatus' comments make it likely that only the phrase explicitly identified is a parody of Ennius.

143 *Rhetorica ad Herennium*

It is likewise faulty when something is taken as certain that is agreed upon by all, which even now is in dispute, in this way:

oh, look you: the gods, who have power over the
    movements of beings above and below,
make peace among themselves, create harmony

nam ita pro suo iure hoc exemplo usum Thesprotum [thes-
protum *codd. pler.*: crespontem *cod.*] Ennius induxit,
quasi iam satis certis rationibus esse demonstrasset.

Cf. Cic. *Inv. rhet.* 1.91.

144

a Cic. *Rosc. Am.* 89–90
verum ego forsitan propter multitudinem patronorum in
grege adnumerer, te pugna Cannensis accusatorem sat
bonum fecit. multos caesos non ad Trasumennum lacum,
sed ad Servilium vidimus. [90]

tr⁷?   quis ibi non est vulneratus ferro Phrygio?

non necesse est omnis commemorare Curtios, Marios,
denique omnes eos [omnes eos *Martin*: mammeos *codd.*]
quos iam aetas a proeliis avocabat, postremo Priamum
ipsum senem Antistium quem non modo aetas, sed etiam
leges pugnare prohibebant.

Phrygio *codd.*: *Enn. forma* "Brugio" *usum esse verisimile (cf.
Trag. F 154)*

For in this manner does Ennius bring Thesprotus on stage,[1] using this example on his own authority, as if he had already demonstrated by sufficiently sure proofs that this was the case.

[1] Most scholars assign these lines to Ennius' play *Cresphontes* and make the speaker Cresphontes (on the authority of a single manuscript); others assign them to the tragedy *Thyestes*, as the words of Thesprotus (as in the majority of manuscripts).

144

a Cicero, *Pro Sexto Roscio Amerino*

But because of the large number of advocates for the defense I perhaps might just be counted as another in the crowd; the battle of Cannae[1] has made you[2] a sufficiently good accuser. We have seen many slain, not near Lake Trasimene,[3] but near the Servilian reservoir.[4] [90]

Who was not wounded there by Phrygian steel?

There is no need to recall all the Curtii, the Marii, and then all those whom advanced age already called away from battles, lastly the aged Priam himself, Antistius, whom not only age, but also the laws prevented from fighting.[5]

[1] The Roman defeat in 216 BC during the Second Punic War.   [2] Erucius, the prosecutor (since the Sullan proscriptions have reduced the number of advocates).   [3] In the battle in 217 BC.   [4] A cistern near the Forum in Rome, where the heads of those killed in the Sullan proscriptions were displayed.   [5] I.e., various professional prosecutors.

b Schol. Gron. ad Cic. *Rosc. Am.* 90 (pp. 311.30–12.3 Stangl)

"ferro Frugio": in Ennio haec fabula inducitur, Achilles quo tempore propter Briseidam cum Graecis pugnare noluit; quo etiam tempore Hector classem eorum incendit. in hac pugna Ulixes vulneratus inducitur et fugiens ‹ad› [*Graevius*] Achillen [Aiacem *Orelli*] venit. cum interrogaretur ab Aiace [Achille *Düntzer*] cur fugisset, ille, ut celaret dedecus inultum: "quis enim vulneratus ferro Frugio?"

145 Cic. *Off.* 1.51–52

omnium autem communia hominum videntur ea quae sunt generis eius quod ab Ennio positum in una re transferri in permultas potest:

ia^6 homo qui erranti comiter monstrat viam
       quasi lumen de suo lumine accendat facit:
       nihilo minus ipsi luce{a}t, cum illi accenderit

b Scholia Gronoviana to Cicero, *Pro Sexto Roscio Amerino*

"Phrygian steel": In Ennius this ‹scene of the› play is brought on stage at the time when Achilles, on account of Briseis, does not wish to fight together with the Greeks; at the time too when Hector sets their fleet on fire. In this battle Ulixes is brought on stage wounded and comes to Achilles in the course of his flight. When he is asked by Aiax why he has fled, he, in order to hide the unavenged dishonor, ‹says›: "For who ‹was› wounded by Phrygian steel?"[1]

---

[1] Scholars attribute this line to Ennius' tragedies *Achilles* or *Hectoris lytra*. But the scene cannot be assigned securely to either, and there is no direct match with scenes in Homer's *Iliad* (Hector setting the ships on fire: Hom. *Il.* 15.716–16.124; Ulixes wounded: Hom. *Il.* 11.401–88; Ulixes flees: Hom. *Il.* 8.92–98). The names in the scholiast's note have sometimes been emended, but the situation is not impossible. On the possible meaning of the quotation in Cicero, the Homeric basis, and the dramatic version(s), see Jocelyn 1972, 55–59; on the text and the potential context, see Ramsey 2014.

145 Cicero, *On Duties*

But those things seem to be shared among all humans that are of the kind that, described by Ennius for one thing, can be transferred to a great many:

> The man who, in a friendly manner, shows the way to
> someone wandering about
> has an effect as if he kindles a light from his own
> light:
> it shines for himself no less, when he has kindled it
> for the other.

una ex re satis praecipit ut quidquid sine detrimento com-
modari possit, id tribuatur vel ignoto. [52] . . . sed quoniam
copiae parvae singulorum sunt, eorum autem qui his
egeant infinita est multitudo, vulgaris liberalitas referenda
est ad illum Enni finem "nihilo minus ipsi lucet," ut facul-
tas sit qua in nostros simus liberales.

Cf. Cic. *Balb.* 36.

146 Cic. *De or.* 1.199–200

quid est enim praeclarius quam honoribus et rei publicae
muneribus perfunctum senem posse suo iure dicere idem,
quod apud Ennium dicat ille Pythius Apollo, se esse eum,
unde sibi, si non populi et reges, at omnes sui cives consi-
lium expetant, suarum [suarum summarum *codd.*: suarum
om. codd. rec., *del. nonnulli edd.*: summarum *om. codd.
rec.*, *del. nonnulli edd.*] rerum incerti;

ia^6?   quos ego mea ope ex
ia^6 incertis certos compotesque consili
              dimitto ut ne res temere tractent turbidas

[200] est enim sine dubio domus iuris consulti totius ora-
culum civitatis.

---

1 Cicero's report of the oracle-giving Apollo's words in Ennius
begins in indirect speech and then turns to direct quotation.
While the section in indirect speech is also almost certainly based
on Ennius' play, the exact wording cannot be restored (despite
many scholarly hypotheses), since the extent of Cicero's interven-
tion is unclear.

On the basis of this one thing he instructs well enough that, whatever can be bestowed without disadvantage, this should be made available even to an unknown person. [52] . . . But since the resources of individuals are small, but of those who lack them there is an infinite multitude, general generosity is to be judged with reference to this limit set by Ennius "it shines for himself no less," so that there is the ability according to which we can be generous toward our people.

146 Cicero, *On the Orator*

For what is more glorious than that an old man, after having carried out offices and services for the republic, is able to say, with full justification for him, the same thing that in Ennius the famous Pythian Apollo says,[1] namely that he is the one from whom, if not nations and kings, all his citizens seek counsel, when uncertain of their affairs;[2]

> those I send away, turned by my help
> from unsure ones to sure and in control of their
>   plans,
> so that they do not treat rashly things in turmoil

[200] For without doubt the house of a lawyer is an oracle for the entire community.

[2] The passage has often been attributed to Ennius' *Eumenides* since Apollo is thought to play a major role in this play. But such a rather generic description of the effect of Apollo's oracle could appear in a variety of contexts.

147 Gell. *NA* 5.15.9

hos aliosque talis argutae delectabilisque desidiae aculeos cum audiremus vel lectitaremus neque in his scrupulis aut emolumentum aliquod solidum ad rationem vitae pertinens aut finem ullum quaerendi videremus, Ennianum Neoptolemum probabamus, qui profecto ita ait:

ia/tr   philosophandum est, paucis; nam omnino haud placet

Cf. Cic. *De or.* 2.155–56; *Rep.* 1.30; *Tusc.* 2.1–2; Apul. *Apol.* 13; Gell. *NA* 5.16.5.

148 Cic. *De or.* 2.221–22

. . . ; quod est hominibus facetis et dicacibus difficillimum, habere hominum rationem et temporum et ea quae occurrant, cum salsissime dici possunt, tenere. itaque nonnulli ridiculi homines hoc ipsum non insulse interpretantur. [222] dicere enim aiunt Ennium, "flammam a sapiente facilius ore in ardente opprimi, quam bona dicta teneat"; haec scilicet bona dicta quae salsa sint; nam ea dicta appellantur proprio iam nomine.

---

[1] Cicero reports words from Ennius in indirect speech. Thus the exact wording of the original remains uncertain, since the extent of Cicero's changes is unclear. The statement is generic so that it could appear in almost any play; such *sententiae* are not uncommon in Roman tragedy.   [2] Cicero's point is that *dicta* originally meant "sayings, statements," but then came to mean also "witty sayings, witticisms."

147 Gellius, *Attic Nights*

When we heard or read these and other similar stimuli to clever and delightful inactivity and did not see in these philosophical problems either some genuine advantage referring to the conduct of life or any purpose to the inquiry, we approved of the Ennian Neoptolemus,[1] who indeed spoke thus:[2]

> one must do philosophy, but in moderation; for it
> does not please completely

[1] The fragment is attributed to a particular speaker, but not to a specific play; no other Ennian fragment is assigned to the same speaker, and the name does not appear in any testimonia. The fragment is often referred to Ennius' *Andromacha*, since Neoptolemus received Andromache as his share of the booty after the capture of Troy. [2] The line is quoted a number of times, but often only in part and/or in indirect speech. The version given at Gell. *NA* 5.15.9 seems closest to the original wording (restored in various ways).

148 Cicero, *On the Orator*

. . . ; what is extremely difficult for funny and sharp-tongued men is to take account of people and circumstances and to forego opportunities that arise when something could be said most wittily. And so some humorous men explain this very point not inelegantly. [222] For they say that Ennius says that[1] "a flame in his burning mouth can be suppressed more easily by a wise man than he can hold back good sayings," obviously those good sayings that are witty; for such sayings are now referred to by that specific name.[2]

149 Cic. *De or.* 3.162

quo in genere primum est fugienda dissimilitudo:

ia/tr   caeli ingentes fornices

quamvis sphaeram in scaenam, ut dicitur, attulerit Ennius, tamen in sphaera fornicis similitudo inesse non potest.

Cf. Varro, *Ling.* 5.19 (cf. Enn. *Trag.* F 34, 83.1–2).

150 Cic. *Off.* 1.26

maxime autem adducuntur plerique ut eos iustitiae capiat oblivio cum in imperiorum honorum gloriae cupiditatem inciderunt. quod enim est apud Ennium:

?   nulla sancta societas nec fides regni est

id latius patet. nam quidquid eius modi est in quo non possint plures excellere, in eo fit plerumque tanta contentio ut difficillimum sit servare "sanctam societatem."

Cf. Cic. *Rep.* 1.49.

149 Cicero, *On the Orator*

In this genre [of metaphor] dissimilarity is the first thing to be avoided:

heaven's immense vaults

Even though Ennius brought the globe to the stage, as is reported, still there can be no similarity to a vault in a globe.[1]

[1] Cicero disapproves of this metaphor, since he believed that the sky can be compared to a globe (*sphaera*), but not to a vault or arch (*fornix*). Varro, on the other hand, does not seem to have problems with this expression. Other metaphors in Ennius (*Trag.* F 173; *Inc.* F 5) suggest that he could describe the sky as vaulted above the earth. Whether Cicero means that Ennius introduced the word *sphaera* to the general public or actually put a globe on stage as a prop is debated. At any rate the famous globe of Archimedes was brought to Rome in Ennius' lifetime (cf. Cic. *Rep.* 1.21, Jaeger 2011, 50–62).

150 Cicero, *On Duties*

But most people are so completely led astray when they rush into desire for power, honor, and glory that forgetfulness of justice catches them. For what is found in Ennius:[1]

there is no sacred fellowship or loyalty in kingship

has a rather wide application. For in any kind of thing in which not many can excel, such competition frequently arises that it is very difficult to preserve "a sacred fellowship."

[1] The fragment is sometimes associated with the tragedy *Thyestes*, since this is a play about power, but such a general statement could also occur in other tragedies.

151

a Cic. *Div.* 1.66–67

inest igitur in animis praesagitio extrinsecus iniecta atque inclusa divinitus. ea si exarsit acrius, furor appellatur, cum a corpore animus abstractus divino instinctu concitatur:

tr^7	sed quid oculis rapere visa est derepente ardentibus?
tr^7?	ubi illa paulo ante sapiens virginali' modestia?—
tr^7	mater, optumatum multo mulier melior mulierum,
	missa sum superstitiosis hariolationibus;
5	namque me Apollo fatis fandis dementem invitam
	ciet.
	virgines vereor aequalis, patris mei meum factum
	pudet,
	optumi viri; mea mater, tui me miseret, mei piget.
	optumam progeniem Priamo peperisti extra me; hoc
	dolet.
	men obesse, illos prodesse, me obstare, illos obsequi.

2 virginis *Turnebus*
5 namque *Hottinger*: neque *codd.*

---

[1] The speech that follows was apparently famous and is often quoted (sometimes only in parts); this is why Cicero nowhere identifies the author explicitly. At *Orat.* 155 (see Enn. *Trag.* F 152) he gives a series of examples from three tragic poets (including a line from this fragment), the second and third ones being Pacuvius and Accius; therefore, in view of Cicero's assessment of Livius Andronicus and Naevius (cf. T 18) and the fact that the three later tragic poets or their works are mentioned together elsewhere in Cicero (cf. T 15, 21, 24, 25), the attribution to Ennius is almost certain. On this fragment, its potential place

151

a Cicero, *On Divination*

There is therefore in human minds foreboding infused from outside and shut in by divine agency. If it has flared up rather sharply, it is called madness, when the mind, drawn away from the body, is excited by a divine impulse:[1]

> But what did she seem to catch suddenly with
>   glowing eyes?
> Where is that maidenly modesty, sane just a short
>   while ago? ::
> Mother,[2] a woman much better than the best women,
> I am driven by prophetic soothsayings;
> for Apollo spurs me against my will in frenzy to   5
>   predict what will happen.
> I am abashed before the young women of my age, I
>   am ashamed of my deeds before my father,
> the best of men; my mother, I have pity for you, I am
>   vexed at myself.
> You have borne the best progeny to Priam except
>   myself; this hurts.
> That I am an obstacle, they are useful; that I stand in
>   the way, they obey!

in a plot and its relation to Euripides, see Grilli 1965, 161–68; Jocelyn 1998, 300–306; Paduano 2000, 261–64.

[2] While Cassandra's prophecies and reflections are addressed to her mother (Hecuba), the introductory lines are more likely to be a comment by the chorus or another third person (if the text is not changed). The time seems to be after the Judgment of Paris and before the outbreak of the Trojan War. Therefore, the attribution to Ennius' *Alexander*, frequently suggested, seems likely.

o poema tenerum et moratum atque molle! sed hoc minus ad rem; [67] illud, quod volumus, expressum est, ut vaticinari furor vera soleat:

tr^7 10   adest, adest fax obvoluta sanguine atque incendio.
          multos annos latuit; cives, ferte opem et restinguite.

deus inclusus corpore humano iam, non Cassandra loquitur.

da^4 iamque mari magno classis cita
          texitur. exitium examen rapit;
          adveniet, fera velivolantibus
15   navibus complevit manus litora.

tragoedias loqui videor et fabulas.

b Cic. *Div.* 1.114

multos . . . quorum furibunda mens videt ante multo, quae sint futura. quo de genere illa sunt:

r^c eheu videte:
tr^8 iudicavit inclitum iudicium inter deas tris aliquis,
          quo iudicio Lacedaemonia mulier, Furiarum una,
              adveniet.

Cf. Cic. *Att.* 8.11.3; *Orat.* 155 (cf. Enn. *Trag.* F 152); *Div.* 2.112–13.

Oh, what a tender poem, in line with her character, and gentle! But this is less relevant to the matter at hand; [67] the thing that we want is the expression that madness tends to prophesy the truth:

> The torch is here, is here, covered in blood and fire.
> It has been hidden for many years; citizens, bring
>   help and extinguish it.

Now a god shut in human body, not Cassandra, is speaking:

> Already a swift fleet is being built for the great sea
>   [i.e., for the Greeks traveling to Troy].
> It hurries along a swarm of deaths;
> it will come, a fierce troop
> has filled the shores with ships with speeding sails.   15

I seem to be talking tragedies and plays.

b Cicero, *On Divination*

many . . . whose furious mind sees much that will happen in advance. Of such a kind is the following:

> Oh, look:
> someone [Paris] has judged a famous judgment
>   among three goddesses,
> by which judgment a Lacedaemonian woman, one of
>   the Furies, will come [Helen].

152 Cic. *Orat.* 155

atque etiam a quibusdam sero iam emendatur antiquitas,
qui haec reprehendunt. nam pro "deum atque hominum
fidem" "deorum" aiunt. ita credo hoc illi nesciebant; an
dabat hanc licentiam consuetudo? itaque idem poeta qui
inusitatius contraxerat [*Trag.* F 151.6] "patris mei meum
factum pudet" pro "meorum factorum" et [*Trag.* F 151.13]
"texitur, exitium examen rapit" pro "exitiorum," non dicit
"liberum," ut plerique loquimur, cum "cupidos liberum"
aut "in liberum loco" dicimus, sed ut isti volunt:

*tr*⁷   neque tuum umquam in gremium extollas liberorum
      ex te genus

et idem [*Trag.* F 153.5]: "namque Aesculapi liberorum."

153 Cic. *Tusc.* 2.38–39

quin etiam videmus ex acie efferri saepe saucios et quidem
rudem illum et inexercitatum quamvis levi ictu ploratus
turpissimos edere; at vero ille exercitatus et vetus ob eam-

152 Cicero, *Orator*

And even ⟨the speech of⟩ antiquity is now being emended somewhat late by certain people, who criticize these things.[1] For instead of "loyalty to gods [*deum*: contracted genitive] and men," they say "to gods" [*deorum*: common, uncontracted genitive]. They [the ancients], I believe, did not know this; did not usage give this license? This is why the same poet, who had rather unusually contracted [*Trag.* F 151.6] "I am ashamed of my deeds [*meum factum*] before my father" instead of "of my deeds" [*meorum factorum*] and [*Trag.* F 151.13] "it is being built, it hurries along a swarm of deaths [*exitium*]" instead of "of deaths" [*exitiorum*], does not say "of children" [*liberum*], as most of us do, when we say "eager for children" or "in place of children," but, as they want [*liberorum*]:[2]

> and you may never lift into your lap offspring of
> children from you

and the same ⟨poet⟩ [*Trag.* F 153.5]: "for of the children of Aesculapius."

[1] Those who argue for rules and the removal of irregularities of language against those who follow usage as a guide.   [2] Since there is talk of the role of offspring, the line has been attributed to the tragedies *Medea* or *Phoenix* (spoken by Amyntor).

153 Cicero, *Tusculan Disputations*

Indeed, we see the wounded often carried away from the battle line and the raw and untrained person in particular pouring forth the most disgraceful wailing as a result even of a light strike; but this man, trained and experienced,

que rem fortior, medicum modo requirens a quo oblige-
tur:

o Patricoles,

inquit

ia^8 ad vos adveniens auxilium et vestras manus
peto, prius quam oppeto malam pestem mandatam
   hostili manu—
neque sanguis ullo potis est pacto profluens
   consistere—
si qui sapientia magis vestra mors devitari potest;
5   namque Aesculapi liberorum saucii opplent porticus;
non potest accedi.

certe Eurypylus hic quidem est. hominem exercitum! [39]
ubi tantum luctus continuatur, vide quam non flebiliter
respondeat. rationem etiam adfert cur aequo animo sibi
ferendum sit:

   qui alteri exitium parat,
eum scire oportet sibi paratum, pestem ut participet
   parem.

abducet Patricoles, credo, ut conlocet in cubili, ut volnus

8 paratum *Bentley*: paratam *codd.*

---

[1] Since Cicero reports a dialogue between the wounded Eu-
rypylus, coming back to the Greek camp from the battle before
Troy, and Patroclus, from whom he seeks help (cf. Hom. *Il.*
11.575–92, 11.807–12.2), and inserts comments of his own, partly
addressed to the characters, it is debatable which sections are to
be attributed to Cicero and which ones to the play. The dia-

and for this reason braver, merely seeking a doctor to bandage him, says:[1]

> Patroclus, coming to you, I ask for help and your
>   hands,
> before I meet evil death, brought about by the hand
>   of the enemy—
> in no way can the blood gushing forth come to a
>   halt—
> if in some way death can rather be avoided by your
>   knowledge;
> for the wounded fill the porches of the sons of   5
>   Aesculapius;[2]
> it is not possible to approach.

Certainly this is Eurypylus. A troubled man! [39] Where so much lament follows in succession, see how he does not respond with weeping. He even puts forward a reason why he must bear it with calm mind:

> He who prepares destruction for another
> must know that it is prepared for him that he
>   may participate in the same ruin.

Patroclus will lead him away, I believe, to lay him down on a bed in order to bind up the wound. If indeed he were a

logue must come from a tragedy connected with the Trojan myth and has often been assigned to *Achilles* or *Hectoris lytra* (on Ennius' authorship, see on *Trag.* F 151). On text and context, see Grilli 1965, 175–80; Jocelyn 1972, 59–70; De Rosalia 1992 [1993]; Koster 2000.   [2] The Greek doctors Podalirius and Machaon (cf. Hom. *Il.* 2.731–32).

obliget, si quidem homo esset; sed nihil vidi minus. quae-
rit enim quid actum sit:

> eloquere, eloquere, res Argivum proelio ut se
> sustinet.
10 non potest ecfari tantum dictis, quantum factis
> suppetit
> laboris.

quiesce igitur et volnus alliga. etiam si Eurypylus posset,
non posset Aesopus:

tr^8? ubi fortuna H{a}ectoris nostram acrem aciem
inclinatam

et cetera explicat in dolore; sic est enim intemperans mili-
taris in forti viro gloria.

Cf. Cic. *Orat.* 155 (cf. Enn. *Trag.* F 152).

154 Cic. *Orat.* 160

"Burrum" semper Ennius, nunquam "Pyrrhum";

ia/tr vi patefecerunt Bruges

non "Phryges." ipsius antiqui declarant libri. nec enim
Graecam litteram adhibebant—nunc autem etiam duas—
et cum "Phrygum" et "Phrygibus" dicendum esset, absur-
dum erat aut etiam in barbaris casibus Graecam litteram

---

1 Since *Phryges* is used for "Trojans" in poetry, the fragment
is likely to come from one of Ennius' tragedies connected with
the Trojan War: it is sometimes assigned to Ennius' *Achilles* or
Hectoris lytra. For the form *Bruges,* cf. Quint. *Inst.* 1.4.15.

human being, but I have seen nothing less like one. For he [Patroclus] asks what has happened:

> Tell me, tell me, how the Argives' cause holds up in
>   the battle.
> Not as much can be said with words, as how much   10
>   work is necessary
> for the deeds.

Now be quiet and bind up the wound [addressed to Patroclus]. Even if Eurypylus could, Aesopus [a famous actor in Cicero's time] could not [bear the pain any longer]:

> where Hector's fortune ⟨made⟩ our brave battle line
>   waver

And he [Eurypylus] sets out the rest in pain; so unrestrained in a brave man is the desire for glory in war.

154 Cicero, *Orator*

Ennius always ⟨uses the form⟩ *Burrus*, never *Pyrrhus*;[1]

> the *Bruges* opened up by force

not *Phryges*. The old books of ⟨the poet⟩ himself demonstrate it. For they were not used to have recourse to a Greek letter [*y*]—but now even to two [*y* and *z*]—and when *Phrygum* and *Phrygibus* [*Phryges* in genitive and dative / ablative] were to be said, there was the absurd situation either in the oblique cases[2] too to have recourse

---

[2] Lit., "barbaric," from a Greek point of view, since formed according to Roman rules.

adhibere aut recto casu solum Graece loqui; tamen et "Phryges" et "Pyrrhum" aurium causa dicimus.

Bruges *Victorius*: fruges *vel* phruges *vel* friges *vel* phry *vel* briges *codd.*

155 Cic. *Fin.* 2.41

nec vero audiendus Hieronymus, cui summum bonum est idem quod vos interdum vel potius nimium saepe dicitis, nihil dolere. non enim, si malum est dolor, carere eo malo satis est ad bene vivendum. hoc dixerit potius Ennius:

tr   nimium boni est cui nihil est mali

nos beatam vitam non depulsione mali sed adeptione boni iudicemus, . . .

156 Cic. *Tusc.* 3.5

at et morbi perniciosiores pluresque sunt animi quam corporis—hi enim ipsi odiosi sunt quod ad animum pertinent eumque sollicitant,

   animusque aeger

ut ait Ennius,

tr   semper errat;

to a Greek letter or to speak Greek in the nominative only; still we say both *Phryges* [nominative / accusative] and *Pyrrhum* [accusative] for the sake of our ears.[3]

[3] That is, we are inconsistent, since *Phryges* is a Greek form, and *Pyrrhum* is a word with a Greek letter and a Latin ending.

155 Cicero, *On Ends*

Nor, to be sure, should one listen to Hieronymus,[1] for whom the chief good is the same as what you say sometimes or rather too often, to feel no pain. For, if pain is an evil, it is not enough to be free from this evil to live well. Let Ennius say this, though:[2]

very much good has he who has nothing ill

We shall judge a happy life not by the avoidance of evil, but by the attainment of good, . . .

[1] A Peripatetic philosopher in the 3rd c. BC.   [2] The line is sometimes assigned to Ennius' *Hecuba*, but for such a general statement many contexts are possible (cf. Publilius Syrus, *Sent.* 430 R.[2]).

156 Cicero, *Tusculan Disputations*

But the diseases of the mind are both more deadly and more numerous than those of the body—for they are themselves hateful since they affect the mind and torment it, and

a sick mind

as Ennius says,

always wanders around;

tr^7 neque pati neque perpeti potest, cupere numquam
desinit

quibus duobus morbis, ut omittam alios, aegritudine et
cupiditate, qui tandem possunt in corpore esse graviores?

157 Cic. *Tusc.* 3.39–44

quid ergo? huiusne vitae propositio et cogitatio aut Thyes-
tem levare poterit aut Aeetam, de quo paulo ante dixi [Cic.
Tusc. 3.26], aut Telamonem pulsum patria, exulantem at-
que egentem? . . . [44] . . . quaerendum igitur quem ad
modum aegritudine privemus eum qui ita dicat:

tr^7? pol mihi fortuna magis nunc defit quam genus.
tr^7 namque regnum suppetebat mi, ut scias quanto e
loco,
quantis opibus, quibus de rebus lapsa fortuna accidat.

quid? huic calix mulsi inpingendus est, ut plorare desinat,
aut aliquid eius modi? ecce tibi ex altera parte ab eodem
poeta [Enn. *Trag.* F 23.3–17] . . .

2 mi{hi} *Manutius*: mihi *codd.*

---

[1] The lines are assigned to a male speaker but not attributed
to any particular figure, play, or poet. The continuation of the
passage with a quotation from Ennius' *Andromacha* proves them
to be Ennian. The speaker is clearly another *exemplum*, i.e.,
someone other than the mythical heroes mentioned. Therefore,
an attribution to Ennius' *Telamo* or *Thyestes*, which has been
suggested, is unlikely (see also Jocelyn 1967, 394–95). Cf. Acc.
Trag. 619–20 R.[2–3].

it can neither endure nor endure to the end, it never
ceases to desire[1]

in comparison with these two diseases, to say nothing of
others, distress and desire, which <diseases> concerning
the body, then, can be more severe?

[1] The words of Ennius that Cicero builds into his argument
can be fairly clearly identified, but their metrical shape is uncer-
tain, as is their attribution to a particular tragedy.

157 Cicero, *Tusculan Disputations*

What then? Could the idea and thought of such a life [a
happy life according to the Epicureans] relieve Thyestes
or Aeetes, about whom I spoke a little earlier [Cic. *Tusc.*
3.26], or Telamon, expelled from his country, an exile, and
in want? . . . [44] . . . Therefore one has to ask in what way
we can free him from distress, who speaks thus:[1]

> by Pollux, good fortune is lacking now for me
>   more than noble descent.
> For I used to have a kingdom, so that you may know
>   from what standing,
> from what power, from what riches fortune may lapse
>   and fall down.

Well, is a cup of wine to be thrust upon him, so that he
stops lamenting, or something of this kind? See, from the
other side you have by the same poet [*Trag.* F 23.3–17]
. . .

158 Cic. *Tusc.* 4.70

quis est enim iste amor amicitiae? cur neque deformem adulescentem quisquam amat neque formosum senem? mihi quidem haec in Graecorum gymnasiis nata consuetudo videtur, in quibus isti liberi et concessi sunt amores. bene ergo Ennius:

tr^7 flagiti principium est nudare inter civis corpora

qui ut sint, quod fieri posse video, pudici, solliciti tamen et anxii sunt, eoque magis quod se ipsi continent et coercent.

flagiti{i} *edd.*: flagitii *codd.*

159 Cic. *Nat. D.* 2.64–65

sed ipse Iuppiter, id est iuvans pater, quem conversis casibus appellamus a iuvando Iovem, a poetis [Inc. *Ann.* F 124] "pater divomque hominumque" dicitur, a maioribus autem nostris optumus maxumus, . . .—[65] hunc igitur Ennius, ut supra dixi [Cic. *Nat. D.* 2.4], nuncupat ita dicens [*Trag.* F 134] "aspice hoc sublime candens, quem {in} vocant omnes Iovem" planius quam alio loco idem

tr^7 cui quod in me est exsecrabor, hoc quod lucet quid-
          quid est

hunc etiam augures nostri cum dicunt "Iove fulgente tonante": dicunt enim "caelo fulgente et tonante."

"sententia parum perspicua" *Vahlen*[2] *in app.; an* exsecrabor *ut* consecrabo *intellegendum et* huic *pro* hoc *legendum?*

158 Cicero, *Tusculan Disputations*

What is this love of friendship then? Why does no one love either an ugly young man or a handsome old man? To me this custom seems to have originated in the gymnastic schools of the Greeks, in which this kind of lovemaking is free and allowed. Well therefore ⟨does⟩ Ennius ⟨say⟩:

> the beginning of disgrace is to bare bodies among
> citizens

Even though this ⟨kind of lovemaking⟩ may be decent, which I see can happen, yet it is accompanied by uneasiness and anxiety, and all the more because it curbs and restrains itself [i.e., there are no rules from outside].

159 Cicero, *On the Nature of the Gods*

But Jupiter himself, i.e. "the helping father," whom we call "Jove" in the oblique cases from "to help" [*iuvare*], is called by the poets [Inc. *Ann.* F 124] "father of gods and men," but by our ancestors the best and the greatest, . . .— [65] him, then, Ennius, as I have said above [Cic. *Nat. D.* 2.4], calls, speaking thus [*Trag.* F 134] "look at this thing shining on high, whom all call Jupiter," more explicitly than the same ⟨poet⟩ elsewhere

> to whom I will vow as an offering whatever is in me,
> this [or: to this?] that shines whatever it is[1]

Him our augurs also ⟨mean⟩ when they say "when Jupiter lights and thunders": for they say "when the sky lights and thunders."

[1] Meaning and construction are obscure; the translation is based on the understanding suggested in the textual note.

160 Cic. *Div.* 1.88

Amphilochus et Mopsus Argivorum reges fuerunt, sed iidem augures, iique urbis in ora marituma Ciliciae Graecas condiderunt; atque etiam ante hos Amphiaraus et Tiresias non humiles et obscuri neque eorum similes, ut apud Ennium est:

tr⁷   qui sui quaestus causa fictas suscitant sententias

sed clari et praestantes viri, qui avibus et signis admoniti futura dicebant; . . .

161 Cic. *Div.* 2.57

Democritus quidem optumis verbis causam explicat, cur ante lucem galli canant; depulso enim de pectore et in omne corpus diviso et mitificato cibo, cantus edere quiete satiatos; qui quidem silentio noctis, ut ait Ennius,

an⁴?   favent faucibus russis
an⁴   cantu plausuque premunt alas

cum igitur hoc animal tam sit canorum sua sponte, quid in mentem venit Callistheni dicere deos gallis signum dedisse cantandi, cum id vel natura vel casus efficere potuisset?

---

¹ The Greek atomist philosopher (5th c. BC).   ² This piece has sometimes been attributed to Ennius' *Iphigenia,* but various other contexts are possible. Since Cicero inserts the quotation into his own sentence, it is not entirely clear where the quotation begins and whether Cicero quotes a continuous sequence.   ³ A Greek historian and philosopher (4th c. BC).

160 Cicero, *On Divination*

Amphilochus and Mopsus[1] were kings of the Argives, but the same men were also augurs, and they founded Greek cities on the maritime coast of Cilicia; and even before them ⟨there were⟩ Amphiaraus and Tiresias,[2] ⟨men⟩ not lowly and obscure and similar to those, as is found in Ennius:[3]

who, for their own gain, call forth made-up maxims

but illustrious and outstanding men, who, admonished by birds and signs, told the future; . . .

[1] Early seers in Greek myths. [2] Well-known seers in mythical stories about Thebes. [3] The criticism of (a particular type of) seer has encouraged attribution of the line to Ennius' *Telamo*, which includes similar sentiments (Enn. *Trag.* F 117). Such general criticism of seers, however, could also appear in other plays.

161 Cicero, *On Divination*

Indeed, Democritus[1] explains in the best words the reason why cocks crow before dawn; for after their food has been pushed down from the chest and has been distributed throughout the entire body and been digested, they pour forth crows, satisfied by sleep; but in the silence of the night, as Ennius says,[2]

they indulge with their red throats
in song and push their wings with flapping;

thus, when this animal is so vocal of its own accord, how has it come into Callisthenes'[3] mind to say that the gods have given the cocks the sign to sing, when either nature or chance could have effected this?

162 Cic. *Off.* 1.61

itaque in probris maxime in promptu est si quid tale dici
potest [*Trag. inc. inc.* 210 R.$^{2-3}$]: "vos enim iuvenes ani-
mum geritis muliebrem, illa virgo viri," et si quid eius-
modi:

ia^6   Salmacida spolia sine sudore et sanguine

sudore et sanguine *Cic.*: sanguine et sudore *Fest.*

Cf. Fest., p. 439.10–18 L.

163 Cic. *Off.* 2.23

omnium autem rerum nec aptius est quicquam ad opes
tuendas ac tenendas quam diligi nec alienius quam timeri.
praeclare enim Ennius:

tr^7   quem metuunt oderunt; quem quisque odit periisse
           expetit

164 Cic. *Off.* 2.62

propensior benignitas esse debebit in calamitosos, nisi
forte erunt digni calamitate. in iis tamen qui se adiuvari

174

162 Cicero, *On Duties*

And so among reproaches this is particularly apposite if something like this can be said [*Trag. inc. inc.* 210 R.$^{2-3}$]: "for you young men bear a woman's mind, that young maiden a man's," and something of this sort:[1]

> spoils of Salmacis[2] without sweat and blood

[1] The fragment has often been attributed to Ennius' *Aiax*, with respect to the assignment of Achilles' arms.   [2] Salmacis is the name of a nymph and a spring at Halicarnassus, whose waters were believed to have an effeminating effect (cf. Ov. *Met.* 4.285–388). *Salmacida spolia* must then be spoils won in an easy way (*Salmacidus* derived from *Salmacis*; *Salmacida* as adjective with *spolia* rather than as an address in the vocative).

163 Cicero, *On Duties*

But of all things nothing is more suitable for protecting and keeping power than to be loved, and nothing more foreign than to be feared. For splendidly ⟨does⟩ Ennius ⟨say⟩:[1]

> whom they fear, they hate; whom one hates, one
>   desires his death

[1] The fragment has sometimes been attributed to Ennius' *Thyestes*, presumably on the basis of the similarity with a line from Accius' *Atreus* (cf. Acc. *Trag.* 203–4 R.$^{2-3}$; cf. also Ov. *Am.* 2.2.10; Hieron. *Ep.* 82.3.2). Such a general *sententia* could come from a variety of plays.

164 Cicero, *On Duties*

Benevolence will need to be more inclined toward those afflicted by disaster, unless, by chance, they deserve the

volent non ne adfligantur sed ut altiorem gradum ascendant, restricti omnino esse nullo modo debemus, sed in deligendis idoneis iudicium et diligentiam adhibere. nam praeclare Ennius:

ia^6 benefacta male locata malefacta arbitror

165 Cic. *Off.* 3.104

sed in iureiurando non qui metus sed quae vis sit debet intellegi. est enim iusiurandum adfirmatio religiosa; quod autem adfirmate et quasi deo teste promiseris, id tenendum est. iam enim non ad iram deorum, quae nulla est, sed ad iustitiam et ad fidem pertinet. nam praeclare Ennius:

tr^7 o Fides alma apta pinnis et ius iurandum Iovis

qui ius igitur iurandum violat, is Fidem violat, quam in Capitolio vicinam Iovis Optimi Maximi, ut in Catonis oratione est [fr. 238 ORF^4], maiores nostri esse voluerunt.

Cf. Apul. *De deo Soc.* 5 (131–32).

166 Cic. *Amic.* 64

quid, haec ut omittam, quam graves, quam difficiles plerisque videntur calamitatum societates? ad quas non est facile inventu qui descendant. quamquam Ennius recte

---

[1] This rhetorically shaped *sententia* is sometimes attributed to Ennius' *Hecuba*, presumably due to a perceived similarity with a line in Euripides' homonymous play (cf. Eur. *Hec.* 1226–27; cf. also Eur. *Or.* 454–55), but such a general statement could appear in various contexts.

disaster. Still, in the case of those who wish to be helped, we ought by no means to hold back altogether, not so that they do not suffer, but so that they may advance to a higher level; but in selecting the worthy we ought to use judgment and diligence. For Ennius splendidly ‹says›:

good deeds badly placed I regard as bad deeds

165 Cicero, *On Duties*

But in swearing an oath, not what the fear ‹in violating it› is, but what the obligation ‹in undertaking it is› should be understood. For an oath is a religious affirmation; and moreover, what you have promised with solemn assertion and as if with a god as witness must be kept. For this has to do not with the wrath of the gods, which does not exist, but with justice and faith. For Ennius splendidly ‹says›:

o Faith, gracious and equipped with wings, and the oath of Jupiter

He who violates the oath therefore violates Faith, which our ancestors wanted to be on the Capitol near Jupiter Optimus Maximus, as it says in Cato's speech [fr. 238 *ORF*⁴].

166 Cicero, *On Friendship*

Well, to pass by other things, how hard, how difficult for most people do associations with misfortune appear? It is not easy to find people who would lower themselves to those. Yet Ennius rightly ‹says›[1]

ia[6]   amicus certus in re incerta cernitur

tamen haec duo levitatis et infirmitatis plerosque convin-
cunt, aut si in bonis rebus contemnunt, aut in malis dese-
runt.

167 Varro, *Ling.* 5.14

locus est, ubi locatum quid esse potest, ut nunc dicunt,
collocatum. veteres id dicere solitos apparet apud Plau-
tum [*Aul.* 191]: . . . apud Ennium:

ia[6]   o terra Thraeca ubi Liberi fanum inclutum
      Maro locavit

   1 T<h>r<a>eca *Fleckeisen* (Threca *iam Gulielmius*): treca
codd.   inclutum *Gulielmius*: inciuiũ *codd.*   2 locavi<t>
Ribbeck[1]: locavi *codd.*

168 Varro, *Ling.* 5.23

terra, ut putant, eadem et humus; ideo Ennium in terram
cadentis dicere:

ia/tr   cubitis pinsibant humum

169 Varro, *Ling.* 7.12

tueri duo significat, unum ab aspectu ut dixi, unde est
Enni illud:

ia/tr   tueor te, senex? pro Iuppiter!

---

   1 Some scholars attribute this line to Ennius' *Hectoris lytra*
and interpret it as Achilles' greeting of Priam.

a certain friend is ascertained in an uncertain
   situation

still, these two things convict most people of unreliability
and inconstancy, either if they neglect ‹friends› in good
circumstances or desert them in bad ones.

167 Varro, *On the Latin Language*

A *locus* ["place"] is where something can be *locatum*
["placed"] or, as they say nowadays, *collocatum* ["estab-
lished"]. That the ancients were accustomed to say this is
clear in Plautus [*Aul.* 191]: . . . In Ennius:

O Thracian Land, where Maro[1] placed a renowned
shrine of Liber [Bacchus]

[1] Maro is a companion of Bacchus and said to have founded
the Thracian town of Maroneia.

168 Varro, *On the Latin Language*

terra ["earth"], as they believe, ‹is› the same as *humus*
["soil"]; therefore ‹they believe that› Ennius denotes men
falling to earth:

with their elbows they beat the soil[1]

[1] Cf. Enn. 10 *Ann.* F 16.

169 Varro, *On the Latin Language*

tueri ["to look at, to protect"] has two meanings, one from
seeing, as I have said, whence that ‹verse› of Ennius:

Do I see you, old man? Oh, Jupiter![1]

et [Inc. *Ann.* F 42] . . . alterum a curando ac tutela, ut
. . .

170 Varro, *Ling.* 7.12–13

quare a tuendo et templa et tesca dicta cum discrimine eo
quod dixi. [13] etiam indidem illud Enni:

ia^6 extemplo acceptum me necato et filium

extemplo enim est continuo, quod omne templum esse
debet continuo septum nec plus unum introitum habere.

> necato *Scaliger*: negato *cod.*

171 Varro, *Ling.* 7.16

Ennius:

tr^7 ut tibi Titanis Trivia dederit stirpem liberum

Titanis Trivia Diana est, ab eo dicta Trivia, quod in trivio
ponitur fere in oppidis Graecis vel quod luna dicitur esse,
quae in caelo tribus viis movetur, in altitudinem et latitu-

and [Inc. *Ann.* F 42] . . . The other meaning is from caring and guardianship, as . . .

170 Varro, *On the Latin Language*

Therefore from *tueri* ["to look at, to protect"] both *templa* ["temples"] and *tesca* ["holy places"] are derived with the difference that I have mentioned.[1] From the same origin ⟨is⟩ also this ⟨expression⟩ of Ennius:[2]

> without delay take and kill me and my son

For *extemplo* ["without delay"] is *continuo* ["without a break"], since every temple must be fenced around without a break and not have more than one entrance.

[1] In what immediately precedes (cf. *Trag.* F 169).   [2] The utterance is sometimes referred to Andromache and Astyanax in *Andromacha* or, with a change to *acceptam . . . filiam*, to Hecuba and Polyxena in *Hecuba*.

171 Varro, *On the Latin Language*

Ennius:[1]

> so that [or: as soon as][2] Trivia, of Titan's family, gave
> [or: will have given] you a line of children

Trivia, of Titan's family, is Diana, called "Trivia" from the fact that she [i.e., an image of her] is generally placed at a meeting place of three roads [*trivium*] in Greek cities or because she is said to be the moon, who moves in the sky in three ways [*tribus viis*], toward the summit, to the side,

[1] This line has been attributed to Ennius' *Medea* or *Andromeda*.   [2] The character of this *ut*-clause is uncertain.

181

dinem et longitudinem. Titanis dicta, quod eam genuit, ut {ni} [*Spengel*] Plautus [*Bacch.* 893], Lato; ea, ut scribit Manilius [Man. F 2 *FPL*[4]], "est Coe<o> creata Titano."

172 Varro, *Ling.* 7.19

Enni{i}:

ia[6]?   Areopagitae quid dedere † quam pudam †

Areopagitae ab Areopago; {h}is [*Laetus*] locus Athenis.

quid *cod.*: quia *Ribbeck*[2]   † quam pudam † *Jocelyn*: quam pudam *cod.*: aequam pilam *Ribbeck*[2]

173 Varro, *Ling.* 7.48

apud Ennium:

an[4]   quaeque in corpore cava caeruleo
an[4c]/   caeli cortina receptat
paroem

cava cortina dicta, quod est inter terram et caelum ad similitudinem cortinae Apollinis; ea a corde, quod inde sortes primae existimatae.

1 cav{s}a *Columna*: causa *cod.*   2 caeli <c>ortina receptat *Turnebus* (<c>ortina receptat *iam Columna*): cęlo orta nare ceptat *cod.*

---

[1] Some scholars regard this fragment as coming from a tragedy, while others assign it to Ennius' *Annals* or are unsure about the genre. Meter and style suggest a tragedy (perhaps including reflections on natural philosophy), but the context remains uncertain.

and into the distance. She is called "of Titan's family" because, as Plautus ‹says› [*Bacch.* 893], Lato [Leto / Latona] brought her into being; she [Lato], as Manilius writes [Man. F 2 *FPL*⁴], "was sired by the Titan Coeus."

172 Varro, *On the Latin Language*

‹A line› of Ennius:[1]

what did the judges of the Areopagus give . . . (?)?

Areopagitae ["judges of the Areopagus"] ‹is derived› from *Areopagus*; this ‹is› a place in Athens.

[1] Mention of the Areopagus (meeting place of that court in Athens) has often encouraged the connection of this fragment with Ennius' *Eumenides*. The precise meaning is uncertain because of the corruption in the second half. The frequently adopted conjecture *aequam pilam* is based on the assumed context and suggests the equality of votes for and against Orestes, achieved by Athena in Aeschylus' version (Aesch. *Eum.* 674–753).

173 Varro, *On the Latin Language*

In Ennius:[1]

and what [or: whatever] the hollow cauldron receives in the blue body of the sky

cava cortina ["hollow cauldron"] ‹is› said because it is between earth and sky in the shape of Apollo's cauldron [the vessel on the oracular tripod at Delphi]; this [*cortina*] ‹is derived› from *cor* ["heart"] because the first fortune-telling lots ‹are› believed ‹to have been taken› from there.

174 Varro, *Ling.* 7.49

apud Ennium:

ia[6]   quin inde invitis sumpserint perduellibus

perduelles dicuntur hostes; . . .

175 Varro, *Ling.* 7.87

‹ . . . lymphata› [*Turnebus e* Cic. *Div.* 1.80] dicta a lympha;
‹lympha› [*L. Spengel*] a Nympha, ut quod apud Graecos
Θέτις, apud Ennium:

?   Thelis illi mater

   Thelis *Delrius*: thetis *cod.*

176 Varro, *Ling.* 7.89

apud Ennium:

tr[7]   si voles advortere animum, comiter monstrabitur

comiter hilare ac lubenter, cuius origo Graeca κῶμος, . . .

174 Varro, *On the Latin Language*

In Ennius:

> that they should not take ‹something / someone›
> from there against the will of their foes

perduelles ["foes"] is used as a term for *hostes* ["enemies"];[1] . . .

[1] For *perduellis* as the old term for "enemy," when *hostis* meant "foreigner," see Cic. *Off.* 1.37; Varro, *Ling.* 5.3.

175 Varro, *On the Latin Language*

‹*lymphata*› ["frantic"] is derived from *lympha* ["water nymph"]; ‹*lympha*› ["water nymph"] from *Nympha* ["nymph"], as, what ‹is› Thetis among the Greeks, ‹is› in Ennius:[1]

> Thelis[2] ‹is› his mother

[1] When understood as a statement about Achilles and his mother, Thetis, the fragment is attributed to Ennius' *Achilles*, *Hectoris lytra*, or *Iphigenia*, as these tragedies are thought to include Achilles. [2] For "Thelis" (or, perhaps, "Telis") as an ancient form of "Thetis," see Varro, *Rust.* 3.9.19.

176 Varro, *On the Latin Language*

In Ennius:

> if you would like to turn your mind here, it will be
> shown willingly

comiter ["courteously"] ‹means› "cheerfully" and "willingly"; its Greek origin ‹is› *komos* ["revelry"], . . .

177 Varro, *Ling.* 7.93

euax verbum ni{c}hil significat, sed effutitum naturaliter
est (ut apud Ennium:

ᵖ   hehae! ipse clipeus cecidit

apud Ennium [*Inc.* F 12]: . . . ; apud . . .); . . .

Cf. Gramm. inc., *GL* V, p. 574.24.

178 Varro, *Ling.* 7.101

apud Ennium:

ia^6 vocibus concide, fac iam musset obrutus

mussare dictum, quod muti non amplius quam MU di-
cunt; a quo idem dicit id quod minimum est [*Inc.* F 13]:
"neque, ut aiunt, μῦ facere audent."

    fac i‹am› mus‹s›et *Warmington*: facimus et *cod.*

Cf. Serv. et Serv. Dan. ad Verg. *Aen.* 12.657.

179 Varro, *Ling.* 10.70

† de † genere multi utuntur non modo poetae, sed etiam
† plerique haec primo omnes † qui soluta oratione loquun-
tur dicebant ut qu‹a›estorem praetorem, sic Hectorem
Nestorem: itaque Ennius ait:

186

177 Varro, *On the Latin Language*

The word *euax* ["hurray"] does not mean anything, but is
something blurted forth spontaneously (as in Ennius:[1]

oh [*hapax legomenon*]! the shield itself fell down

in Ennius [*Inc.* F 12]: . . . ; in . . .); . . .

[1] This exclamation is attributed to Ennius' tragedies by almost
all editors; only Spengel suggests that it might be from a comedy,
where someone ridicules a soldier. It could come from any of the
tragedies including battles.

178 Varro, *On the Latin Language*

In Ennius:[1]

thrash him with words, see to it that he will just
    mutter (?), crushed[2]

mussare ["mutter"] <is> said, because *muti* ["the mute"]
do not say more than "*mu*"; hence the same <poet> says
this that is least [*Inc.* F 13]: "and, as they say, they do not
dare to utter *mu*."

[1] This line is mostly attributed to Ennius' tragedies, although
a few editors consider comedies: Wright (1974, 67) attributes the
line to a *flagitatio* scene in a comedy.   [2] The middle of the
line is corrupt; the translation is based on the adopted conjecture.

179 Varro, *On the Latin Language*

Not only do many poets use this form, but also almost all
(?) who speak in prose initially used to say, like *quaestorem*,
praetorem ["quaestor," "praetor": Roman words with
Latin form of accusative], thus *Hectorem*, *Nestorem*
["Hector," "Nestor": Greek words with Latin form of ac-
cusative]: hence Ennius says:

P   Hectoris natum de Troiano muro iactari

Accius [*Trag. inc.* XXXVI R.[2–3]] haec in tragoediis largius a prisca consuetudine movere coepit et ad formas Graecas verborum magis revocare, . . .

    Troiano *del. Scaliger et multi edd.*   iactarier *Scaliger et multi edd.*

180 Rut. Lup., *RLM*, p. 8.14–19

διαφορά. hoc schema ‹est›, cum verbum iteratum aliam sententiam significat, ac significavit primo dictum. id est huius modi: . . . item in Enni versu [*Halm sec. Meineke*: item universum *codd.*]:

tr[7]   mulierem: quid potius dicam aut verius quam
        mulierem?

181 Fronto, Ad M. Caesarem et invicem libri, *Ep.* 8.1 (p. 28.7–9 van den Hout)

† adfinitate sociatum neque tutelae subditum, praeterea in ea fortuna constitutum in qua, ut Q. Ennius ait,

tr[7]   omnes dant consilium vanum atque ad voluptatem
        omnia

Hector's son be thrown from the Trojan wall[1]

Accius [*Trag. inc.* XXXVI R.[2-3]] in his tragedies began to move these ⟨forms⟩ to quite a large extent away from the ancient usage and to return them rather to the Greek forms of the words [i.e., used the Greek form of the accusative], . . .

[1] Most editors attribute this fragment to Ennius' *Andromacha*, and some connect it with Enn. *Trag.* F 23. The piece must come from a tragedy dealing with the aftermath of the capture of Troy, which could also be *Hecuba*.

180 Rutilius Lupus

diaphora ["difference," in Greek]. This figure ⟨exists⟩ when a word, when repeated, expresses a different meaning from what it expressed when used for the first time. This is of this kind: . . . . Likewise in Ennius' line:

woman [*acc.*]: what could I say better or more truly than "woman"?[1]

[1] The grammarian's interpretation implies that the second instance of the word *mulier* has different connotations.

181 Fronto, *Correspondence* [Marcus Aurelius to Fronto]

(?) a man ⟨not⟩ bound by kinship and not subject to guardianship, moreover set up in such a social position in which, as Ennius says,

all give empty counsel and everything directed to pleasing

182 Fronto, Ad M. Caesarem et invicem libri, *Ep.* 2.3 (p. 55.15–16 van den Hout)

de Herode quod dicis, perge, oro te, ut Quintus noster [i.e., Ennius] ait,

*ia*⁶   pervince pertinaci pervicacia

183 Paul. *Fest.*, p. 110.16–17 L.

METUS feminine dicebant. Ennius:

ia/tr   vivam an moriar, nulla in me est metus

Cf. Fest., p. 364.2–5 L.

184 Fest., p. 166.11–24 L.

NAUCUM ait Ateius Philologus poni pro nugis. . . . quidam ex Graeco, quod sit ναὶ καὶ οὐχί, levem hominem significari. . . . sed ⟨et⟩ Ennius:

*ia*⁶   illic est nugator, nihili, non nauci homo

illic *Ursinus*: illuc *cod.*   nihil⟨i⟩ *Ursinus*: nihil *cod.*

182 Fronto, *Correspondence* [Marcus Aurelius to Fronto]

As regards what you say about Herodes [Herodes Atticus], carry on, I pray you, as our Quintus[1] says,

> prevail with persevering persistence![2]

[1] The collocation *Quintus noster* denoting a poet can refer only to Ennius (cf. Enn. *Trag.* F 181; cf. T 8, 9, 31, 44, 50, 102: *noster Ennius / pater Ennius*; cf. Enn. *Trag.* F 49, 73, 84, 101, 109, 181: *Quintus Ennius*).   [2] On the meaning of the terms see also Acc. *Trag.* 4–9 R.[2–3].

183 Paul the Deacon, *Epitome of Festus*

They used to say *metus* ["fear"] in feminine gender. Ennius:

> whether I live or die, there is no fear in me

184 Festus

Ateius the philologist[1] says that *naucum* ["a thing of trifling value"] is used instead of *nugae* ["trifle"]. . . . Some, from the Greek, because it is *nai kai ouchi* ["yes and no," in Greek], that it denotes a shallow man. . . . But ⟨also⟩ Ennius:[2]

> this person is a fool, a nothing, a man of not even a
> little worth

[1] L. Ateius Praetextatus, a grammarian (1st c. BC).
[2] The fragment has been attributed to Ennius' tragedies, comedies, or satires.

185 Fest., p. 218.2–6 L.

OBSIDIONEM potius dicendum esse, quam obsidium, ad-
iuvat nos testimonio suo Ennius [Pacuvius *unus cod.*] in
Telamone cum ait [*Trag.* F 118]: . . . item alio loco:

*ia*⁶   Hector, qui haud cessat obsidionem obducere

186

a Fest., p. 388.25–32 L.

SOSP⟨ES⟩ . . . Enn⟨ius⟩

?   . . . parentem et pa . . . sospitem

. . . Ennius [Inc. *Ann.* F 129] vid⟨*etur servatorem
signi*⟩ficare cum dix⟨it⟩ [*Ursinus ex Epitoma*] ". . . liber."

pa⟨triam di servate⟩ *Scaliger et multi edd.*

b Paul. *Fest.*, p. 389.6–7 L.

SOSPES salvus. Ennius tamen "sospitem" pro servatore
posuit.

192

185 Festus

In that one should say *obsidio* ["blockade"] rather than *obsidium* ["blockade": less common form, mainly ante- and post-class.] Ennius supports us by his testimony in *Telamo*, when he says: [*Trag.* F 118]: . . . Likewise elsewhere:[1]

Hector, who does not hesitate to lead ⟨troops⟩
    against the blockade

[1] Since this fragment mentions Hector, it has often been attributed to Ennius' *Hectoris lytra*, but the play *Achilles* is equally possible.

186

a Festus

sospes ["safe and sound"] . . . Ennius

    . . . father and . . . (?) preserver[1]

. . . Ennius [Inc. *Ann.* F 129] ⟨seems to mean "preserver" when he said⟩ ". . . free."

[1] Since text is missing in the middle, and presumably at the beginning, of the fragment, construction and context must remain uncertain. The widely accepted conjecture by Scaliger makes sense if *sospes* is assumed in its ordinary sense.

b Paul the Deacon, *Epitome of Festus*

sospes ["safe and sound"], "unharmed." Yet Ennius has put *sospes* ["safe and sound"] instead of "preserver."

187 Fest., p. 488.12–23 L.

⟨TESCA sun⟩t loca augurio desig⟨nata⟩ . . . ⟨*Cic*⟩ero aspera, difficilia aditu . . .

?   loca aspera, saxa, tesca tuor

       ⟨lo⟩ca *Scaliger*

Cf. Paul. *Fest.*, p. 489.7–8 L.

188 Fest., p. 494.12–20 L.

TAM significationem habet, cum ponimus propositivam quandam, cui subiungimus quam, aut cum dicimus tam egregium opus tam parvo pretio venisse, id est sic, ita, . . . at antiqui tam etiam pro tamen usi sunt, ut Naevius [*Com.* 130/31 R.$^{2-3}$]: . . . Ennius:

?   ille meae tam potis pacis potiri

TRAGEDIES: INCERTA

187 Festus

⟨*tesca* ["holy places"] are⟩ sites marked out for augury. . . .
Cicero ⟨says that they are⟩ rough and difficult to access
. . .

rough sites, rocks, holy places I see[1]

[1] The section in Festus is lacunose and thus unclear; in his
epitome, Paul the Deacon merely transmits part of the lemma.
The quotation can be attributed to Ennius only by reference to
liber Vaticanus n. 2731 (S) (quoted by Mommsen 1865, 276):
*templa antiqua tesca esse ait cuero aspera difficilia aditu. Ennius:
ardua aspera saxa tuos.* Still, reconstructing the precise wording
of what should be attributed to Ennius remains difficult.

188 Festus

tam ["so"] has a meaning, when we put it as some kind of
proposition, to which we add *quam* ["as"], or when we say
"such a great work has been bought for such a small price,"
that is *sic, ita* ["so," "thus": other Latin words with the
same meaning], . . . But the ancients also used *tam* in-
stead of *tamen* ["still"], as Naevius [*Com.* 130/31 R.[2-3]]: . . .
Ennius:[1]

still, this person ⟨is⟩ able to gain my amity

[1] This quotation is generally attributed to Ennius' dramas,
though some scholars have doubted whether the piece is tragic.
The meter and line division, and also the context, must remain
uncertain.

195

189 Schol. ad Hor. *Carm.* 3.11.18

"muniant angues caput eius": ut ait Ennius:

ia/tr　　angue villosi canis

190 Donat., *GL* IV, p. 398.24–26

homoeoteleuton est cum simili modo dictiones plurimae finiuntur, ut

tr[7]　　eos reduci quam relinqui, devehi quam deseri
　　　　malui

Cf. Charis., *GL* I, p. 282.9–11 = p. 370 B.; Diom., *GL* I, p. 447.5–8 ("ut apud Ennium").

191 Non., p. 196.29–32 M. = 289 L.

CAEMENTA neutri, ut est usu. . . . feminini Ennius:

ia[6]　　labat, labuntur saxa, caementae cadunt

　　lab{ab}untur *edd.*: lababuntur *codd.*　　caementa⟨e⟩ *Iunius*: caementa *codd.*

192 Non., pp. 197.28–98.4 M. = 290 L.

QUIS et generi feminino adtribui posse veterum auctoritas voluit. . . . Ennius:

ia　　et quis illaec est quae lugubri succincta est stola?

189 Scholia to Horace, *Odes*

"‹though› snakes fortify his head": as Ennius says:[1]

of a dog shaggy with a snake

[1] These words are generally seen as coming from a tragedy by Ennius. If the commentator on Horace correctly noted a close parallel (Hor. *Carm.* 3.11.17–20), this would be a description of Cerberus and presumably come from a tragedy in which someone enters the underworld.

190 Donatus

A homoeoteleuton is when many words end in a similar way, like

I have wanted them rather to be led back than left behind, to be taken away than abandoned

191 Nonius

caementa ["stones"] ‹is› of neuter ‹gender›, as it is customary. . . . of feminine ‹gender› [*hapax legomenon*] Ennius:

it totters, the rocks drop, the stones fall

192 Nonius

quis ["who"], the authority of the ancients wanted it to be able to be assigned also to the feminine gender. . . . Ennius:

and who is this woman who is clothed in a garment of mourning?

193 Non., p. 205.23–30 M. = 302 L.

FRETUM neutri tamen generis esse volumus. . . . masculini
. . . Ennius:

*tr*⁷   crassa pulvis oritur, omnem pervolat caeli fretum

194 Hieron. *Ep.* 60.14.4

Naevius poeta [*Com.* 106 R.²⁻³]: "pati," inquit, "necesse est
multa mortalem mala." unde . . . , prudenterque Ennius:

   plebes

ait

*ia*⁶   in hoc regi antestat loco: licet
       lacrimare plebi, regi honeste non licet.

ut regi, sic episcopo. immo minus regi quam episcopo. ille
enim nolentibus praeest, hic volentibus; . . .

195 Serv. Dan. ad Verg. *G.* 1.12

nonnulli vero ob hoc "cui prima frementem fudit aquam"
legunt, quod veteres murmura aquae fremitum dicebant:
Ennius

ia/tr   ager oppletus imbrium fremitu

et denuo [Inc. *Ann.* F 62] . . . , Vergilius in XI [*Aen.* 11.299]
. . .

---

¹ The fragment has often been ascribed to Ennius' *Androm-
eda,* but the reference is not clearly to sea water. Kessissoglu
(1990, 72–73) attributes the line to *Euhemerus.*

193 Nonius

Nevertheless, we want *fretum* ["strait"] to be of neuter gender.... of masculine [rarer and mainly ante-class.] ... Ennius:

> thick dust rises, it flies through the entire strait of the sky

194 Jerome, *Letters*

The poet Naevius says [*Com.* 106 R.[2–3]]: "it is necessary that a mortal bears many evils." Hence ..., and wisely Ennius says:[1]

> the common people are superior to the king in this:
> the common people are allowed to shed tears, a king
>   is not allowed to do so, with honor.

As for a king, thus for a bishop. In fact, less so for a king than for a bishop. For the former is in charge of those who are not willing, the latter of those who are willing; ...

[1] This general statement could come from any of Ennius' tragedies involving "kings"; it has often been attributed to *Iphigenia*.

195 Servius Danielis, *Commentary on Virgil*

But some read [in Virgil] "to whom she [the earth] first sent forth rumbling water [*frementem ... aquam*, while others read: *frementem ... equum*, 'a horse']" for this reason, namely that the ancients called the murmur of water "rumble" [*fremitus*]: Ennius[1]

> a field filled with the rumble of downpours

and again [Inc. *Ann.* F 62] ..., Virgil in ‹Book› 11 [*Aen.* 11.299] ...

196 Serv. Dan. ad Verg. *Aen.* 9.399

"pulchram properet per vulnera mortem": aut deest
"adire," aut deest "ad," ut sit "ad mortem properet": aut
certe antique "properet mortem," ut Plautus [F 165 L.]
"properate prandium." Ennius:

ia/tr   festivum festinant diem

Cf. Serv. Dan. ad Verg. *G.* 4.170.

197 Serv. ad Verg. *Aen.* 1.4

"saevae": cum a iuvando dicta sit Iuno, quaerunt multi, cur
eam dixerit saevam, et putant temporale esse epitheton,
quasi saeva circa Troianos, nescientes quod saevam dice-
bant veteres magnam. sic Ennius:

ia/tr   induta fuit saeva stola

198 Serv. Dan. ad Verg. *Aen.* 2.62

"occumbere morti": novae locutionis figura et penitus re-
mota. Ennius:

tr⁷?   ut vos nostri liberi
tr⁷   defendant, pro vostra vita morti occumbant obviam

1 nostri *cod.*: vestri *cod.²*   2 vostra *cod.*: vestra *cod.²*

196 Servius Danielis, *Commentary on Virgil*

"should he hasten a beautiful death through wounds": either "to go toward" is missing, or "toward" is missing, so that it would be "should hasten toward death": or certainly ⟨he uses⟩ "he should hasten death" in an old-fashioned way, as Plautus [F 165 L.] "make haste over a meal." Ennius:[1]

they make haste over the festive day

[1] The example from Ennius has a verb different from the one used in Virgil, but the verb in Ennius seems to have a similar meaning and use. The discussion distinguishes between intransitive (with indication of direction) and transitive uses of these verbs.

197 Servius, *Commentary on Virgil*

saevae ["ferocious"]: since Juno is derived from *iuvare* ["to help"], many ask why he [Virgil] has called her *saeva* ["ferocious"], and they believe that it is an occasional epithet, as if she were "ferocious" as regards the Trojans, not knowing that the ancients used *saeva* for *magna* ["large, great"]. Thus Ennius:

she was clothed in a large garment

198 Servius Danielis, *Commentary on Virgil*

occumbere morti ["to meet death"]: A form of a novel expression and far removed ⟨from ordinary usage⟩. Ennius:

that our sons defend you, meet death for the sake of your life

199 Serv. ad Verg. *Aen.* 6.686

"genis": palpebris: Ennius de dormiente:

ia/tr   imprimitque genae genam

200 Serv. ad Verg. *Aen.* 7.320

"Cisseis": regina Hecuba filia secundum Euripidem [cf. Eur. *Hec.* 3] Cissei, quem Ennius et Pacuvius et Vergilius sequuntur: nam Homerus [*Il.* 16.718] Dymantis dicit. haec se facem parere vidit et Parin creavit, qui causa fuit incendii.

201 Paul. *Fest.*, p. 507.12–13 L.

VITULANS: laetans gaudio, ut partu. Ennius:

ia⁶   is habet coronam vitulans victoria

202

199 Servius, *Commentary on Virgil*

genis ["from the eyes"]: "from the eyelids." Ennius about someone sleeping:

and s/he presses eyelid to eyelid

200 Servius, *Commentary on Virgil*

"Cisseis":[1] queen Hecuba, daughter of Cisseus, according to Euripides [cf. Eur. *Hec.* 3], whom Ennius and Pacuvius and Virgil follow: for Homer [*Il.* 16.718] says ⟨that she is the daughter⟩ of Dymas. She saw that she was giving birth to a torch and brought forth Paris, who was the cause of a fire.

[1] Some scholars assign the word *Cisseis* ("daughter of Cisseus") to Ennius, but the passage does not imply that it is a quotation; this section is rather a testimonium on the genealogy of Hecuba followed by various poets (cf. Eur. *Hec.* 3–4; Apollod. *Bibl.* 3.12.5 – 3.148, Hyg. *Fab.* 91.1). Most scholars refer the reference to Ennius' *Hecuba.*

201 Paul the Deacon, *Epitome of Festus*

vitulans ["uttering a cry of joy": rare and mainly anteclass.]: "rejoicing with joy," as about birth. Ennius:[1]

he has the crown, uttering a cry of joy in victory

[1] This extract is often attributed to Ennius' *Alexander* and referred to a description of Alexander's (= Paris') victory.

PRAETEXTAE (F 1–5)

Like his predecessor Naevius, Ennius wrote serious dra-
mas not only on Greek myths (tragedies) but also on Ro-
man history (fabulae praetextae), *a specifically Roman*
dramatic genre. The fragments provide evidence of two
plays, each one representing one of what appear to be the

AMBRACIA (F 1–4)

Marcus Fulvius Nobilior waged war against the Aetolians
in 189 BC and captured the city of Ambracia (Liv. 38.3.9–
11.9; Polyb. 21.25–30). Ennius accompanied him on that
campaign and described his achievement in literary works,
presumably in Annales 15 *and in this* praetexta *(cf. T 10,*
29, 88, 92, 95, 96). A possible occasion for the play was the

1 Non., pp. 87.28–88.2 M. = 125 L.

CLUET: nominatur. . . . Ennius Ambracia:

tr^7 per gentes esse cluebat omnium miserrimus

PRAETEXTAE (F 1–5)

main types: plays on contemporary history and plays on the foundation stories of Rome.

Bibl.: Suerbaum 1994, 361; 2002, 129; 2003, 222; Manuwald 2001 [2004], 75–78, 148–50. Lit.: Manuwald 2001; Kragelund 2002; Boyle 2006, 83–87.

AMBRACIA (F 1–4)

games vowed to Iuppiter Optimus Maximus at Ambracia und celebrated in 186 BC (Liv. 39.5.7–10, 39.22.1–2).

Bibl.: Suerbaum 1994, 361; 2002, 129; 2003, 222; Manuwald 2001 [2004], 149. Lit.: Suerbaum 1994, 361; 2002, 129; Manuwald 2001, 162–72; Boyle 2006, 83–85.

1 Nonius

cluet ["he is said": ante-class. word]: "he is spoken of." . . . Ennius in *Ambracia*:

> among the peoples he was said to be the most
>   wretched of all

2 Non., pp. 183.1–5 M. = 268–69 L.

VEGET, pro vegetat vel erigit vel vegetum est. . . . Ennius Ambracia:

da⁶/an?   et aequora salsa veges ingentibus ventis

3 Non., p. 469.25–29 M. = 753 L.

CUNCTANT, pro cunctantur. . . . Ennius Ambracia:

tr⁷   bene mones tute: ipse cunctat: o vide fortem virum!

   cuncto *codd. nonnulli*: cunctato *codd. rell.*: cunctato o *Vahlen*

4 Non., p. 471.11–18 M. = 756 L.

POPULAT: est et passivum populatur. . . . Ennius Ambracia:

tr⁷?   agros audaces depopulant servi dominorum domi

   domi{nis} *Buecheler*: dominis *codd.*: domini *Bothe*: minis *Ribbeck olim*

SABINAE (F 5)

The title suggests a play representing the famous abduction of the Sabine women after the foundation of Rome (e.g., Liv. 1.9–13; Ov. Fast. 3.187–228; Plut. Rom. 14–19; Dion. Hal. Ant. Rom. 2.30–46). The surviving fragment may represent the women intervening in the fight between their fathers and husbands.

2 Nonius

veget ["enlivens": archaic word], instead of "invigorates" or "causes to rise" or "it is vigorous." . . . Ennius in *Ambracia*:

> and you [Neptune?] enliven the salty seas with immense winds

3 Nonius

cunctant ["they hesitate": active], instead of *cunctantur* [deponent form]. . . . Ennius in *Ambracia*:

> you advise well: he hesitates: o, see the brave man!

4 Nonius

populat ["plunders"]: there is also a passive [i.e., deponent form] *populatur*. . . . Ennius in *Ambracia*:

> bold slaves lay waste the fields of their masters at home

SABINAE (F 5)

Bibl.: Suerbaum 1994, 361; 2002, 129; 2003, 222; Manuwald 2001 [2004], 149–50. Lit.: Lentano 1989; Suerbaum 1994, 361; 2002, 129; Manuwald 2001, 172–79; Boyle 2006, 85–87.

5 Iulius Victor, *Ars* 6.4, *RLM*, p. 402.28–31

ab eventu in qualitate, ut: "qualia sunt ea, quae evenerunt aut quae videantur eventura, tale illud quoque existimetur, ex quo evenerunt," ut Sabinis Ennius dixit:

ia⁶　cum spolia generi‹s› detraxeritis, quam ‹, patres,›
　　　inscriptionem dabitis?

1 generi‹s› *Jan*: generi *cod.*　　‹patres› *Mueller*

5 Iulius Victor

From the result with regard to quality, as: "of what kind are those that have resulted or that seem about to result, of that kind too will be regarded that from which they have resulted," as Ennius said in *Sabinae*:

> when you have dragged ⟨us as?⟩ spoils away from
> ⟨your?⟩ sons-in-law ⟨, fathers,⟩ what
> inscription will you put up?[1]

[1] The reference is to a dedicatory inscription as on a triumphal monument.

COMOEDIAE (F 1–6)

Ennius wrote comedies in the palliata *tradition best known from the plays of Plautus and Terence, but little remains, and he was apparently not regarded as very successful in the genre (T 4). A plot cannot be determined for any play.*

CAUPUNCULA (F 1)

The title of this play, corrupted in transmission, does not refer to a figure or an event from myth or history; the play is therefore generally regarded as a comedy. The common restoration now is Caupuncula, *presumably derived from* copa *("a woman who provides entertainment in taverns, a dancing girl") rather than from* caupona *("a landlady; an*

1 Non., p. 155.30–31 M. = 229 L.

PROPITIABILIS, a propitiando [ad propitiandum *codd. nonnulli*]. Ennius Caupuncula [*Ribbeck*: cupiuncula *codd.*: Cupuncula *Vahlen*: Coponicula *Onions*]:

ia/tr hinc est animus propitiabilis

COMEDIES (F 1–6)

Bibl.: Suerbaum 1994, 361–62; 2002, 129; 2003, 223. *Lit.*: Traina 1960, 94–96; Wright 1974, 62–67; Suerbaum 1994, 361–62; 2002, 129; 2003, 223.

CAUPUNCULA (F 1)

inn, tavern, lodging house"). *The character of this woman was probably central to the plot, but no details can be inferred from the single, fairly general fragment.*

Bibl.: Suerbaum 2002, 129; 2003, 223. *Lit.*: Wright 1974, 63; Suerbaum 1994, 361.

1 Nonius

propitiabilis ["able to be propitiated"], from "propitiate" [adjective derived from verb]. Ennius in *Caupuncula*:

hence the mind is able to be propitiated

211

PANCRATIASTES (F 2–4)

The title and the fragments identify this play as a comedy.
The title (lit., "a combatant in the pancratium") may be
metaphorical ("the all-round champion"), referring to the
typical comic slave (cf. Palaestrio of Plaut. Mil.*). The frag-*

2 Non., pp. 505.35–6.3 M. = 813 L.

AUDIBO, pro audiam. Ennius Telamone [*Trag.* F 124]: . . .
idem Pancratiaste:

ia^8 quo nunc me ducis? :: ubi molarum strepitum audibis
    maximum

3 Non., p. 513.12–13 M. = 825 L.

PROTERVITER: Ennius Pancratiaste:

ia^6 quis est qui nostris foribus tam proterviter?

Cf. Plaut. *Rud.* 414; *Truc.* 256.

4 Non., p. 517.10–13 M. = 832 L.

DESUBITO: . . . Ennius Pancratiaste:

tr^7 cum desubito me orat mulier lacrimansque ad genua
    accidit

PANCRATIASTES (F 2–4)

ments suggest stock comic elements: slave punishment (F 2), door-knocking (F 3), pathetic narrative (F 4).

Bibl.: Suerbaum 2002, 129; 2003, 223. Lit.: Wright 1974, 63–66; Suerbaum 1994, 361–62.

2 Nonius

audibo ["I will hear"], instead of *audiam* [class. form of future tense]. Ennius in *Telamo* [*Trag.* F 124]: . . . The same ‹poet› in *Pancratiastes*:

> where are you leading me now? :: where you will hear
>   the noise of millstones loudest

3 Nonius

proterviter ["boldly": unique form of adverb]: Ennius in *Pancratiastes*:

> who is he who ‹knocks› so boldly at our door?

4 Nonius

desubito ["suddenly"]: . . . Ennius in *Pancratiastes*:

> when suddenly the woman entreats me and falls
>   down at my knees, shedding tears.

INCERTUM (F 5)

The second line of this fragment recalls a line of Naevius'
Tarentilla *(Paul. Fest., p. 26.14–15 L.:* ADNICTAT saepe et
leviter oculo adnuit. Naevius in Tarentilla: alii adnutat, alii
adnictat, alium amat, alium tenet.*), which has since Sca-*
liger encouraged attribution of this play to Naevius, but
the evidence of Isidore is unambiguous, and the fragment
should be retained for Ennius (thus Jocelyn 1972, 1002
and n. 149; von Albrecht 1975, 237; Suerbaum 1994, 362;

5 Isid. *Orig.* 1.26.1–2

sunt quaedam et digitorum notae, sunt et oculorum, qui-
bus secum taciti proculque distantes conloquuntur. sicut
mos est militaris, ut quotiens consentit exercitus, quia
voce non potest, manu promittat. alii quia voce non pos-
sunt, gladiorum motu salutant. [2] Ennius de quadam
impudica:

ia^6?	quasi in choro pila
ia^6	ludens datatim dat se et communem facit.
	alium tenet, alii adnutat, alibi manus
	est occupata, alii pervellit pedem,
5	alii dat anulum spectandum, a labris
	alium invocat, cum⟨que⟩ alio cantat; adtamen
	aliis dat digito litteras.

2 dadatim *unus cod.*: datim *duo codd.*   se *Otto*: sese
codd.   5 expectandum *nonnulli codd.*: spectandum *codd.*
rel.   6 cum⟨que⟩ *Ribbeck*

INCERTUM (F 5)

2002, 129; 2003, 223). The similarity of language probably reflects the uniform diction of the palliata *tradition (cf. Plaut.* Asin. *774–86), while the parallel with Naevius further supports identification of the line with comedy, not satire (both considered by von Albrecht 1975, 237). On the fragment, and its implications for the comedies of Naevius and Ennius, see von Albrecht 1975, 235–39.*

5 Isidore, *Origins*

There are also some signs of the fingers, and there are some of the eyes, by which they converse with each other silently and at a great distance. Such is the military custom, so that, whenever the army agrees, it makes assurances by hand because it cannot do so by voice. Others, since they cannot do so by voice, make a greeting with a movement of swords. [2] Ennius ‹says› about some unchaste girl:

> As if playing with a ball in a group
> she offers herself from hand to hand and makes
>   herself common.
> She holds one, nods to another, elsewhere a hand
> is busy, one she pinches at the foot,
> to another she gives a ring to look at, from her lips   5
> she summons one, and she sings with yet another;
>   still
> she makes letters with her finger for others.

DUBIUM (F 6)

*The late-antique writer Fulgentius (6th c. AD) cites this
fragment as from an otherwise unknown Ennian comedy
(evidence in Baldwin 1988, 44). Since many of his quota-
tions are problematic, Fulgentius is considered an unreli-
able source: whether this testimony is trustworthy and
sufficient to posit a play called* Telestis *thus remains in
doubt. He does, however, also transmit genuine material.
The piece could be authentic even though this is the only*

6 Fulg. *Serm. ant.* 19

QUID SIT FRIGUTTIRE: friguttire dicitur subtiliter adgar-
rire. unde et Plautus in Casina ait [Plaut. *Cas.* 267]: "quid-
nam friguttis?" et Ennius [Hennius *unus cod.*] in Telestide
[tellestide *vel* celestide *codd. rel.*] comoedia sic ait:

tr^4	haec anus admodum friguttit,
$cr^2 + tr^{4c}$	nimirum sauciavit se flore Liberi

DUBIUM (F 6)

mention of Ennius in Fulgentius and the only record of this play. Scholars now seem increasingly willing to accept it as an Ennian fragment.

Telestis is also the name of the virgo *in Plautus'* Epidicus. *If this is a true fragment, it could be designed to be sung aside to a companion or to the audience (Jocelyn 1972, 1003).*

Bibl.: Suerbaum 1994, 361–62; 2002, 129; 2003, 223.

6 Fulgentius

What is *friguttire* ["to speak indistinctly"]: *friguttire* is said for "to speak in a restrained manner." Whence Plautus says in *Casina* [Plaut. *Cas.* 267]: "Why, pray, are you speaking so indistinctly?," and Ennius puts it thus in the comedy *Telestis*:[1]

> this old woman speaks indistinctly at a high rate [i.e., slurs];
> she has surely wounded herself with the flower of Liber[2]

[1] The different meters in the two lines suggest a lyric section.

[2] Bacchus or Dionysus, the expression standing metonymically for "wine." Drunkenness is characteristic of old women in comedy (cf. Leaena, Plaut. *Curc.* 96–142).

MINOR WORKS

EPICHARMUS (F 1–5)

The Sicilian poet Epicharmus (ca. 540–450 BC) is best known as a writer of comedies based on Greek myths and contemporary themes, but a significant body of gnomic material and philosophical sayings also circulated under his name. Whether he actually composed separate philosophical works is uncertain: the authenticity of this philosophical corpus was already challenged in antiquity (Pseudepicharmeia). *He did, however, come to be seen as an exponent of neo-Pythagorean views (remains in* PCG, *vol. I, pp. 8–173, including fragments from the comedies and* Pseudepicharmeia *as well as Ennius' version; "philosophical" works in DK 23, B 47–54; discussion of* Pseudepicharmeia *in, e.g., Kerkhof 2001, 79–115).*

The work of Ennius called Epicharmus *seems to have been based on these philosophical writings: one fragment suggests the poet dreaming (F 1), another explains the etymology of a name (F 3); others deal with the four elements and their relation to mind and body. It is possible that, as in the proem to the* Annals, *an encounter between Ennius and his Greek predecessor explained how he came*

EPICHARMUS (F 1–5)

to narrate Epicharmus' doctrine, perhaps drawing upon Pythagorean views on the migration of souls. Epicharmus may also have appeared speaking in his own voice, if Varro's introductions, "Epicharmus says" or "Ennius' Epicharmus says" (F 2, 3), refer to the text and not simply to the work's title.

Various metrical patterns appear in the fragments, though the text is often uncertain, and since observations on the nature of the universe and the relationship among gods, humans, and the natural world can also be found in the Annals *and tragedies, attribution of unidentified fragments to the* Epicharmus *can be problematic. Vahlen and Courtney, for example, ascribe* Inc. F 9, 40, *and* 56 *to this work.*

Bibl.: Suerbaum 2002, 130–31; 2003, 225. Edd./Comm.: Garbarino 1973, 130–32, 276–89; Courtney 1993, 30–38. Lit.: Kerényi 1950, 73–80; Suerbaum 1968, 92–94 (on the dream motif); Brink 1972, esp. 562–64 (on the role of Homer); Liuzzi 1973–74 (on Ennius' Pythagorism); Bettini 1979, 31–51; Feeney 1991, 120–22.

1 (= T 27) Cic. *Acad.* 2.51

eadem ratio est somniorum. num censes Ennium, cum in
hortis cum Ser. Galba vicino suo ambulavisset, dixisse
visus sum mihi cum Galba ambulare? at cum somniavit
ita narravit: "visus Homerus adesse poeta" [1 *Ann.* F 3],
idemque in Epicharmo:

> nam videbar somniare med ego esse mortuum

> med ego *Manutius, Lambinus*: me et ego *codd.*

2 Varro, *Ling.* 5.59–60

haec duo Caelum et Terra, quod anima et corpus. humi-
dum et frigidum terra, sive [1 *Ann.* F 7] . . . sive, ut Zenon
Cit⟨ie⟩us [Zeno, F 126 Arn.], animalium semen ignis is
qui anima et mens, qui caldor e caelo, quod huic innume-
rabiles et immortales ignes. itaque Epicharmus [⟨cum⟩
add. Spengel] dicit de mente humana. ait:

> istic est de sole sumptus ignis

idem ⟨de⟩ sole{m} [*Spengel*]:

> isque totus mentis est

ut humores frigidae sunt humi, ut supra ostendi [Varro,
Ling. 5.24]. [60] quibus iuncti caelum et terra omnia ex
⟨se⟩ [*Laetus*] genuerunt, quod per hos natura

> frigori miscet calorem atque humori aritudinem

Cf. Non., p. 71.17–20 M. = 99 L.

---

[1] The founder of the Stoic school of philosophy (ca. 333/2–262
BC).   [2] The quotations described as statements by "Epi-

1 (= T 27) Cicero, *Prior Academics*

The same principle applies to dreams. Do you suppose that Ennius, when he had gone for a walk in the garden with his neighbor Servius Galba[1] said, "I seemed to go for a walk with Galba"? But when he dreamed, he reported thus: "the poet Homer seemed to be present" [1 *Ann.* F 3], and the same poet says in *Epicharmus*:

> for I seemed to dream that I was dead

[1] Ser. Sulpicius Galba (aedile 189, praetor 187 BC).

2 Varro, *On the Latin Language*

These two, Heaven and Earth, are a pair like life and body. Earth is damp and cold, whether [1 *Ann.* F 7] . . . , or, as Zeno of Citium[1] says [Zeno, F 126 Arn.], the seed of living things is that fire, which is life and mind; this heat is from the sky, since it has countless and immortal fires. And thus Epicharmus speaks about the human mind. He says,

> that is fire taken from the sun

the same poet says about the sun:

> and that is entirely mind

as liquids belong to the cold earth, as I have shown above [Varro, *Ling.* 5.24]. [60] Joined with these, the sky and the earth gave birth to everything out of themselves, since through these nature

> mixes heat with cold and dryness with moisture[2]

charmus" are in Latin verse, and since Varro elsewhere speaks of "Ennius' Epicharmus," it appears justified to assign them to Ennius' poem (see Introduction to *Epicharmus*).

223

3 Varro, *Ling.* 5.68

hinc Epicharmus Enni{i} "Proserpinam" quoque appellat, quod solet esse sub terris. dicta Proserpina, quod haec ut serpens modo in dexteram modo in sinisteram partem late [late<ns> *Bettini*] movetur. serpere et proserpere idem dicebant, ut Plautus quod scribit [*Poen.* 1034; *Stich.* 724] "quasi proserpens bestia."

4 Varro, *Rust.* 1.4.1

eius [i.e., agri culturae] principia sunt eadem, quae mundi esse Ennius scribit:

aqua terra anima et sol

et *del. Politianus*

3 Varro, *On the Latin Language*

Hence Ennius' Epicharmus also calls her [the moon] "Proserpina" because she is accustomed to being under the earth.[1] She is called Proserpina since she, like a serpent [*serpens*], moves now to the right, now to the left side over a large area. "To creep" [*serpere*] and "to creep forward" [*proserpere*] mean the same, as Plautus shows, when he writes [*Poen.* 1034; *Stich.* 724] "like an animal creeping forward [*proserpens*]."[2]

[1] The mythical Proserpina spent time in the underworld with Hades.   [2] Varro's derivation of the name Proserpina (Greek Persephone, daughter of Zeus and Demeter) from Latin cognates is now regarded as folk etymology; the name is rather thought to be a Latin version of the Greek (see Cic. *Nat. D.* 2.66), which may have entered Latin via Etruscan. Only the fact that the name Proserpina appeared in Ennius' *Epicharmus*, not the precise wording, can be recovered from Varro's report.

4 Varro, *On Agriculture*

Its [agriculture's] basic elements are the same as those that, as Ennius writes, are those of the world:

water, earth, air and sun [fire][1]

[1] This list of the four elements does not use the standard terminology, but the wording is reminiscent of other fragments and thus likely to reflect Ennius' own terms. This may corroborate attribution of the fragment, transmitted without indication of the work, to *Epicharmus* (since Columna), but some scholars have suggested the *Annals*, since the phrase can be scanned as the end of a hexameter. Cf. the similar list at 7 *Ann.* F 10. Varro may have taken the words from different parts of the work, where they might have occurred in different cases.

5 Prisc., *GL* II, p. 341.18–22

sciendum tamen, quod etiam "hic" et "haec concordis" et
"hoc concorde" dicebant, "hic" et "haec amentis" et "hoc
amente." nec mirum, cuius simplex quoque "mentis" En-
nius protulit in Epicharmo:

terra corpus est, at mentis ignis est

pro "mens."

5 Priscian

Nevertheless, one must note that they also said *concordis* masculine and feminine and *concorde* neuter ["like-minded"; unusual forms of nominative instead of *concors*], *amentis* masculine and feminine and *amente* neuter ["out of one's mind"; unusual forms of nominative instead of *amens*]. Nor is it strange when Ennius put forward also its simple form, *mentis* ["mind": nominative; cf. F 2], in *Epicharmus*:

the body is earth, but the mind is fire

instead of *"mens"* [usual nominative].

EPIGRAMMATA (F 1–3)

*Ennius is said to have introduced to Rome not only the
hexameter, but also the elegiac distich (T 109). The pre-
served couplets allude to the death and lasting achieve-
ments of either Ennius himself or Scipio. They are all be-
lieved to be separate epigrams, a genre for which the
Saturnian meter had previously been used. They may have
been influenced by (near-)contemporary Greek epigram-
matic poetry. There is no evidence for when Ennius' epi-
grams were written and for what particular contexts, but*

1

a Cic. *Leg.* 2.56–57

Gai Mari sitas reliquias apud Anienem dissipari iussit
Sulla victor acerbiore odio incitatus quam si tam sapiens
fuisset quam fuit vehemens; [57] quod haud scio an timens
⟨ne⟩ [*suppl. Lambinus*] suo corpori possit accidere pri-
mus e patriciis Corneliis igni voluit cremari. declarat enim
Ennius de Africano:

> hic est ille situs

vere, nam "siti" dicuntur ii qui conditi sunt.

---

[1] C. Marius (ca. 157–86 BC), the opponent of Sulla.
[2] A river in Italy, tributary of the Tiber. The story is told by
Val. Max. 9.2.1.   [3] P. Cornelius Scipio Africanus and L. Cor-
nelius Sulla Felix were both members of the *gens Cornelia*.

228

EPIGRAMS (F 1–3)

they are often linked to the persistent, though unfounded, tradition that Ennius was buried in the tomb of the Scipiones (having produced the appropriate epigrams before his death) and that a statue of him was erected there besides those of the Scipiones (T 9, 49, 53, 56, 62, 99).

Bibl.: Suerbaum 2002, 132; 2003, 226. Edd./Comm.: Garbarino 1973, 138; Courtney 1993, 39–43. Lit.: Walbank 1967, 57–58; Suerbaum 1968, 167–78, 208–14, 333–36 (on epigrams for Ennius and their reception); Lausberg 1984, 275–77; Skutsch 1985.

1

a Cicero, *On the Laws*

Sulla, when victorious, ordered the remains of Gaius Marius,[1] which had been buried, to be scattered about the Anio,[2] provoked by a hatred more bitter than if he had been as wise as he was violent. [57] Perhaps fearing that this might happen to his own body, Sulla was the first among the patrician Cornelii[3] who wanted to be cremated by fire. For Ennius declares about Africanus:

> here he is laid to rest

rightly, for those who are buried are said to be "laid to rest."

b Sen. *Ep.* 108.33

deinde Ennianos [*Pincianus*: inanes *codd.*] colligit [i.e., grammaticus] versus et in primis illos de Africano scriptos:

> cui nemo civis neque hostis
> quivit pro factis reddere opis pretium

ex eo se ait intellegere ⟨opem⟩ [*Korsch*] apud antiquos non tantum auxilium significasse sed operam. ait {opera} [*Vahlen*] enim Ennius [*Haase*: in eius *vel* eius *codd.*] neminem potuisse Scipioni neque civem neque hostem reddere operae pretium.

    2 quivit *Muretus*: quivult *codd.*   opis *Vahlen*: operae *codd.*

2

a Cic. *Tusc.* 1.34

loquor de principibus; quid poetae? nonne post mortem nobilitari volunt? unde ergo illud?

> aspicite, o cives, senis Enni imaginis formam:
> hic vestrum panxit maxuma facta patrum

mercedem gloriae flagitat ab is quorum patres adfecerat gloria. idemque:

    2 panxit *Victorius*: pinxit *codd.*

---

[1] Whether these epitaphs are genuine or derive from a later source is unknown. They should not be associated with the representation of Ennius in the tomb of the Scipiones (T 9, 49, 56, 62), whose identity would not have been debated if accompanied by an epitaph.

b Seneca, *Epistles*

Then he [a grammarian] collects Ennian lines and in particular those written about Africanus:

> to whom nobody, neither citizen nor foreigner,[1]
> was able to render recompense for his efforts in
> proportion to his deeds[2]

On that basis he says that he understands that among the ancients the term *ops* meant not only "help" [*auxilium*], but also "effort" [*opera*]. For Ennius says that nobody, neither citizen nor foreigner, could have rendered Scipio recompense for his efforts.

[1] Understanding *hostis* as "non-citizen." If it means "enemy," *pretium* becomes "due return" (for good or ill).   [2] The two quotations, first joined by Turnebus, form a plausible couplet, though there is no explicit connection in the sources. The elegiac meter identifies these fragments as belonging to epigrams, presumably written after Scipio's death in 183 BC.

2[1]

a Cicero, *Tusculan Disputations*

I am speaking about leading citizens; what about poets? Do they not want to gain renown after death? Where then does this come from?

> Look, fellow citizens, at the form and image of aged
> Ennius:
> he set to verse your fathers' greatest deeds.

He demands the reward of glory from those whose fathers he had equipped with glory. And the same poet:

231

nemo me lacrimis <decoret nec funera fletu
    faxit>. cur? volito vivos per ora virum

sed quid poetas? opifices post mortem nobilitari volunt.

b Cic. *Tusc.* 1.117

nam si supremus ille dies non <vitae> extinctionem, sed
commutationem adfert loci, quid optabilius? sin autem
perimit ac delet omnino, quid melius quam in mediis vitae
laboribus obdormiscere et ita coniventem somno conso-
piri sempiterno? quod si fiat, melior Enni quam Solonis
oratio. hic enim noster:

    nemo me lacrimis decoret

inquit,

                    nec funera fletu
    faxit.

at vero ille sapiens [Cic. F poet. 84 Traglia; cf. Sol. F 22.5–6
Diehl; Cic. *Cato* 73]: "mors mea ne careat lacrimis: linqua-
mus amicis / maerorem, ut celebrent funera cum gemitu."

Let nobody honor me with tears or perform my
   funeral with weeping.
  Why? I live, flying about upon the lips of men.[2]

But why talk only about poets? Craftsmen want to be re-
nowned after death.

[2] The notion that a poet does not die because his works live
on was taken up by later poets (e.g., Hor. *Carm.* 3.30). For verbal
reminiscences, cf. Verg. *G.* 3.8–9; *Aen.* 12.235.

b Cicero, *Tusculan Disputations*

For if that final day brings not the extinction ⟨of life⟩, but
a change of place, what is more desirable? If, however, it
annihilates and destroys completely, what is better than to
fall asleep in the middle of the toils of life and thus, closing
one's eyes, to be sent to a deep ever-lasting sleep? If this
should happen, the statement of Ennius is better than that
of Solon. For our man [Ennius] says:

"Let nobody honor me with tears or perform my
   funeral with weeping."

But that wise man [Solon] says [Cic. F poet. 84 Traglia; cf.
Sol. F 22.5–6 Diehl; Cic. *Cato* 73]: "Let my death not lack
tears: let us leave grief to friends, / so that they celebrate
my funeral with lamentation."

3

a Cic. *Tusc.* 5.49

atque hoc sic etiam concluditur: nec in misera vita quic-
quam est praedicabile aut gloriandum nec in ea quae nec
misera sit nec beata. et est in aliqua vita praedicabile ali-
quid et gloriandum ac prae se ferendum, ut Epaminondas:
"consiliis nostris laus est attonsa Laconum," ut Africanus:

> a sole exoriente supra Maeotis paludes
>   nemo est qui factis aequiperare queat

quod si <est> [*Lambinus*], beata vita glorianda et praedi-
canda et prae se ferenda est; nihil est enim aliud quod
praedicandum et prae se ferendum sit.

1 supra *codd. Cic.*: adusque *cod. Mamertini*: usque ad *Livi-
neius ad Mamertinum*

b Lactant. *Div. inst.* 1.18.10–13

si quis unum hominem iugulaverit, pro contaminato ac
nefario habetur nec ad terrenum hoc domicilium deorum
admitti eum fas putant. ille autem qui infinita hominum
milia trucidarit, cruore campos inundaverit, flumina infe-
cerit, non modo in templum sed etiam in caelum admitti-
tur. [11] aput Ennium sic loquitur Africanus [Cic. *Rep.*
F inc. 2 Powell]:

> si fas endo plagas caelestum ascendere cuiquam est,
>   mi soli caeli maxima porta patet

3

a Cicero, *Tusculan Disputations*

And this can also be concluded in the following way: neither in a wretched life is there anything deserving of renown or worthy of glory nor in one that is neither wretched nor happy. And in some lives there is something deserving of renown and worthy of glory and to be put on display, like Epaminondas: "by our counsels the glory of the Lacedaemonians was trimmed,"[1] like Africanus:

> from the sun rising over the marches of Maeotis[2]
> there is nobody who can become equal in deeds

If it exists, a happy life is worthy of glory and deserving of renown and to be put on display; for there is nothing else that is deserving of renown and to be put on display.

[1] A line inscribed on a statue of Epaminondas (cf. Paus. 9.15.6: ἡμετέραις βουλαῖς Σπάρτη μὲν ἐκείραιο δόξαν).
[2] The Sea of Azov.

b Lactantius, *Divine Institutions*

If anyone has killed a single person, he is regarded as polluted and a scoundrel, and they believe it is not right that he be admitted to this earthly dwelling place of the gods. But he who has killed countless thousands of men, flooded fields with blood and dyed rivers is admitted not only into the sacred building, but also into heaven. [11] In Ennius, Africanus speaks thus [Cic. *Rep.* F inc. 2 Powell]:

> if it is allowed for anyone to ascend to the realms of
> the heaven dwellers,
> for me alone heaven's greatest gate lies open

235

scilicet quia magnam partem generis humani extinxit ac perdidit. [12] o in quantis tenebris, Africane, versatus es vel potius o poeta, qui per caedes et sanguinem patere hominibus ascensum in caelum putaveris! [13] cui vanitati etiam Cicero adsensit [Cic. *Rep.* F inc. 3 Powell]. "est vero" inquit "Africane: nam et Herculi eadem ista porta patuit"; tamquam ipse plane, cum id fieret, ianitor fuerit in caelo.

Cf. Sen. *Ep.* 108.34; Mamertinus, *Genethl. Maximiani* (= *Pan. Lat.* 11) 16.3–4.

obviously, because he has extinguished and destroyed a large part of the human race. [12] In what great darkness, Africanus, have you dwelled or rather you, poet, who believe that the ascent to heaven is open to men through murder and blood! [13] To this foolishness even Cicero agreed [Cic. *Rep.* F inc. 3 Powell]. "It is indeed," he says, "Africanus: for this same door stood open for Hercules too"; as if obviously he himself, when this happened, was the doorman in heaven.[1]

[1] The poet quoted at *Tusc.* 5.49 is almost certainly Ennius; Lactantius' quotations derive, at least ultimately, from Cic. *Rep.* Scaliger joined the two couplets, but without any specific justification, and there may be a lacuna between the two lines of (a). The elegiac meter encourages assignment to the epigrams rather than to *Scipio*.

EUHEMERUS SIVE SACRA
HISTORIA (F 1–11)

Euhemerus of Messene, active around 300 BC, wrote an influential travelogue describing a fictitious voyage to certain uncharted islands in the Indian Ocean. There he discovered a gold column describing the deeds of Uranus, Kronos, and Zeus, who were revealed to have been originally great kings subsequently worshipped as gods in honor of their achievements. That narrative gave Euhemerus' work the title Sacred History *and advanced the concept of "euhemerism" (the human origin of the gods) that proved of interest to the Hellenistic world for justifying the establishment of ruler cults. The work is best known through excerpts preserved by Diodorus Siculus (5.41–46, 6.1) and an epitome by Eusebius* (Praep. evang. 2.52–62).

Ennius' Euhemerus *was a Latin version of this narrative: what survives deals mainly with stories about the genealogy and life of Jupiter. These sometimes differ from other mythological accounts and from the official Roman state cult, but the work's focus on the origin of the gods rather than natural philosophy does not squarely contradict views expressed in* Epicharmus *(see Feeney 1991, 120–22). Cicero suggests that Ennius was not the only Roman to engage with Euhemerus' theories (T 31). He may thus represent contemporary interests: the idea that out-*

EUHEMERUS, OR THE *SACRED HISTORY* (F 1–11)

standing individuals might win divine honors could be reflected in Ennius' glorification of Roman aristocrats in his praetextae, Annals, *and* Scipio *and in his tendency to represent their achievements as benefiting all the Roman people.*

Cicero (T 31) and Lactantius (F 2) say that Ennius "translated and recounted" Euhemerus, which may suggest something beyond verbatim translation. Indeed, the inclusion of explanations of Greek names and information on Roman matters suggest a freer treatment and the adjustment to Roman interests that also characterizes the Hedyphagetica. *Nevertheless, the fragments attributed to Ennius are often used to establish the structure and content of Euhemerus' original work.*

Ennius' version seems to have consisted of several books (F 1). Most of its fragments are transmitted by the Christian author Lactantius, who refers to Euhemerus' views in his discussion of pagan gods. His sources are not entirely clear, nor is it certain to what extent he may have inserted his own comments, fitted an originally chronological narrative to his own systematic argument, and altered Ennius' original phrasing. Only F 2, 3, 4, 5, 8, 9 are likely to approximate verbatim quotation, as suggested by their

style and the way they are introduced (Laughton 1951; Fraenkel 1951). Lactantius' quotations, however, probably do accurately suggest that Ennius' work was in prose, not verse, and is thus, together with Cato's De agricultura, *one of the oldest surviving prose texts in Latin literature.*
  Bibl.: Suerbaum 2002, 131–32; 2003, 225–26. Edd./

1 Varro, *Rust.* 1.48.1–2 = T 83 Wi. = *FGrH/BNJ* 63 F 26

in segetibus autem, frumentum quo culmus extulit, spica{m}. ea, quae mutilata non est, in hordeo et tritico tria habet continentia, granum, glumam, aristam (et etiam primitus, spica cum oritur, vaginam). granum dictum quod est intimum soldum [soldum *vel* solidum *codd.*], gluma qui est folliculus eius; arista quae ut acus tenuis longa eminet e gluma, proinde ut grani apex sit gluma et arista. [2] arista et granum omnibus fere notum, gluma paucis. itaque id apud Ennium solum scriptum scio esse in Euhemeri libris versis. videtur vocabulum etymum habere a glubendo, quod eo folliculo deglubitur granum.

2 Lactant. *Div. inst.* 1.11.32–34 = T 65 + 70 Wi. = *FGrH/ BNJ* 63 T 3a + F 19

de Neptuni sorte manifestum est: cuius regnum tale fuisse dicimus, quale Marci Antoni fuit infinitum illud imperium, cui totius orae maritimae potestatem senatus decreverat, ut praedones persequeretur ac mare omne pacaret. sic Neptuno maritima omnia cum insulis obvenerunt. [33]

EUHEMERUS

Comm.: FGrH/BNJ 63 (*Euhemerus' texts and fragments, including Ennius' version, with commentary*); Garbarino 1973, 133–37, 289–308; Winiarczyk 1991; Courtney 1999, 27–39. *Lit.*: Liuzzi 1973–74; Bryce 1990, 328–47; Winiarczyk 1994; Romano 2008.

1 Varro, *On Agriculture*

Now as for grain crops, where the stem has brought forth the grain there is the spike. This, when it is not beardless, in barley and wheat, has three components: seed, husk, beard (and also at first, when the spike emerges, sheath). What is the hard part on the inside is called the seed, the husk what is its shell; the beard is what protrudes far out of the husk like a slender needle, as if husk and beard formed a peaked top for the grain. [2] "Beard" and "seed" are known to almost everyone, "husk" to few. Thus only in Ennius do I know this is written, in the books translated from Euhemerus. The word "husk" [*gluma*] seems to have its etymology from "removing the bark" [*glubendo*] because the seed is stripped [*deglubitur*] of this skin.

2 Lactantius, *Divine Institutions*

As regards Neptune's lot it is clear: we say that his reign was such as that unlimited dominion of Marcus Antonius, to whom the senate had given by decree command over the entire coast so he could pursue the pirates and pacify the sea as a whole.[1] Thus everything maritime together with the islands fell to the lot of Neptune. [33] In what

[1] M. Antonius (cos. 99, censor 97 BC, the great orator) campaigned against the Cilician pirates as *praetor pro consule* in 102 BC.

quomodo id probari potest? nimirum veteres historiae docent. antiquus auctor Euhemerus, qui fuit ex civitate Messene, res gestas Iovis et ceterorum qui dii putantur collegit historiamque contexuit ex titulis et inscriptionibus sacris quae in antiquissimis templis habebantur maximeque in fano Iovis Triphylii, ubi auream columnam positam esse ab ipso Iove titulus indicabat, in qua columna sua gesta perscripsit, ut monumentum posteris esset rerum suarum. [34] hanc historiam et interpretatus est Ennius et secutus. cuius haec verba sunt:

> ubi Iuppiter Neptuno imperium dat maris ut insulis omnibus et quae secundum mare loca essent omnibus regnaret

ubi *unus cod. corr.*: ibi *codd. aliqui*   ut *edd.*: hoc est ut *codd. aliqui*: et *codd. rel.*   in insulis *edd.*

3 Lactant. *Div. inst.* 1.11.35 = T 67 Wi. = *FGrH/BNJ* 63 F 20

potest et mons Olympus figuram poetis dedisse ut Iovem dicerent caeli regnum esse sortitum, quod Olympus ambiguum nomen est et montis et caeli. in Olympo autem Iovem habitasse docet eadem historia quae dicit:

> ea tempestate Iuppiter in monte Olympo maximam partem vitae colebat et eo ad eum in ius veniebant, si quae res in controversia erant. item si quis quid novi invenerat quod ad vitam humanam utile esset, eo veniebant atque Iovi ostendebant.

---

[1] Although the passage does not mention Euhemerus, "the same history" must refer to the *Sacred History* quoted elsewhere (cf. also August. *Ep.* 17.1 [*CCSL* XXXI, p. 40] = T 59 Wi.).

way can this be proved? Old histories of course demonstrate it. The ancient author Euhemerus, who was from the community of Messene, collected the deeds of Jupiter and others who are regarded as gods and composed a history from the commemorative tablets and sacred inscriptions that are found in the most ancient temples and particularly in the shrine of Jupiter Triphylius, where a commemorative tablet showed that a golden column had been put in place by Jupiter himself on which he recorded his achievements, to be a memorial of his deeds for posterity. [34] This history was translated and recounted by Ennius. His words are as follows:

> where Jupiter gives Neptune command over the sea
> so that he would rule over all islands and all places
> that were along the sea

3 Lactantius, *Divine Institutions*

Mount Olympus can also have given poets this manner of speaking, so they could say that Jupiter obtained by lot the kingdom of the sky, since Olympus is ambiguous, the name of both the mountain and the sky. But that Jupiter lived on Olympus the same *History* shows, which says:[1]

> In this period Jupiter used to spend the greatest part of his life on Mount Olympus, and there they came to him for legal procedures if any matters were controversial. Likewise, if anyone had found out anything new that was useful to human life, they came there and showed it to Jupiter.

4 Lactant. *Div. inst.* 1.11.44–47 = T 69A Wi. = *FGrH/BNJ* 63 F 24

quare si Iovem et ex rebus gestis et ex moribus hominem fuisse in terraque regnasse deprehendimus, superest ut mortem quoque eius investigemus. [45] Ennius in Sacra Historia descriptis omnibus quae in vita sua gessit ad ultimum sic ait:

> deinde Iuppiter postquam quinquies terras circuivit omnibusque amicis atque cognatis suis imperia divisit reliquitque hominibus leges mores frumentaque paravit multaque alia bona fecit, inmortali gloria memoriaque adfectus sempiterna monumenta sui{s} reliquit. [46] aetate pessum acta in Creta vitam commutavit et ad deos abiit eumque Curetes filii sui curaverunt decoraveruntque eum; et sepulchrum eius est in Creta in oppido Gnosso et dicitur Vesta hanc urbem creavisse; inque sepulchro eius est inscriptum antiquis litteris Graecis ΖΑΝ ΚΡΟΝΟΥ id est Latine Iuppiter Saturni.

[47] hoc certe non poetae tradunt, sed antiquarum rerum scriptores.

sui{s} *L. Mueller*: suis *codd.*

Cf. *Epitome Div. inst.* 13.4–5 = T 69B Wi.

4 Lactantius, *Divine Institutions*

Therefore, if we understand that, both on account of his deeds and on account of his character, Jupiter was a human being and reigned on earth, it remains for us to investigate his death as well. [45] Ennius in the *Sacred History*, after having described everything that he did in his life, toward the end says this:

> Then after Jupiter had walked round the earth five times and had distributed power among all his friends and relatives and left human beings laws and customs and provided grain and did many other good things, he was stirred by the immortal glory of his memory and left eternal monuments of himself. [46] After his life fell into decline, he passed away on Crete and went away to join the gods, and the Curetes, his sons, cared for him and honored him; and his sepulcher is on Crete in the town of Knossos, and Vesta is said to have created this town;[1] and on his sepulcher there is inscribed in ancient Greek letters "Zeus, son of Kronos," which is in Latin "Jupiter, son of Saturnus."

[47] This at any rate is not what the poets transmit, but the writers about events from the past.

---

[1] Euhemerus would have said Hestia, whose association with Crete goes back to her birth from Kronos and Rhea. Cf. Hes. *Th.* 453–54; *H. Aphr.* 22–23.

5 Lactant. *Div. inst.* 1.11.60–65 = T 62 + 57 + 52 Wi. =
FGrH/BNJ 63 F 21 + 18

non ergo mirandum si nomina eorum caelo terraeque at-
tributa essent, qui reges genuerant potentissimos. [61]
apparet ergo non ex caelo esse natum, quod fieri non pot-
est, sed ex homine cui nomen Urano fuit. . . . [62] . . . nunc
dicam quomodo, ubi, a quo sit hoc factum: non enim Sa-
turnus hoc, sed Iuppiter fecit. [63] in Sacra Historia sic
Ennius tradit:

> deinde Pan eum deducit in montem, qui vocatur
> Caeli stel{l}a. postquam eo ascendit, contemplatus
> est late terras ibique in eo monte aram creat Caelo
> primusque in ea ara Iuppiter sacrificavit. in eo loco
> suspexit in caelum quod nunc nos nominamus, ei-
> que quod supra mundum erat, quod aether vocaba-
> tur, de sui avi nomine caelum nomen indidit idque
> Iuppiter quod aether vocatur placans primus cae-
> lum nominavit eamque hostiam quam ibi sacrifica-
> vit, totam adolevit.

nec hic tantum sacrificasse Iuppiter invenitur. [64] Caesar
quoque in Arato refert [Schol. ad Caes. Germ. *Arat.* 318]
Aglaosthenen [*FGrH/BNJ* 499 F 2] dicere Iovem cum ex
insula Naxo adversus Titanas proficisceretur et sacrificium
faceret in litore, aquilam ei in auspicium advolasse, quam

5 Lactantius, *Divine Institutions*

Hence it is no surprise if the names of those who had begotten the most powerful kings have been attributed to heaven and earth. [61] Therefore it is obvious that he [Saturn] was not born of the sky, which cannot happen, but of a human being whose name was Uranus. . . . [62] . . . Now I will say in what way, where, by whom this [naming] was done: for it was not Saturn who did this, but Jupiter. [63] In the *Sacred History* Ennius reports the following:

> Then Pan led him [Jupiter] to a mountain, which is called the Stele of Caelus [~ Pillar of Heaven]. After he ascended it, he surveyed the lands far and wide, and there on that mountain he creates an altar for Caelus, and Jupiter was the first to sacrifice on that altar. In that place he looked up to heaven, as we now call it, and to that which was above the world, which used to be called aether, he gave the name heaven [*caelum*] from the name of his grandfather [Caelus ~ Uranus], and appeasing that which is called aether, Jupiter was the first to call it heaven, and that victim he sacrificed there he burned completely.

And not only here is Jupiter found to have sacrificed. [64] Caesar [Germanicus] too reports in *Aratus* [Schol. ad Caes. Germ. *Arat.* 318] that Aglaosthenes [*FGrH/BNJ* 499 F 2] says that, when Jupiter set off from the isle of Naxos against the Titans and made sacrifice on the shore, an eagle flew to him as a sign, which the victor [later] took

victor bono omine acceptam tutelae suae subiugarit. [65]
Sacra vero Historia etiam ante

> consedisse illi aquilam in capite atque ei regnum
> portendisse

testatur. cui ergo sacrificare Iuppiter potuit nisi

> Caelo avo

quem dicit Euhemerus

> in Oceania mortuum et in oppido Aulacia sepul-
> tum?

Pan eum *vel* pauenium *vel* pane udeducit *codd.*: Panchaeum
vel Panchaeum eum *vel* Panchaiam *viri docti*   stel{l}a *Cia-*
conius: stella *codd.*: sella *Krahner*   eique *Brandt*: idque
codd.   sacravit *edd.*   aulacia *vel* aut lacia *vel* aulatia
codd.

6 Lactant. *Div. inst.* 1.13.2 = T 66 Wi. = *FGrH/BNJ* 63
F 22

idem [i.e., Saturnus] sororem suam Rheam quam latine
Opem dicimus cum haberet uxorem, responso vetitus esse
dicitur mares liberos educare, quod futurum esset ut a
filio pelleretur. quam rem metuens natos sibi filios non
utique devorabat ut ferunt fabulae, sed necabat, quam-
quam scriptum sit in Historia Sacra

> Saturnum et Opem ceterosque tunc homines hu-
> manam carnem solitos esitare: verum primum Io-
> vem leges hominibus moresque condentem edicto
> prohibuisse, ne liceret eo cibo vesci.

under his wing as a good omen. [65] But the *Sacred History* testifies that even before[1]

an eagle had sat down on his head and predicted the kingdom for him.

To whom then could Jupiter sacrifice if not

to Caelus, his ancestor,

of whom Euhemerus says that

he died in Oceania[2] and was buried in the town of Aulacia?[3]

[1] How close the following quotations in indirect speech are to Ennius' original wording is uncertain.   [2] A place on Euhemerus' mythical island Panchaia.   [3] Perhaps Huracia, another place on Panchaia (cf. Diod. Sic. 5.45.2).

6 Lactantius, *Divine Institutions*

When the same [Saturn] had his sister Rhea, whom we call Ops in Latin, as his wife, he is said to have been forbidden by an oracle to bring up male children, since it would come about that he would be driven out by a son. In fear of this, he absolutely did not devour the sons born to him, as stories tell, but killed them, although it is written in the *Sacred History*:

that Saturn and Ops and the other humans of that time were accustomed to eat human flesh, but Jupiter, establishing laws and customs for humans, was the first to forbid by an edict that it was permitted to feed oneself with that food.[1]

[1] How close this quotation in indirect speech is to Ennius' original wording is uncertain.

7 Lactant. *Div. inst.* 1.13.14–15 = T 51A Wi. = *FGrH/BNJ* 63 F 12

Ennius quidem in Euhemero non primum dicit regnasse Saturnum, sed Uranum patrem.

> initio

inquit

> primus in terris imperium summum Caelus habuit.
> is id regnum una cum fratribus suis sibi instituit
> atque paravit

[15] non magna dissensio, siquidem maximorum auctorum de filio ac patre dubitatio est. sed tamen utrumque fieri potest, ut primus Uranus eminere inter ceteros potentia coeperit et principatum habere, non regnum, postea Saturnus maiores sibi opes comparaverit ac regium nomen adsciverit.

Cf. *Epitome Div. inst.* 14.2–4 = T 51B Wi.

8

a Lactant. *Div. inst.* 1.14.1–8 = T 54 Wi. = *FGrH/BNJ* 63 F 14 + 15

nunc, quoniam ab iis quae rettuli aliquantum Sacra Historia dissentit, aperiamus ea quae veris litteris continentur, ne poetarum ineptias in accusandis religionibus sequi ac probare videamur. [2] haec Ennii [enni *vel* enim *codd.*] verba sunt:

> exim Saturnus uxorem duxit Opem. Titan, qui maior
> natu erat, postulat ut ipse regnaret. ibi Vesta mater
> eorum et sorores Ceres atque Ops suadent Saturno,
> uti de regno ne concedat fratri. ibi Titan, qui facie

7 Lactantius, *Divine Institutions*

Ennius indeed says in *Euhemerus* that it was not Saturn who was the first to reign, but his father Uranus.

In the beginning,

he says,

Caelus was the first to have the greatest power in the world. He set up and provided this kingdom for himself together with his brothers.

[15] Not a great disagreement, if there is doubt about son and father among the greatest writers.[1] But still both can happen, that first Uranus began to stand out among others in power and have a preeminent position, not the kingdom, later that Saturn gathered greater power for himself and obtained the title of king.

[1] Ennius and others mentioned in what precedes.

8

a Lactantius, *Divine Institutions*

Now since the *Sacred History* disagrees somewhat with those things I have reported, let's reveal that which is contained in truthful documents, so that we do not seem to recount and approve the foolishness of poets in upbraiding religion. [2] These are the words of Ennius:

Then Saturn took Ops as his wife. Titan, who was older [than Saturn], demanded that he himself should reign. Thereupon Vesta, their mother, and the sisters Ceres and Ops persuaded Saturn not to yield to his brother concerning the kingdom. There-

251

deterior esset quam Saturnus, idcirco et quod vide-
bat matrem atque sorores suas operam dare uti
Saturnus regnaret, concessit ei ut is regnaret. itaque
pactus est cum Saturno, uti si quid liberum virile
secus ei natum esset, ne quid educaret. id eius rei
causa fecit, uti ad suos gnatos regnum rediret. tum
Saturno filius qui primus natus est, eum necave-
runt. deinde posterius nati sunt gemini, Iuppiter
atque Iuno. tum Iunonem Saturno in conspectum
dedere atque Iovem clam abscondunt dantque eum
Vestae educandum celantes Saturnum. item Neptu-
num clam Saturno Ops parit eumque clanculum
abscondit. ad eundem modum tertio partu Ops
parit geminos, Plutonem et Glaucam. Pluto Latine
est Dis pater, alii Orcum vocant. ibi filiam Glaucam
Saturno ostendunt, at filium Plutonem celant atque
abscondunt. deinde Glauca parva emoritur. haec, ut
scripta sunt, Iovis fratrumque eius stirps atque cog-
natio: in hunc modum nobis ex sacra scriptione tra-
ditum est.

[7] item paulo post haec infert:

deinde Titan postquam rescivit Saturno filios pro-
creatos atque educatos esse clam se, seducit secum
filios suos qui Titani vocantur, fratremque suum
Saturnum atque Opem conprehendit eosque muro
circumegit et custodiam iis apponit.

---

[1] It seems to be rather the fourth.   [2] Elsewhere in Lac-
tantius the work is quoted as *Sacra Historia*; only here is it
referred to as *sacra scriptio*. This probably indicates that the
sentence including this expression belongs to the quotation from

upon Titan, who was less handsome than Saturn, for that reason and because he saw that his mother and sisters were making an effort for Saturn to reign, yielded to him so that he reigned. And so he made an agreement with Saturn, that if any male offspring were born to him, he would not bring him up. That he did for this reason, so that the kingdom would return to his own sons. Then they killed the son who was the first to be born to Saturn. Then later twins were born, Jupiter and Juno. Then they gave Saturn Juno to see and secretly hid Jupiter and gave him to Vesta to bring him up, concealing him from Saturn. Likewise Ops bears Neptune in secret from Saturn and hides him secretly. In the same way in a third[1] birth Ops bears twins, Pluto and Glauca. Pluto is in Latin Dis pater, others call him Orcus. There they show the daughter Glauca to Saturn, but hide the son Pluto and conceal him. Then Glauca dies as a young girl. This, as is written, is the origin and kinship of Jupiter and his brothers: in this way it was handed down to us from the *Sacred Writing* [= *Sacred History*].[2]

[7] Likewise a little later he mentions this:

Then Titan, after he found out that sons had been begotten by Saturn and brought up in secret from him, led away with him his own sons, who are called Titans, and seized his brother Saturn and Ops and surrounded them by a wall and set a guard over them.

Ennius (as the *Epitome* paraphrases), rather than being a comment by Lactantius himself.

[8] haec historia quam vera sit, docet Sibylla Erythraea eadem fere dicens, nisi quod in paucis quae ad rem non attinent discrepat.

b Epitome *Div. inst.* 13.3 = T 10 Wi.

quam historiam vertit Ennius in Latinam ‹linguam› [*Davisius*], cuius haec verba sunt:

> haec, ut scripta sunt, Iovis fratrumque eius stirps atque cognatio: in hunc modum nobis ex sacra scriptione traditum est.

9 Lactant. *Div. inst.* 1.14.10–12 = T 56 + 58 Wi. = *FGrH/ BNJ* 63 F 16

reliqua historia sic contexitur:

> Iovem adultum, cum audisset patrem atque matrem custodiis circumsaeptos atque in vincula coniectos, venisse cum magna Cretensium multitudine Titanumque ac filios eius pugna vicisse, parentes vinculis exemisse, patri regnum reddidisse atque ita in Cretam remeasse. post haec deinde Saturno sortem datam, ut caveret ne filius eum regno expelleret; illum elevandae sortis atque effugiendi periculi gratia insidiatum Iovi, ut eum necaret; Iovem cognitis insidiis regnum sibi denuo vindicasse ac fugasse

[8] The Erythraean Sibyl,[3] saying roughly the same things, shows how true this history is, except that she differs on a few items that are not relevant to the matter.[4]

[3] One of the canonical Sibyls (from Erythrae, a city in Ionia).

[4] J. N. Adams, *An Anthology of Informal Latin, 200 BC–AD 900* (Cambridge: Cambridge University Press, 2016), pp. 7–26, provides detailed linguistic commentary on this text, sections 2–6.

b Epitome of Lactantius, *Divine Institutions*

This history was turned into the Latin language by Ennius, whose words are as follows:

> this, as is written, is the origin and kinship of Jupiter and his brothers: in this way it has been handed down to us from the *Sacred Writing* [= *Sacred History*].

9 Lactantius, *Divine Institutions*

The remainder of the *History* is composed as follows:

> that the grown-up Jupiter, when he had heard that his father and mother had been surrounded by guards and thrown in fetters, came with a great number of Cretans and defeated Titan and his sons in battle, freed his parents from the fetters, returned the kingdom to his father, and so returned to Crete. Then, after that, an oracle was given to Saturn that he should beware that his son not drive him out of the kingdom; in order to thwart the oracle and avoid the danger, he ambushed Jupiter in order to kill him; Jupiter, having recognized the ambush, once again claimed the kingdom for him-

Saturnum. qui cum iactatus esset per omnes terras
persequentibus armatis, quos ad eum conprehen-
dendum vel necandum Iuppiter miserat, vix in Ita-
lia locum in quo lateret invenit.

10 Lactant. *Div. inst.* 1.17.9–10 = T 75A Wi. = *FGrH/BNJ*
63 F 25

quid loquar obscenitatem Veneris omnium libidinibus
prostitutae non deorum tantum, sed et hominum? haec
enim ex famoso Martis stupro genuit Harmoniam, ex Mer-
curio Hermaphroditum, qui est natus androgynus, ex Iove
Cupidinem, ex Anchise Aenean, ex Bute Erycem; ex Ado-
nio quidem nullum potuit, quod etiamtum puer apro ictus
occisus est. [10] quae

prima

ut in Historia Sacra continetur,

artem meretriciam instituit auctorque mulieribus in
Cypro fuit, uti vulg⟨at⟩o corpore quaestum face-
rent: quod idcirco imperavit, ne sola praeter alias
mulieres inpudica et virorum adpetens videretur.

vulg⟨at⟩o *Crenius*: vulgo *codd.*

Cf. *Epitome Div. inst.* 9.1 = T 75B Wi.

11 Lactant. *Div. inst.* 1.22.21–27 = T 64A Wi. = *FGrH/
BNJ* 63 F 23

Historia vero Sacra testatur ipsum Iovem postquam rerum
potitus sit, in tantam venisse insolentiam, ut ipse sibi fana
in multis locis constituerit. [22] nam cum terras circum-

self and put Saturn to flight. When he had been driven about over all lands by armed pursuers, whom Jupiter had sent to seize or kill him, he barely found a place in Italy where he could hide.

10 Lactantius, *Divine Institutions*

What shall I say about the indecency of Venus, devoted to prostitution for the lusts not only of all the gods, but also of men? For she bore from the notorious adultery with Mars Harmonia; from Mercury Hermaphroditus, who was born androgynous; from Jupiter Cupid, from Anchises Aeneas; from Butes Eryx. From Adonis she could not bear anybody, since he was struck by a boar and killed when still a boy. [10] She was

the first

as it is said in the *Sacred History*,

to introduce the profession of prostitution, and she was its instigator for women in Cyprus, that they made profit from prostituting their bodies: she ordered this so that she did not appear to be the only one, surpassing other women, to be unchaste and solicitous of men.

11 Lactantius, *Divine Institutions*

Indeed, the *Sacred History* bears witness that Jupiter himself, after he had come to power, went to such a level of arrogance that he himself founded shrines for himself in many places. [22] For when he went round the lands,

iret, ut in quamque regionem venerat, reges principesve populorum hospitio sibi et amicitia copulabat et cum a quoque digrederetur, iubebat sibi fanum creari hospitis sui nomine, quasi ut posset amicitiae ac foederis memoria conservari. [23] sic constituta sunt templa Iovi Ataburio, Iovi Labryandio: Ataburus enim et Labryandus hospites eius atque adiutores in bello fuerunt; item Iovi Laprio, Iovi Molioni, Iovi Casio et quae sunt in eundem modum. quod ille astutissime excogitavit, ut et sibi honorem divinum et hospitibus suis perpetuum nomen adquireret cum religione coniunctum. [24] gaudebant ergo illi et huic imperio eius libenter obsequebantur et nominis sui gratia ritus annuos et festa celebrabant. [25] simile quiddam in Sicilia fecit Aeneas, cum conditae urbi Acestae hospitis nomen inposuit, ut eam postmodum laetus ac libens Acestes diligeret augeret ornaret. [cf. Verg. *Aen.* 5.708–78] [26] hoc modo religionem cultus sui per orbem terrae Iuppiter seminavit et exemplum ceteris ad imitandum dedit. [27] sive igitur a Melisseo, sicut Didymus tradidit, colendorum deorum ritus effluxit, sive ab ipso Iove, ut Euhemerus, de tempore tamen constat quando dii coli coeperint.

Cf. *Epitome Div. inst.* 19.4 = T 64B Wi.

---

[1] A cult of Zeus Atabyrios existed on Mount Atabyris on Rhodes and of Zeus Labryandios at Labranda in Caria. Cults of Zeus Laprios and Zeus Molio cannot be connected to any specific sites. A cult of Zeus Kasios existed on Mount Kasios, near Antioch, in Egypt, and on Corcyra.

[2] A mythical king of Crete (cf. Lactant. *Div. inst.* 1.22.19–20).

whenever he came into each region, he bound the kings or leaders of their peoples to him in hospitality and friendship, and whenever he left each, he ordered a shrine to be set up for him in the name of his host, as if a memory of friendship and alliance could be preserved. [23] Thus temples to Jupiter Ataburius, to Jupiter Labryandius were founded: for Ataburus and Labryandus were his hosts and supporters in war; likewise to Jupiter Laprius, to Jupiter Molio, to Jupiter Casius and other temples that are named in this way.[1] He devised this very cleverly, so that he could acquire divine honor for himself and a perpetual name for his hosts connected with religious cult. [24] Therefore they were happy and followed his orders willingly and celebrated annual rituals and festivities for the sake of their names. [25] In Sicily Aeneas did something similar, when he bestowed on the town being founded the name of his host Acestes, so that later Acestes, happily and willingly, would love, expand and beautify it [cf. Verg. *Aen.* 5.708–78]. [26] In this way Jupiter sowed the religious celebration of his cult all over the world and gave others an example to imitate. [27] Hence, be it that the ritual of honoring the gods originated from Melisseus,[2] as Didymus[3] transmitted, be it from Jupiter himself, as Euhemerus says, nevertheless, it is clear concerning the time when the gods began to be honored.[4]

[3] Presumably Didymus the Blind, a theologian who produced commentaries on large parts of the Bible (ca. AD 313–398).

[4] No verbatim quotation can be gained from this passage; it reports only what Euhemerus said, presumably in Ennius' version. There are likely to be additions by Lactantius.

HEDYPHAGETICA (F 1)

The surviving fragment suggests that Ennius' Hedyphage-
tica was based on a gastronomic poem by Archestratos
of Gela (second half of the fourth century BC), which
was known by various names: Hedypatheia, Gastronomia,
Deipnologia, Opsopoiia. *What is left of Ennius' version is*
a section on fish, detailing where the best varieties of each
can be found.

Part of Archestratos' treatment of the same fish is
preserved by Athenaeus (Athen. 3.92d, 7.300de, 7.318f,
7.320a = Supplementum Hellenisticum, *F 132–92). While*
Ennius' debt to it is obvious, he has clearly not produced
a straightforward translation. He substitutes Italian place
names for Greek ones, choosing locations in southern Italy
that must have been familiar to him. He also makes more
specific the general indication "Ambracia" if, as is now
generally accepted, the transmitted caradrum *in line 3 re-*
fers not to a type of fish, but to a place on the Ambracian
gulf (a misunderstanding that triggered the textual cor-
ruption). Ennius could presumably describe the area more
precisely because he had been there with Fulvius Nobilior
in 189 BC, which suggests a terminus post quem *for the*
composition (Skutsch 1948, 99; but cf. Fucarino 1991/93,
195–96).

The text, with its many place-names and rare words for

HEDYPHAGETICA
(DELIKATESSEN) (F 1)

types of fish, is rather corrupt, but the general structure and most names can be restored with some confidence. Nevertheless, identification of the different types of seafood is not entirely clear and must be regarded as tentative (on ancient names for types of fish see de Saint-Denis 1947; Thompson 1947; app. on Supplementum Hellenisticum, F 193), *even though many of them are also mentioned in other ancient authors, sometimes with divergent views of their provenance. The translation uses roughly equivalent English names.*

The work is in hexameters, yet the metrical practice differs from the Annals *(unless major changes to the transmitted text of* Hedyphagetica *are made): all lines are end-stopped, and hiatus, iambic shortening, hypermetric lines, and elision are not found to the same extent elsewhere. The changes are most likely due to the generic difference between* Hedyphagetica *and* Annals *rather than to any kind of poetic development.*

Bibl.: Suerbaum 2002, 133; 2003, 228. Edd./Comm.: Montanari 1983, 129–31; Supplementum Hellenisticum, F 193; *Courtney 1993, 22–25; Hunink 1997, II 120–22. Lit.: Bo 1956; Bettini 1979, 53–76; Mariotti 1991, 17–21 (on text, date, and meter); Fucarino 1991/93; Kruschwitz 1998 (on text and relation to model).*

1 Apul. *Apol.* 39.2–4

Q. Ennius hedyphagetica {a} versibus scribsit; innume-
rabilia genera piscium enumerat, quae scilicet curiose
cognorat. paucos versus memini, eos dicam: [3]

> omnibus ut Clipea praestat mustela marina!
> mures sunt Aeni aspra ostrea plurima Abydi{mus}.
> Mytilenae est pecten Caradrumque apud Ambraciai,
> Brundisii sargus bonus est (hunc magnus si erit,
>   sume).
> 5   apriculum piscem scito primum esse Tarenti;
> Surrenti elopem fac emas, glaucumque aput Cumas.
> quid scarum praeterii cerebrum Iovis paene supremi
> (Nestoris ad patriam hic capitur magnusque bonus-
>   que),
> melanurum, turdum merulamque umbramque
>   marinam.
> 10   polypus Corcyrae, calvaria pinguia, acarnae,
> purpura, muriculi, mures, dulces quoque echini.

2 Aeni aspra Helm (*hiatum in caesura putat Ennio concedi posse; de forma aspra cf. Verg. Aen. 2.379*): aeniaſpera *cod. descr.*: aeniasſp̃a *cod.*: alia alii   Abydi{mus} *Casaubon, codd. det. et edd.*: abidim; *cod. descr.*

3 caradrumque (= fossam) Ambraciai *Salmasius, van der Vliet*: caradrumquę apud ūbracię finiſ *cod. descr.*

5 Tarenti *edd.*: targenti *cod., corr. manus posterior*

6 Surrenti <t>u elopem fac emas, glaucum face Cumis *Baehrens*: ſurrentia elopê *cod.*

10 Corcyrae<st> *Bergk*: corcirę *cod.*   acarnae *Salmasius, Vahlen*: carne *cod.*

1 Apuleius, *Apologia*

Ennius wrote *Hedyphagetica* in verses; he lists innumer-
able kinds of fish, which he had obviously got to know
assiduously. I remember a few lines; I will quote these: [3]

How the sea weasel from Clupea[1] surpasses all!
There are mussels at Aenus[2] and plentiful scaly oys-
ters at Abydus.[3] At Mytilene[4] there is scallop and
near Charadrus[5] on the gulf of Ambracia. At Brun-
disium the sargue is good (if it is big, get it). Know
that the little boar fish is first-rate at Tarentum; take
care to buy sturgeon at Surrentum and blue shark
at Cumae.[6] What of the parrot wrasse? I almost
passed over it, the brain of all-high Jupiter[7] (this is
caught, big and good, by Nestor's homeland[8]), the
oblade, the wrasse, the sea merle, and the sea mai-
gre. At Corcyra[9] there is octopus, fat flounders,
basses, the purple shellfish and the little purple
shellfish, mussels, and sweet sea urchins, too.

[1] A town on the east coast of North Africa, east of Carthage,
also called Aspis.

[2] A city just east of the river Hebrus on the coast of Thrace.

[3] A town on the southeast side of the Hellespont.

[4] A town on Lesbos.

[5] A town on the gulf of Ambracia in Epirus.

[6] Four places in the south of Italy.

[7] The *scarus* seems to have been regarded as a particular
delicacy (Hor. *Sat.* 2.2.22).

[8] Pylos.

[9] Modern Corfù.

[4] alios etiam multis versibus decoravit, et ubi gentium quisque eorum, qualiter assus aut iurulentus optime sapiat, nec tamen ab eruditis reprehenditur; ne ego reprehendar, qui res paucissimis cognitas Graece et Latine propriis et elegantibus vocabulis conscribo.

Cf. Schol. ad Petron. 119.

[4] Others too he embellishes with many lines, saying where in the world each of these can be found, how they taste best, roasted or stewed; and yet he is not criticized by learned people; so I should not be criticized either for writing down things known to very few people in Greek and Latin in correct and stylish language.

PRAECEPTA (F 1)

This work, apparently written in trochaic septenarii, is likely to have contained a series of doctrines or guidelines, perhaps connected with moral philosophy. See below for its possible identification with Protrepticus.

1 Prisc., *GL* II, p. 532.16–20

vetustissimi tamen etiam in simplici "serui" protulisse inveniuntur, pro "ordinavi" et pro "sevi." Ennius in praeceptis:

> ubi videt avenam lolium crescere inter triticum,
> selegit, secernit, aufert; sedulo ubi operam addidit,
> qu⟨oni⟩am tanto studio seruit

1 vidēt   3 qu⟨oni⟩am *Vahlen*: quam *codd., ante* quam *lacunam ponunt multi*

PRAECEPTA (F 1)

Bibl.: Suerbaum 2002, 133; 2003, 227. Edd./Comm.: Garbarino 1973, 137–38; Courtney 1993, 38–39; Russo 2007, 39–47.

1 Priscian

Very ancient writers, however, are found to have used *serui* [perfect] even with the noncompound ‹verb›, for "I have arranged" and for "I have sown."[1] Ennius in *Praecepta*:

> as soon as he sees oat and darnel growing among the
>   wheat,
> he weeds it out, eliminates it, removes it; as soon as
>   he has diligently attended the task,
> since he sowed with such eagerness, ‹he . . .›[2]

[1] The grammarian claims that *serui* was used as the perfect tense for two verbs, "to arrange" (*sero, serui, sertum*) and "to sow" (*sero, sēvi, satum*), but this alternative perfect of the second verb is very rare. The same applies to compounds.   [2] This praise of diligence, presumably with the promise of a reward to come, could be understood literally as agricultural advice, but may well be a metaphor for the elimination of vices.

PROTREPTICUS (F 1)

The titles Protrepticus *and* Praecepta, *both attested for Ennius, are often thought to refer to the same work, but with only one mention and one fragment for each that is impossible to confirm.*

Protrepticus *is the title of a work by the late Roman poet Ausonius and also appears in Greek literature, for instance*

1 Charis., *GL* I, p. 54.16–20 = p. 68 B.

at cum nulla causa cogente quid tale dicitur, tunc nimirum confitendum est de errore, ut idem Gellius in XCVII "portabus," et mox "oleabus" [Cn. Gellius, F 10, 11 *FRHist*], et Plautus in Curculione [506] "hibus," et Ennius in Protreptico:

    pannibus

quae notanda videntur.

PROTREPTICUS (F 1)

as a work ascribed to Aristotle. The pieces are "exhortations," usually to philosophy. The single word transmitted for Ennius is too vague to establish the content of his Protrepticus.

Bibl.: Suerbaum 2002, 133; 2003, 227. Edd./Comm.: Garbarino 1973, 137–38; Russo 2007, 39–47.

1 Charisius

But when, with no compelling reason, something like this [unnecessary and unusual forms of dative and ablative plurals] is said, then one must evidently confess an error, as the same Gellius[1] says [Cn. Gellius, F 10, 11 *FRHist*] "doors" in <Book> 97 and a little later "olive trees," and Plautus in *Curculio* [506] "these," and Ennius in *Protrepticus*:

rags

which seems noteworthy.

[1] The Republican historian Cn. Gellius, mentioned a few lines above.

SATIRES (t 1; F 1–19)

Although literary historians generally follow Horace (Sat. 2.1.62–64) and Quintilian (Inst. 10.1.93) in regarding Lucilius as the "inventor" of Roman verse satire, posterity knew four books of miscellaneous Ennian poems under the collective title Satires *(T 40b, 94). Whether Ennius himself was responsible for the compilation and gave it that title is beyond recall. Barely thirty lines survive, and with only about a third of these identified by book number, whatever organizing principles shaped the collection are impossible to determine. Enough remains, however, to preserve the voice of a good-natured, somewhat garrulous moralizer, who sounds rather more like Horace than Lucilius (F 7, 12, 13). The fragments include strong suggestions of comic diction (F 1, 4, 11) and comic character (F 9) and hint at the use of fables (t 1, F 10, 14, 16), proverbs (F 17, 18), and autobiographical vignette (F 13). Indeed, details pre-*

TESTIMONIUM

t 1 Quint. *Inst.* 9.2.36

sed formas quoque fingimus saepe . . . ut Mortem et Vitam, quas contendentes in satura tradit Ennius.

SATIRES (t 1; F 1–19)

served in the later biographical tradition likely derive from Ennius' own satirical narratives (T 14, 27, 83, 97), and his apparent parodies of epic diction would in effect be self-parodies (F 3, 5, 15, 19; cf. Sota F 2, 5). The collection seems to have employed primarily iambic and trochaic rhythms, but hexameters and Sotadeans also appear. Some hexameter fragments often ascribed to the Annals (e.g., Inc. Ann. F 16, 44, 82, 87, 111) may belong instead to the satires.

Useful discussions are provided by Van Rooy 1965, 30–49; Waszink 1972; Muecke 2005; Goldberg 2018; text and brief commentary in Courtney 1993, 7–21; full discussion with bibliography and detailed commentary in Russo 2007, 49–185, now the authoritative edition. The order of presentation follows Russo: note that F 12–19 are attributed to the Satires only by conjecture.

TESTIMONIUM

t 1 Quintilian, *The Orator's Education*

We also often invent personifications . . . like Death and Life, which Ennius represents debating in a satire.

FRAGMENTS

1 Non., p. 474.22–25 M. = 761 L.

CONVIVANT, pro convivantur . . . Ennius satyrarum lib. I:

ia[6]   malo hercle magno suo convivat sine modo

magno suo *Bothe*: suo magno *codd.*

2 Non., p. 510.7–10 M. = 820 L.

CELERE, pro celeriter . . . Ennius satyrarum lib. I:

ia[6]   dum quicquid ⟨des⟩ des celere

⟨des⟩ *codd. recc.*

3 Serv. Dan. ad Verg. *Aen.* 12.121–22

"pilataque plenis / agmina": hoc est pilis armata. . . . vel certe "pilata" fixa et stabilia . . . nam et Graeci res densas et artas πιλωτά dicunt. Ennius satyrarum II:

da[6]   contemplor
   inde loci liquidas pilatasque aetheris oras

cum firmas et stabiles significaret quasi pilis fultas.

SATIRES

FRAGMENTS

1 Nonius

convivant [active], for *convivantur* [deponent, "they carouse"] . . . Ennius, *Satires*, Book 1:

> let him carouse without restraint—and be throughly damned![1]

[1] Punctuation after *convivat* creates a line of dialogue with a somewhat different meaning: "Let him party 'til he drops! :: Hold on a minute."

2 Nonius

celere, for *celeriter* ["quickly"] . . . Ennius, *Satires*, Book 1:

> so long as whatever you give, you give quickly

3 Servius Danielis, *Commentary on Virgil*

"and columns javelined to the full": i.e., armed with javelins . . . or at the least *pilata* means "fixed and steady" . . . for the Greeks too call things dense and thick πιλωτά ["compressed"]. Ennius, *Satires* 2:

> I gaze
> from there on the clear and dense regions of the
> ether

since he means they are firm and steady, as if supported by javelins.

273

4 Non., p. 147.8–9 M. = 214 L.

OBSTRIGILLARE: obstare. Ennius satyrarum lib. II:

*tr*⁷   restitant occurrunt obstant obstrigillant obagitant

5 Non., p. 33.4–9 M. = 48 L.

PROPINARE a Graeco tractum, post potum tradere . . .
Ennius satyrarum lib. III:

*ia*⁶   Enni poeta, salve, qui mortalibus
versus propinas flammeos medullitus

6 Non., p. 66.18–21 M. = 92 L.

POLITIONES: agrorum cultus diligentes ut polita omnia
dicimus exculta et ad nitorem deducta . . . Ennius satyra-
rum lib. III:

*da*⁶   testes sunt
lati campi quos gerit Africa terra politos

4 Nonius

obstrigillare: "to stand in the way." Ennius, *Satires* Book 2:

> they hang back, run up, stand around, stand in the
> way, harass[1]

[1] The string of verbs in asyndeton is in the comic style, e.g., Plaut. *Curc.* 291: *obstant obsistunt incedunt* ("they stand in the way, block the road, move along"). Cf. Lucil. 264–65 M. = 276–77 W.

5 Nonius

propinare is derived from Greek, "to pass on after drinking" . . . Ennius in Book 3 of his *Satires*:

> greetings, poet Ennius, who pass flaming verses
> from your very marrow[1] on to mortal men[2]

[1] Cf. 9 *Ann.* F 6, hailing the orator Cornelius Cethegus as *Suadai medulla*, "the marrow [i.e., essence] of Persuasion."
[2] A term of high style: so Cato in his oratory prefers *mortales* to *homines*. The governing image is of a cup passed around at a symposium.

6 Nonius

politiones: the diligent cultivation of fields, just as we call all things *polita* that are carefully made and brought to a high gloss . . . Ennius in *Satires*, Book 3:

> the broad plains
> that the African land bears neatly cultivated are
> witnesses

7 Non., p. 470.19–20 M. = 754 L.

CRIMINAT: Ennius satyrarum lib. III:

ia[6]   nam is non bene vult tibi qui falso criminat
apud te

8 Macrob. *Sat.* 6.5.5

"tristis" pro amaro translatio decens est ut "tristisque
lupini" [Verg. *G.* 1.75], et ita Ennius in libro saturarum
[saturarum *Colonna*: Sabinarum *codd.*] quarto:

ia[7]?   neque ‹ille› triste quaeritat sinapi
neque cepe maestum

neque ill‹e› triste *Burman*: neque triste *Macrobius*: neque ill
‹lac. c. 8 lett.› te *Serv. Dan.*

Cf. Serv. Dan. ad Verg. *G.* 1.75: Ennius, neque ill‹e tris›te quaeri.
ad sinapi.

9 Donat. ad Ter. *Phorm.* 339–41

"ten asymbolum venire unctum atque lautum e balineis, /
otiosum ab animo, quom ille et cura et sumptu absumitur!
/ dum tibi fit quod placeat, ille ringitur. tu rideas . . .": haec
non ab Apollodoro sed e sexto satirarum Ennii translata
sunt omnia:

7 Nonius

criminat ["makes accusations"]: Ennius, *Satires* Book 3:

> for he does not wish you well, who spreads false
>   accusations
> among your household

8 Macrobius, *Saturnalia*

"grim" is a deft substitution for "bitter," like "grim lupine."
[Verg. *G.* 1.75]. So too Ennius in his fourth book of *Satires*:

> he seeks neither the grim mustard
> nor the mournful onion

9 Donatus, *Commentary on Terence*

"You come without a contribution, oiled and washed from
the baths, / entirely at ease, while he is consumed with
worry and expense! / While things go your way, he gnashes
his teeth. You laugh . . .": All this is taken not from Apol-
lodorus but from the sixth [book of?] satires of Ennius:[1]

---

[1] Terence's *Phormio* was based on a Greek play by Apol-
lodorus of Carystos. The manuscripts of Donatus preserve the
following lines as prose: their reconstruction as iambic senarii
is problematic. See Welsh 2013. Only four books of satires are
otherwise attested (T 40b): either Donatus or his text is likely in
error.

ia[6]   quippe sine cura laetus lautus cum advenis,
           infestis malis, expedito bracchio,
           alacer celsus lupino expectans impetu
           quam mox bona alterius abligurrias,
5   quid censes domino esse animi? pro divum fidem,
           ill' tristist dum cibum servat, tu ridens voras.

> 2 infestis *Ritschl*: infertis *codd.*   4 quam mox . . . abli-
> gurrias *Welsh*: *alia alii*   6 voras *edd.*: vorans *codd.*

10 Gell. *NA* 2.29.17–20

haec quidem est Aesopi fabula de amicorum et propin-
quorum levi plerumque et inani fiducia. . . . [19] hunc
Aesopi apologum Q. Ennius in satiris scite admodum et
venuste versibus quadratis composuit. [20] quorum duo
postremi isti sunt, quos habere cordi et memoriae operae
pretium esse hercle puto:

tr[7]   hoc erit tibi argumentum semper in promptu situm:
           ne quid exspectes amicos, quod tute agere possies.

So when you come along carefree, cheerful,
     scrubbed,
jaws at the ready, arm poised for action,
eager, confident, waiting like a wolf to pounce
as soon as you can gobble up the goodies of another,
what do you suppose your host is thinking? Good   5
     God!
He's glum while minding the provisions you,
     laughing, devour.[2]

[2] This is the first appearance of the comic parasite in satire.
See Damon 1997, 105–8.

10 Gellius, *Attic Nights*

This, at any rate, is Aesop's fable about trust in friends and
relatives being usually idle and in vain.[1] . . . [19] Ennius
wrote up this parable of Aesop quite cleverly and elegantly
using trochaic verse in his satires. [20] These are its last
two lines, which I really think worth remembering and
taking to heart:

Always have this moral ready to hand:
Don't expect anything from friends that you yourself
     can do.

[1] The fable of the lark and its young also appears as Babrius
88 and Avianus 21. Gellius' version, reprinted in its entirety by
Vahlen and Courtney, may incorporate echoes of Ennian phrase-
ology throughout, but only these last two lines are explicit and
deliberate quotations.

11 Gell. *NA* 18.2.7

nuper quaesita esse memini numero septem, quorum
prima fuit enarratio horum versuum, qui sunt in saturis Q.
Enni uno multifariam verbo concinniter inplicati. quorum
exemplum hoc est:

Sot.?   nam qui lepide postulat alterum frustrari,
        quem frustratur, frustra eum dicit frustra esse;
        nam qui sese frustrari quem frustra sentit,
        qui frustratur is frustrast, si non ille est frustra.

12 Gell. *NA* 6.9.2

Q. Ennius in saturis "memorderit" dixit per *e* litteram, non
"momorderit":

ia⁶   meum non est, ac si me canis memorderit

13 Prisc., *GL* II, p. 434.8–10

nos quoque philosophor architector poetor in usu habui-
mus. Ennius,

ia⁶?   numquam poetor nisi si podager

11 Gellius, *Attic Nights*

Recently, I remember, we posed seven questions, the first of which was an explanation of those verses in Ennius' *Satires* that are deftly entangled with one word in multiple senses. This is an example of them:

> for one who seeks cleverly to deceive another
> is deceived in saying the one deceived is deceived;[1]
> for if one is deceived in thinking he is deceiving
>   someone,
> the one deceiving is deceived, if the other is not
>   deceived.

[1] Ennius plays on *frustra* ("unsuccessfully") and *frustrari* ("to be in error"). Cf. the analogous wordplay in Lucil. 203–5 M. = 208–10 W.; 1284–86 M. = 1250–52 W.

12 Gellius, *Attic Nights*

Ennius in his satires said *memorderit* ["has bitten"] with the letter *e*, not *momorderit*:

> it's not my way, as if a dog has bitten me

13 Priscian

We have also had in use the verbs *philosophor, architector, poetor.* Ennius:

> I'm never poetic unless I'm rheumatic[1]

[1] This may well be the source of the report that Ennius died of gout (T 99, 102). For his claim to be a drinker, cf. T 44a.

14 Fest., p. 402.2–5 L.

SUBULO Tusce tibicen dicitur, itaque Ennius:

tr[7]   subulo quondam marinas propter adstabat plagas

Cf. Varro, *Ling.* 7.35.

15 Paul. *Fest.*, p. 51.25–28 L.

idem [Ennius] cum dicit:

da[6]   propter stagna ubi lanigerum genus piscibus pascit

esse paludem demonstrat in qua nascuntur pisces similes ranunculis, quos oves consectatae edunt.

16 Varro, *Ling.* 7.71

apud Ennius:

da[6]   decem coclites quas montibus summis
    Ripaeis fodere

ab oculo cocles ut ocles dictus qui unum haberet oculum.

---

[1] The antecedent may be *massas* ("nuggets"). Whether "ten" refers to the nuggets or the miners is unclear.   [2] The one-eyed Arimaspians lived on the Scythian frontier, says Herodotus 4.13–14, citing the *Arimaspea* ("The Tale of the Arimaspians") by Aristeas of Proconnesus. The Coclites reappear at Plaut. *Curc.* 393.   [3] Varro appears to derive *cocles* from *co* + *ocles*, though in fact it comes into Latin via Etruscan from κύκλωψ.

SATIRES

14 Festus

subulo is the Etruscan word for a tibia player. Thus Ennius:

> a piper once was standing by the seashore[1]

[1] The fable of the fisherman with the pipe appears in Herodotus 1.141, Aesop 11, Babrius 9.

15 Paul the Deacon, *Epitome of Festus*

The same one [Ennius], when he says:

> by pools, where the wool-bearing race[1] feeds on
>   fishes[2]

points to the existence of a swamp where fish are born like small frogs, which sheep pursue and eat.

[1] At 1 *Ann.* F 43.76 birds are the *genus altivoltantum* ("race of high-flyers"); sheep are the *pecus lanigerum* at Accius, *Praet.* 20 R.[2-3]. The tone here may be ironic, as with F 5.

[2] Piscivorous sheep? Warmington understood Festus' gloss *ranunculi* to refer to the plant described by Plin. *HN* 25.172, the water crowfoot (*ranunculus batracium*), though this does not explain why Ennius explicitly says "fish." The compound adjective suggests epic parody.

16 Varro, *On the Latin Language*

In Ennius:

> ten which[1] the One-Eyed men[2] mined
> on the Ripaean mountain peaks

cocles, a person with one eye, is derived from *oculus* ["eye"], as if *ocles*.[3]

17 Cic. *Nat. D.* 1.97

ipsa vero quam nihil ad rem pertinet quae vos delectat maxime similitudo. quid? canis nonne similis lupo atque ut Ennius:

*da*⁶   simia quam similis, turpissima bestia, nobis

at mores in utroque dispares.

18 Fest., p. 444.15–20 L.

scirpus est id quod in palustribus locis nascitur leve et procerum unde tegetes fiunt. inde proverbium est in eas natum res quae nullius impedimenti sunt, in scirpo nodum quaerere. Ennius:

*da*⁶   quaerunt in scirpo, soliti quod dicere, nodum

Cf. Isid. *Orig.* 17.9.97.

19 (= T 58) Pers. 6.9–11

*da*⁶   Lunai portum, est operae, cognoscite, cives:

cor iubet hoc Enni, postquam destertuit esse / Maeonides Quintus pavone ex Pythagoreo.

17 Cicero, *On the Nature of the Gods*

How completely beside the point is that argument from similarity that so delights you! Why, isn't a dog like a wolf? And as Ennius says:

> how like us is the ape,[1] that most vile beast

but the habits of the two differ.

[1] Ennius puns on *sīmia* ("ape") and *sĭmilis* ("like").

18 Festus

The bulrush is that smooth, tall plant that grows in swamps, from which mats are made. From that comes the proverb said of things that present no obstacle, "to look for a knot on a bulrush." Ennius:

> they look, as the saying goes, for a knot on a bulrush[1]

[1] Cf. Plaut. *Men.* 247; Ter. *An.* 941; Lucil. 36 M. ⌐ 34 W.

19 (= T 58) Persius, *Satires*

"Get to know the port of Luna, citizens. It's worth it!"[1]

So urged Ennius' soul, after he snored off being / Quintus Maeonides [Homer, cf. T 63] via a Pythagorean peacock.

[1] The line is attributed to Ennian satire by Housman 1934, endorsed by Skutsch 1985, 750–51. Its ascription to the proem of 1 *Ann.*, traced back to Columna by Suerbaum 1968, 50–55, is supported by Kissel 1990, 776–87, and Gildenhard 2007, 77–79, who understand Ennius' *Lunai portum* to be not the town in Liguria but a location beyond the moon. Persius' *cor . . . Enni* may also echo an Ennian expression: cf. 13 *Ann.* F 3.

SCIPIO (F 1–7)

Later generations associated Ennius so closely with the Cornelii Scipiones that his portrait bust was said to have been displayed at the family tomb on the Via Appia (T 9, 49, 56, 62, and more generally T 42, 47b, 53, 90; cf. the stories at T 14, 27). Although the great P. Cornelius Scipio Africanus (ca. 236–183 BC) must have figured prominently in Ennius' account of the Hannibalic war in the Annals, *explicit evidence of that treatment remains elusive, and extraordinary praise of any one individual seems uncharacteristic of this epic. There is, however, evidence for a separate work entitled* Scipio, *though no quotation of it supplies a context. Its form, content, date, and purpose remain unknown. T 113, if indeed it refers to this work, may imply a date before composition of* Annals 1, *where Ennius claimed actually to be Homer reincarnate, but that may be reading too much into this problematic witness. Scipio's victory at Zama (202 BC) and subsequent triumph (201 BC) are often assumed to have provided the occasion for the poem, but F 1 and 7 might as easily suit the notorious trial of the Scipiones in 187 BC.*

The genre is uncertain. The predominance of trochaic rhythms would be consistent with some sort of staged entertainment, but the invocation of Homer (T 113) may tell against that possibility. An occasional poem, perhaps a

286

SCIPIO (F 1–7)

*panegyric, is therefore more often suspected. The choice
of meter may itself then be significant, since the elegiac
couplet was the established meter for encomium in the
Hellenistic tradition (Barbantani 2001, 3–31; cf. T 109b;
Enn. Epig. F 1, 3). If, as argued by Morgan 2014, Ennius
deliberately cast this work in trochaic septenarii to play
off the meter's Roman associations, the* Scipio *stands as an
important, if problematic witness to the complexity of his
relationship to Greek literary forms.*

*Whether the poem maintained a separate existence or
was eventually included in the collection called* Satires *is
unknown. Its fragments may be difficult to distinguish
from fragments of the* Annals*. F 1–3, which can be scanned
as hexameters, perhaps belong to the epic. F 4, 5, and 7 are
more certainly trochaic septenarii, and so quite possibly
was F 6, the dactylic form that survives being a conse-
quence of Lucilius' parody. Additional fragments some-
times assigned to this work are 8 Ann. F 3 and Inc. Ann.
F 17, 45, 55, 114.*

*Text and commentary in Russo 2007, 187–42; Courtney
1993, 26–30. Discussion by Suerbaum 1968, 103–6, 239–
48; Bettini 1979, 161–67; Scholz 1984; Winiarczyk 1994,
280–82; Morgan 2014; Morelli 2016.*

1 Cic. *Fin.* 2.106

effluit igitur voluptas corporis et prima quaeque avolat saepiusque relinquit causam paenitendi quam recordandi. itaque beatior Africanus cum patria illo modo loquens:

> desine, Roma, tuos hostes

reliquaque praeclare:

> nam tibi moenimenta mei peperere labores

laboribus hic praeteritis gaudet, tu iubes voluptatibus, et hic se ad ea revocat, e quibus nihil umquam rettulerit ad corpus, tu totus haeres in corpore.

2 Cic. *De or.* 3.167

ornandi causa proprium proprio commutatum: "desine, Roma . . ." [F 1],

> testes sunt Campi magni . . .

gravis est modus in ornatu orationis et saepe sumendus.

---

[1] Site of the battle southwest of Utica, where Hasdrubal and Syphax were defeated (Liv. 30.8.3; App. *Lib.* 68; Polyb. 14.7.9, 14.8.2).

SCIPIO

1 Cicero, *On Ends*

Bodily pleasures, then, are transient: each in turn evaporates, leaving cause for regret more often than for recollection. Thus Africanus must be counted happier [than Sardanapalus] when he addresses his country in this way:

cease, Rome, your enemies . . .

and the rest brilliantly:[1]

for my labors have brought forth a great monument
for you

He delights in his past labors, whereas you [Torquatus, the Epicurean] bid us dwell upon our past pleasures; and he recalls experiences that never had any connection with the body, but you are completely concerned with the body.

[1] Cicero's allusive quotations imply his readers' familiarity with the passage. Either the *Scipio* was better known than its remnants now suggest, or the allusion is to the *Annals*. If Scipio's speech is the one mentioned by Liv. 38.50.11, the occasion is not the African triumph but the trial of 187 BC.

2 Cicero, *On the Orator*

For the sake of ornament one proper name is substituted for another: "cease, Rome . . ." [F 1],

the Great Fields[1] are witnesses . . .

This is an effective way to ornament a speech and should often be adopted.

3 Cic. *Orat.* 152–53

nobis ne si cupiamus quidem distrahere voces conceditur. indicant orationes illae ipsae horridulae Catonis, indicant omnes poetae praeter eos qui, ut versum facerent, saepe hiabant, ut Naevius [*Trag.* 65 R.$^{2-3}$ = F 41 *TrRF*] . . . et ibidem [*Trag.* 64 R.$^{2-3}$ = F 42 *TrRF*] . . . at Ennius semel [*consensus codd.*: saepe *unus cod.*]:

Scipio invicte

. . . [153] hoc idem nostri saepius non tulissent, quod Graeci laudare etiam solent.

4 Gell. *NA* 4.7.1–5

Valerius Probus grammaticus inter suam aetatem praestanti scientia fuit. [2] is "Hannibalem" et "Hasdrubalem" et "Hamilcarem" ita pronuntiabat, ut paenultimam circumflecteret, et est epistula eius scripta ad Marcellum, in qua Plautum et Ennium multosque alios veteres eo modo pronuntiasse affirmat. [3] solius tamen Ennii versum unum ponit ex libro, qui *Scipio* inscribitur. [4] eum versum quadrato numero factum subiecimus, in quo nisi tertia syllaba de Hannibalis nomine circumflexe promatur, numerus clausurus est. versus Enni, quem dixit, ita est: [5]

⟨×⟩ qua propter Hannibalis copias considerat

---

[1] Understanding *considerat* from *consido* ("I make camp"), not *considero* ("I observe"). A syllable is missing at the beginning of the line.

3 Cicero, *Orator*

We are not permitted to force a separation between vowels, even should we wish to do so. Those famous, though slightly uncouth speeches of Cato themselves illustrate this; all the poets illustrate this except those who for metrical reasons often permitted hiatus, for example Naevius [*Trag.* 65 R.$^{2–3}$ = F 41 *TrRF*] . . . and again [*Trag.* 64 R.$^{2–3}$ = F 42 *TrRF*] . . . , but Ennius uses it only once:

Invincible Scipio!

. . . [153] Our poets would not very often have tolerated this thing, which the Greeks are actually accustomed to praise.

4 Gellius, *Attic Nights*

The grammarian Valerius Probus stood out in his day [later 1st century AD] for learning. [2] He pronounced "Hannibal" and "Hasdrubal" and "Hamilcar" by lengthening the next to last syllable, and there is a letter from him written to Marcellus, in which he claims that Plautus and Ennius and many other ancients pronounced it this way. [3] He nevertheless cites only one verse of Ennius alone, from the book entitled *Scipio*. [4] I have appended that verse below, created as a *versus quadratus* [lit., "square verse," a trochaic septenarius] in which, unless the third syllable of Hannibal's name is lengthened, the rhythm will limp. The verse of Ennius he quoted runs thus: [5]

. . . where (?) near Hannibal's forces he had made camp[1]

5 Macrob. *Sat.* 6.2.26 (Verg. *Aen.* 10.100–103 "tum pater omnipotens, rerum cui prima potestas, / infit: eo dicente deum domus alta silescit / et tremefacta solo tellus, silet arduus aether, / tum venti posuere, premit placida aequora pontus")

Ennius in *Scipione*:

> ‹× ×› mundus caeli vastus constitit silentio
> et Neptunus saevos undis asperis pausam dedit.
> Sol equis iter repressit ungulis volantibus,
> constitere amnes perennes, arbores vento vacant.

4 constitere *ed. Ven 1528*: consistere *codd.*

6 Macrob. *Sat.* 6.4.6 (Verg. *Aen.* 11.601–2 "tum late ferreus hastis / horret ager")

. . . et Ennius . . . in *Scipione*:

> sparsis hastis longis campus splendet et horret

sed ante omnes Homerus [*Il.* 13.339]: ἔφριξεν δὲ μάχη φθισίμβροτος ἐγχείῃσιν.

Cf. Serv. ad Verg. *Aen.* 11.601

"horret ager": terribilis est. est autem versus Ennianus vituperatus a Lucilio dicente per inrisionem debuisse eum dicere "horret et alget" [1190 M. = 413 W].

5 Macrobius, *Saturnalia* (on Virgil, "then the almighty father, whose power is in all things supreme / speaks: and as he speaks the gods' lofty house falls quiet, / the earth is shaken to its foundation, high heaven is silent, / then the west winds fall, the sea holds its calm surface in check")

Ennius in *Scipio*:

> . . . the vast vault of heaven stood still in silence,
> and fierce Neptune gave the rough waves a respite.
> The Sun checked his horses' course even as their
>   hooves flew,
> the ceaseless rivers stood still, the trees lacked wind.

6 Macrobius, *Saturnalia* (on Virgil, "then the field, full of iron, / bristles with spears")

. . . also Ennius . . . in *Scipio*:

> the field shimmered and bristled with long spears
>   spread

but Homer before all the others [*Il.* 13.339]: "the man-destroying battle bristled with spears."

Cf. Servius, *Commentary on Virgil*

"the field bristles": It is terrifying. It is moreover an Ennian verse faulted by Lucilius, who said in mockery that he ought to have said "shivers and grows cold" [1190 M. = 413 W.].[1]

---

[1] For the likelihood of trochaic rather than dactylic scansion of the Ennian original, see Mackay 1963 and Scholz 1984, 189–92.

7 *SHA*, Claud. (25) 7.7

dicit Ennius de Scipione:

> quantam statuam faciet populus Romanus, quantam
>   columnam,
> quae res tuas gestas loquatur?

1 faciet *codd.*: statuet *Lachmann*

7 *Historia Augusta*

Ennius says about Scipio:

> How great a statue will the Roman people make, how
>   great a column
> to speak of your deeds?[1]

[1] Scipio's defense in 187 BC has again been suggested as the
context (Liv. 38.56.12; Val. Max. 4.1.6a).

SOTA (F 1–5)

Ennius' Sota is named for the third-century Greek poet Sotades (using a short version of the name), who was credited with inventing a particular meter, the Sotadeus *or* ionicus quaternarius a maiore: $- - \cup \cup - - \cup \cup - - \cup \cup$ $- \times \parallel$, *with various resolutions permitted (Bettini 1982, esp. 71–75). The lines attributed to Sotades cover a wide variety of topics; some have philosophical content and a looser linguistic and metrical structure (remains in Powell 1925, 238–45). All lines preserved from Ennius' Sota are*

1 Varro, *Ling.* 5.62

ipsa Victoria ab eo quod superati vinciuntur. . . . ideo haec cum corona et palma, quod corona vinclum capitis et ipsa a vinctura dicitur vieri, ⟨id⟩ est vinciri; a quo est in Sota Enni:

> ibant malaci viere Veneriam corollam

iba . . . *vel* ibant *codd. Fest.*   mala civiere *cod. Varr.*:
mala cluere *vel* mala viere *codd. Cens.*   corollam *cod. Varr.*,
Fest.: coronam *codd. Cens.*

Cf. Fest., p. 514.15–18 L.; *Fragm. de metris*, *GL* VI, p. 613.14–15.

SOTA (F 1–5)

in the characteristic meter, but the scarcity of evidence leaves unclear how closely he followed the Greek model beyond that; in any case, Ennius seems to have addressed a number of topics. If the reference in Fronto's correspondence to Ennius' Sota in a volumen is to be taken literally (T 75), the work was of considerable length. Sotadicorum libri are also attested for Accius (F 19 FPL[4]).

Bibl.: Suerbaum 2002, 133; 2003, 227. Comm.: Courtney 1993, 4–7; Russo 2007, 243–71.

1 Varro, *On the Latin Language*

Victory herself ⟨is named⟩ from the fact that the defeated are "bound" [*vinciuntur*]. . . . Therefore she is connected with the garland and the palm branch since a garland is a "binder" [*vinclum*] of the head and is itself, from "binding" [*vinctura*], said "to be woven" [*vieri*], i.e., "to be bound" [*vinciri*]; whence there is in Ennius' *Sota*:[1]

the softies went along to weave Love's little garland[2]

[1] [Censorinus] identifies the meter as the *ionicus septenarius* (another term for *Sotadeus*).　　[2] *malacus* (lit. "soft") implies effeminacy, as at Plaut. *Mil.* 668; *Venerius* will thus suggest "erotic" rather than "sacred to Venus."

297

2 Fest., pp. 488.32–90.1 L.

TONSAM Ennius significat remum, quod quasi tondeatur ferro, cum ait lib. VII [7 *Ann.* F 8] . . . ; item [7 *Ann.* F 9] . . . ; et in {na} Sota:

> alius in mari vult magno tenere tonsam

3 Paul. *Fest.*, p. 489.5–6 L.

TONGERE nosse est, nam Praenestini tongitionem dicunt notionem. Ennius:

> alii rhetorica tongent

Cf. Fest., p. 488.7–10 L.

4 Paul. *Fest.*, p. 51.23–25 L.

> Cyprio bovi merendam

Ennius sotadico versu cum dixit, significavit id, quod solet fieri in insula Cypro, in qua boves humano stercore pascuntur.

2 Festus

Ennius uses *tonsa* for "oar" because it is as if cut by a knife, as he says in Book 7 [7 *Ann.* F 8] . . . ; likewise [7 *Ann.* F 9] . . . ; and in *Sota*:

> another wishes to hold an oar in the great sea[1]

[1] This and the following fragment may come from a sequence listing different human preferences in priamel form. The language is mock-epic (see Bettini 1982, 74).

3 Paul the Deacon, *Epitome of Festus*

tongere is *nosse* ["to know"]; for the people of Praeneste call *notio* ["idea"] *tongitio* ["knowledge"]. Ennius:

> others know rhetoric[1]

[1] Though not attributed to a particular work, the similarity to the preceding fragment encourages assignment to the *Sota*, which is metrically possible, although the incomplete line could be scanned in other ways (Bettini 1982, 71–73). The people of Praeneste were a frequent butt of jokes in Roman comedy (Wright 1974, 54–55).

4 Paul the Deacon, *Epitome of Festus*

> for a Cyprian ox a light meal

When Ennius said this in a Sotadic line,[1] he meant what often happens on the island of Cyprus, where cattle are pastured on human dung.[2]

[1] The meter makes attribution to Ennius' *Sota* almost certain.   [2] For this practice cf. Plin. *HN* 28.266: *boves in Cypro contra tormina hominum excrementis sibi mederi* ("cattle in Cyprus cure themselves from colic by the excrements of men").

5 *Fragm. de metr.*, *GL* VI, p. 613.16–17

ionicus <a> maiore:

> ille ictus retro rec<c>idit in natem supinus

habet vitium in tertia syllaba.

retro rec<c>idit *Lachmann*: retro recidit *vel* retrorecedit *vel* retrocecidit *codd.*

5 *Anonymous metrical treatise*

"Ionic a maiore":[1]

hit, he fell backward flat on his bum

It has a fault in the third syllable.[2]

[1] The discussion makes clear that the fragment is a Sotadic line (also called *ionicus a maiore*); hence attribution to Ennius' *Sota* is likely. The content is reminiscent of comedy or mock-epic. [2] If the final *s* of *ictus* is not disregarded, as was common in archaic Latin, to make the syllable short.

UNIDENTIFIED WORKS

OPERA INCERTA
(F 1–59)

This section includes material attested for Ennius by the usual range of transmitting authors, but without indication of its source. Because these extracts are generally short and often cited in indirect speech, there is insufficient in-

1 *Rhet. Her.* 4.18

conpositio est verborum constructio quae facit omnes partes orationis aequabiliter perpolitas. ea conservabitur, si . . . et si vitabimus eiusdem litterae nimiam adsiduitatem, cui vitio versus hic erit exemplo—nam hic nihil prohibet in vitiis alienis exemplis uti [1 *Ann.* F 54]: "o Tite, tute, Tati, tibi tanta, tyranne, tulisti!" et hic eiusdem poetae:

> quicquam quisquam cuiquam quemque quisque
> conveniat neget

cuiquam *Columna*: quemquam *vel* quemque *codd.*

UNIDENTIFIED WORKS
(F 1–59)

formation about content or meter to identify them with specific works or even genres. Attributions occasionally suggested by earlier scholars are indicated in the notes.

1 Rhetorica ad Herennium

Artful composition is an arrangement of words that makes every part of the discourse equally polished. It will be maintained if . . . and if we shun excessive repetition of the same letter, for which fault this verse will be an example— for here nothing prevents using examples from the faults of others [1 *Ann.* F 54]: "you, O Titus Tatius, tyrant, took on yourself such great troubles." And this line of the same poet:

> let anyone deny anyone anything, whoever meets whomever[1]

[1] Wordplay with repetition of the same word occurs elsewhere in Ennius (e.g., *Trag.* F 84, 111; *Sat.* F 11). This line, corrupt and of uncertain meaning, is most often attributed to a tragedy, although comedy and satire are possible.

2 (= T 8) Cic. *Arch.* 18

atque sic a summis hominibus eruditissimisque accepimus
ceterarum rerum studia et doctrina et praeceptis et arte
constare, poetam natura ipsa valere et mentis viribus exci-
tari et quasi divino quodam spiritu inflari. quare suo iure
noster ille Ennius "sanctos" appellat poetas, quod quasi
deorum aliquo dono atque munere commendati nobis
esse videantur.

3 (cf. T 109)

a Cic. *Leg.* 2.68

extrui autem vetat [Plato; cf. Plat. *Leg.* 12.958e] sepul-
crum altius, quam quod ⟨quinque homines⟩ [*Turnebus*]
quinque diebus absolverint, nec e lapide excitari plus nec
inponi quam quod capiat laudem mortui incisam ne plus
quattuor herois versibus (quos "longos" appellat Ennius).

b Isid. *Orig.* 1.39.6

hexametros autem Latinos primum fecisse Ennius tradi-
tur; eosque "longos" vocat.

Cf. Atilius Fortunatianus, *GL* VI, pp. 283.28–84.7; Gell. *NA*
18.15.1; Diom., *GL* I, pp. 494.31–95.1.

2 (= T 8) Cicero, *Pro Archia*

And thus we have gathered from the greatest and most learned men that the study of other things is based on learning, rules, and art, but that a poet is proficient by nature itself and aroused by the powers of the mind and inspired as if by some kind of divine spirit. For that reason, our famous Ennius with full justification calls poets "sacred,"[1] since they seem to be entrusted to us as if by some gift and present from the gods.

[1] Context is unknown. The sentiment itself is not necessarily an Ennian coinage: at *Arch.* 31 Cicero casts the same claim as a general truth.

3 (cf. T 109)

a Cicero, *On the Laws*

But he [Plato; cf. Plat. *Leg.* 12.958e] forbids a tomb to be erected higher than what five men can complete in five days, nor that more stone be put up or placed upon it than what captures the glory of the dead, incised in no more than four heroic verses (which Ennius calls "long").

b Isidore, *Origins*

Ennius, moreover, is said to have composed Latin hexameters for the first time, and he calls them "long."[1]

[1] The statement may have appeared in one of the *prooemia* attached to books of the *Annals* or in a satire—or may instead belong to the grammarian Ennius (*Inc.* F 10, 24; T 69, 114).

4 Cic. *Tusc.* 4.52

an est quicquam similius insaniae quam ira? quam bene
Ennius initium dixit insaniae. color, vox, oculi, spiritus,
inpotentia dictorum ac factorum quam partem habent
sanitatis?

5 Cic. *Nat. D.* 2.49

quae si bis bina quot essent didicisset Epicurus certe non
diceret; sed dum palato quid sit optimum iudicat, "caeli
palatum," ut ait Ennius, non suspexit.

6 Cic. *Div.* 2.111

non esse autem illud carmen furentis cum ipsum poema
declarat (est enim magis artis et diligentiae quam incita-
tionis et motus), tum vero ea, quae ἀκροστιχὶς dicitur,
cum deinceps ex primis versus litteris aliquid conectitur,
ut in quibusdam Ennianis: Q. Ennius fecit. id certe magis
est attenti animi quam furentis.

4 Cicero, *Tusculan Disputations*

Is there really anything more similar to madness than anger? How well has Ennius called it the beginning of madness. Complexion, voice, eyes, spirit, powerlessness of words and deed, which part of sanity do they have?

5 Cicero, *On the Nature of the Gods*

If Epicurus had learned how much is twice two, he surely would not speak this way; but when he judges what is best by his palate, he did not look up at "the palate of the sky,"[1] as Ennius says.

[1] For the metaphorical application of *palatum* to *caelum*, see August. *De civ. D.* 7.8; Isid. *Orig.* 11.1.55.

6 Cicero, *On Divination*

Moreover, that this [certain Sibylline verses] is not the poetry of a madman the poem itself declares, for it shows more art and diligence than excitement and movement, and is especially evident from what is called an acrostic,[1] when some meaning is constructed from the initial letters of the verses, as in certain lines of Ennius: "Q. Ennius made ⟨this⟩." That is surely the work of an attentive mind rather than a mad one.

[1] This is the first explicit reference in Latin to acrostic composition, an established feature of Hellenistic Greek style that becomes well established in Latin poetry by the first century BC. The Ennian acrostic does not survive, though pieces of it have been suspected elsewhere. See Herrmann 1928.

7 Cic. *Div.* 2.127

iam vero quis dicere audeat vera omnia esse somnia?

aliquot somnia vera

inquit Ennius, sed omnia non necesse est. quae est tandem ista distinctio? quae vera, quae falsa habet?

8 Cic. *Amic.* 22

principio qui potest esse "vita vitalis," ut ait Ennius, quae non in amici mutua benivolentia conquiescit?

9 Varro, *Ling.* 5.64–65

terra Ops, quod hic omne opus et hac opus ad vivendum, et ideo dicitur Ops mater, quod terra mater. haec enim:

terris gentis omnis peperit et resumit denuo,

quae:

dat cibaria

ut ait Ennius, quae:

quod gerit fruges, Ceres

7 Cicero, *On Divination*

And besides, who dares to say that all dreams are true?

> some dreams are true

says Ennius, but not necessarily all.[1] What then is this distinction? Which ones does he consider true, which ones false?

[1] Cicero's quotation is sometimes emended to form a complete trochaic tetrameter: *aliquot somnia vera sed omnia noenum necesse est* or *aliquot somnia vera sunt, noenum necesse est omnia.*

8 Cicero, *On Friendship*

First of all, how can there be a "life worth living," as Ennius says, which does not rest on mutual goodwill among friends?

9 Varro, *On the Latin Language*

The Earth <is called> Ops, because here [i.e., on earth] is every "work" [*opus*] and she is "necessary" [*opus*] for living, and therefore Ops is called "mother," since the earth is a mother. For she:

> has given birth to all races on earth and takes them
> back again,

she who:

> provides food,

as Ennius says, she who is:

> Ceres, because she bears [*gerit*] the crops

antiquis enim quod nunc G C. [65] idem hi dei Caelum et
Terra Iupiter et Iuno, quod ut ait Ennius:

> istic est is Iuppiter quem dico, quem Graeci vocant
> aerem, qui ventus est et nubes, imber postea,
> atque ex imbre frigus, ventus post fit, aer denuo.
> † haec propter † Iuppiter sunt ista quae dico tibi
> 5   † qua † mortalis atque urbes beluasque omnis iuvat.

7 † haec propter † *Jocelyn*: haec propter *cod.*: haec‹e›propter
Vahlen (*cf. Skutsch ad Enn.* Ann. *268*)   8 † qua † *Jocelyn*:
qua *cod.*: qu‹i›a Laetus

10 Varro, *Ling.* 5.86

fetiales, quod fidei publicae inter populos praeerant: nam
per hos fiebat ut iustum conciperetur bellum et † inde
desitum, ut foedere fides pacis constitueretur. ex his mit-
tebantur, ante quam conciperetur, qui res repeterent, et
per hos etiam nunc fit foedus, quod "fidus" Ennius scribit
dictum.

---

[1] A college of priests who determined the laws and proce-
dures for declaring war and making peace (cf. Liv. 1.24).

since for the ancients what is now G was written C. [65]
These deities Caelum ["Sky"] and Terra ["Earth"] are the
same as Jupiter and Juno, since, as Ennius says:

> That is this Jupiter, of whom I speak, whom the
>   Greeks call
> *aer* ["air"], who is wind and clouds, later rain,
> and cold from rain, then becomes wind [*aer*] again.
> Therefore (?) these things that I mention to you are
>   Jupiter,
> because (?) he strengthens [*iuvat*] all mortals and
>   cities, and animals.[1]

[1] These lines have been variously assigned to tragedies or to
the *Epicharmus*: Varro's incorporation of the quotations into his
own argument makes restoration and attribution especially prob-
lematic. On the fragment, its attribution, and etymologies, see
Bettini 1979, 35–38; Kessissoglu 1990, 75–80.

10 Varro, *On the Latin Language*

The fetials[1] [are so called] because they were in charge of
the public's good name [*fides*] in dealing with other peo-
ples: for through them it came about that a war was de-
clared to be a just one and . . . (?) that trust in a peace was
established by treaty. Some of them used to be sent before
war was declared to demand restitution, and through them
even now a treaty [*foedus*] is made which, as Ennius
writes, was pronounced *"fidus."*[2]

[2] Ennius may have been punning on *fidus* (i.e., *foedus*) and
fides, or Varro's source may instead be the grammarian Ennius
(cf. *Inc.* F 3, 24; T 69, 114).

11 Varro, *Ling.* 6.61

dico originem habet Graecam, quod Graeci δεικνύω. hinc
Ennius:

> dico qui hunc dicare

hinc iudicare, quod tunc ius dicatur; . . .

Cf. Fest., p. 138.10–11 L.

12 Varro, *Ling.* 7.93

euax verbum nichil significat, sed effutitum naturaliter est
(ut apud Ennium [*Trag.* F 177]: "hehae! ipse clipeus ceci-
dit"; apud Ennium:

> heu, mea puella, † spe † quidem id succenset tibi

apud . . .); . . .

   † spe *Goetz* / *Schoell*: spe *codd.*: <i>stequidem *Goetz* / *Schoell*
in app.

13 (cf. *Inc.* F 35) Varro, *Ling.* 7.101

apud Ennium [*Trag.* F 178]: "vocibus concide, fac i‹am›
mus‹s›et obrutus." mussare dictum, quod muti non am-
plius quam MU dicunt; a quo idem dicit id quod minimum
est:

> neque, ut aiunt, μῦ facere audent

Cf. Charis., *GL* I, p. 240.8–10, 28–29.

11 Varro, *On the Latin Language*

"I say" [*dico*] has a Greek origin, since the Greeks say "I show" [*deiknuo*]. Hence Ennius says:

> I say who ‹can (?)› show him[1]

hence "to pronounce a judgment" [*iudicare*], since then a "judicial pronouncement" [*ius*] is announced . . .

[1] The form and meaning of *dicare* in the fragment are uncertain.

12 Varro, *On the Latin Language*

The word *euax* ["hurrah"] does not mean anything, but is something blurted forth spontaneously (as in Ennius [*Trag.* F 177]: "oh! the shield itself fell down"; in Ennius:

> oh, my girl, he is indeed (?) angry with you about
>   that[1]

in . . .); . . .

[1] The text is partly corrupt; the translation reflects the conjecture in the textual note (one of the many proposed). The interjection is also attested at Inc. *Ann.* F 13.

13 (cf. *Inc.* F 35) Varro, *On the Latin Language*

In Ennius [*Trag.* F 178]: "thrash him with words, see to it that he will just mutter (?), crushed." *mussare* ["mutter"] is said because *muti* ["the mute"] do not say more than "*mu*"; hence the same poet says this that is the least:

> and, as they say, they do not dare make a *mu*

14 (cf. Inc. *Ann.* F 85, 126) Varro, *Ling.* 7.103–4

multa ab animalium vocibus tralata in homines, partim
quae sunt aperta, partim obscura; perspicua ut Ennii . . .
[Inc. *Ann.* F 34]: minus aperta, ut . . . Ennii a vitulo:

tibicina maximo labore mugit

15 Varro, *Ling.* 9.107

sed consuetudo alterum utrum cum satis haberet, in toto
corpore potius utitur lavamur, in partibus lavamus, quod
dicimus lavo manus, sic pedes et cetera. quare e balneis
non recte dicunt lavi, lavi manus recte. sed quoniam in
balneis lavor lautus sum, sequitur, ut contra, quoniam est
soleo, oporteat dici "solui," ut Cato et Ennius scribit, non
ut dicit volgus, solitus sum, debere dici; . . .

16 (= T 83) Gell. *NA* 17.17.1

Quintus Ennius tria corda habere sese dicebat, quod loqui
Graece et Osce et Latine sciret.

14 (cf. Inc. *Ann.* F 85, 126) Varro, *On the Latin Language*

Many terms are transferred from the cries of animals to people, some which are obvious, some obscure. Clear terms, as Ennius' . . . [Inc. *Ann.* F 34]: less obvious like . . . this of Ennius, from a calf:

the female flute player bellows with maximum effort[1]

[1] Blänsdorf (*FPL*[4]), scanning as the end and the beginning of a Sotadean, assigns the fragment to Ennius' *Sota*.

15 Varro, *On the Latin Language*

But since common usage accepts each of the two equally, for the entire body it prefers to use "we wash ourselves" [*lavamur*: middle-passive], for parts of the body "we wash" [*lavamus*: active], because we say "I wash my hands" and so too of feet and the rest. Therefore, with respect to baths they do not say correctly "I have washed," but correctly "I have washed my hands." But since in baths we say "I wash myself, I have washed myself," it follows that, by contrast, since it is "I am accustomed," one ought to say "I have been accustomed" [*solui*], as Cato and Ennius write, not, as people commonly say, "I have been accustomed" [*solitus sum*: different, more common form of the perfect tense, passive form with active meaning] should be said . . .

16 (= T 83) Gellius, *Attic Nights*

Quintus Ennius used to say that he had three hearts, because he knew how to speak Greek, Oscan, and Latin.

17 Gell. *NA* 19.8.6

". . . ac fortassean de "quadrigis" veterum auctoritati concessero, "inimicitiam" tamen, sicuti "inscientiam" et "inpotentiam" et "iniuriam," quae ratio est, quamobrem C. Caesar vel dictam a veteribus vel dicendam a nobis non putat, . . . ? . . . "inimicitiam" autem Q. Ennius in illo memoratissimo libro dixit:

> eo ⟨ego⟩

inquit

> ingenio natus sum:
> amicitiam atque inimicitiam in frontem promptam
>   gero

. . ."

1 ego *codd. Non.*: *om. codd. Gell.*

Cf. Non., p. 129.24–26 M. = 188 L.

18 Fest., p. 128.22–23 L.

MOENE singulariter dixit Ennius [Naevius *C. O. Mueller*; *cf. Naev. F 68 FPL*⁴]:

> apud emporium in campo hostium pro moene

17 Gellius, *Attic Nights*

". . . And perhaps, concerning *quadrigae* ["four-horse chariot"; plural form] I [the speaker, an anonymous learned poet] might yield to the authority of the ancients, but as regards *inimicitia* ["enmity"; singular, usually plural], like *inscientia* ["ignorance"] and *inpotentia* ["lack of self-restraint"], and *iniuria* ["injustice"], why does Caesar[1] not think that this [i.e., the singular forms] was said by the ancients or should be said by us. . . ? . . . Furthermore, Ennius in that very famous work said *inimicitia*:

> I was born with this disposition: I bear friendship and enmity readily visible on my forehead[2]

. . ."

[1] The dictator C. Iulius Caesar in his lost work *De analogia*.
[2] The meter is uncertain. The lines are most commonly attributed to a tragedy, but by some to the *Scipio* (so Timpanaro, Blänsdorf, Courtney). A satire is equally possible. For the conceit, cf. Cic. *Cat.* 1.32.

18 Festus

moene ["wall"] in the singular [normally *moenia* in the plural] was said by Ennius:

> near Emporium in enemy territory before the wall[1]

[1] Meter and context are unknown. (Some attribute the line to Naevius.) The reference may be to the Spanish town Empúries, typically called *Emporion* in Greek and *Emporiae* in Latin.

19

a Fest., pp. 186.31–88.2 L.

‹. . . ob praepositio alias› ponitur . . . ‹. . . ; alias pro ad ponitur, ut Ennius [8 *Ann.* F 18]: "ob Romam noc›tu legiones ducere coepit," et alibi:› "ob Troiam duxit."

b Paul. *Fest.*, p. 133.6–8 L.

mortem obisse ea consuetudine dicitur, qua dixerunt antiqui ob Romam legiones ductas, et

ob Troiam duxit exercitum

pro ad . . .

Cf. Paul. *Fest.*, p. 187.7–12 L. ad Enn. 8 *Ann.* F 18.

20 Fest., p. 278.8–16 L.

‹. . . "philo›logam" Ennius in praet‹exta› . . . ‹culpa li›brariorum qui ea quae fem‹inini sunt, dici nolebant mascu›lino. etiam ipsi Gra‹eci ita locuti sunt, qui mulieres philolo›gos, philargyros ‹dixerunt. sed feminam videns libra›rius appellari, mut‹avit› . . . vox explanata non . . . nomina etiam in vi . . . dicimus tam hic lapis q‹uam haec lapis. . . .›

---

[1] If the restoration is correct, the word *philologa* (in whichever case) appeared in the text of a praetexta by Ennius (the *Sabinae?*). Festus suggests that Ennius treated *philologus* as a word that, like the Greek examples provided, was applicable to both genders, the form only later changed to provide a Latin feminine.

19

a Festus

The preposition *ob* ["in front of"] is sometimes used . . . ;
sometimes it is used in place of *ad* ["toward"], as Ennius
[8 *Ann.* F 18]: "he began leading his legions toward [*ob*]
Rome at night," and elsewhere "he led toward [*ob*] Troy."

b Paul the Deacon, *Epitome of Festus*

"to have met one's death" [*ob-isse*] is said according to that
usage by which the ancients said that legions were led
toward [*ob*] Rome, and

> he led the army toward Troy

in place of *ad* . . .

20 Festus

"Female philologist" was used by Ennius in a praetexta[1]
. . . due to the fault of copyists, who did not want things
that are feminine to be called by a masculine word. Yet the
Greeks themselves spoke thus, as they called women "lov-
ing words" [*philo-logos*] or "loving money" [*phil-argyros*].
But a copyist, seeing that a woman was meant, changed it
. . . [*followed by further discussion in very corrupt form
on the use of single gender nouns*]

Ennius famously rendered *philologus* (referring to himself) as
dicti studiosus at 7 *Ann.* F 1. It is possible, however, that *philologa*
(lit., "speech lover") in this context had nothing to do with learn-
ing but meant simply "chatterbox," a suggestion we owe to Katha-
rina Volk.

21 Fest., p. 346.5–7 L.

‹RE›MORBESCAT En‹nius:› . . . ‹in mor›bum reccidat.

22 Fest., pp. 412.35–14.14 L.

‹. . . STIPES fustis terra›e defixus: . . . Ennius . . . ‹stip›ites abiegno . . . ae stipitem . . . mit eum, qua . . . arripit.

23 Fest., p. 478.12–13 L.

TAPPETE ex Graeco sum . . . tae Ennius cum ait: "t . . ."
. . .

24 Fest., p. 482.7–21 L.

topper significare ait Artorius cito, fortasse, celeriter, te-mere. . . . Sinnius [*C. O. Mueller*: iras ennius *cod.*] vero sic: topper fortasse valet in Enni et Pacui scriptis; apud Ennium est:

topper quam nemo melius scit

21 Festus

"s/he falls ill again" [*remorbescat*] in Ennius: . . . s/he falls back into illness.[1]

[1] The verb is subjunctive, but its force cannot be determined without a context.

22 Festus

A "stake" is a stick fixed by being thrust down into the earth: . . . Ennius . . . stakes out of silver fir . . . [*remaining text too corrupt to be translated*]

23 Festus

"cloth used as covering" [*tappete*], taken [?] from the Greek . . . "cloths" [*tapetae?*], when Ennius says: "c<loths> . . ." . . . [1]

[1] The text is very corrupt: Ennius may have used the word *tapete* in the form *tapetae*.

24 Festus

Artorius[1] says that *topper* ["at once"] means "quickly," "perhaps," "fast," "heedlessly." . . . Sinnius[2] however explains thus: *topper* has the force of "perhaps" in the writings of Ennius and Pacuvius; in Ennius there is:

whom [*fem.*] perhaps nobody knows better[3]

[1] Perhaps the grammarian C. Artorius [possibly Cartorius] Proculus, cited by Quint. *Inst.* 9.1.2. [2] Or perhaps S. Ennius (cf. *Inc.* F 3, 10; T 69, 114). [3] The fragment is often attributed to a tragedy. The adverb *topper*, which first appears in Livius Andronicus, is generally taken to mean "at once."

25 Fronto, Ad M. Caesarem et invicem libri, *Ep.* 4.3
(p. 59.12–15 van den Hout)

neque id reprehendo, te verbi translatione audacius pro-
gressum, quippe qui Enni sententia oratorem audacem
esse debere censeam. sit sane audax orator, ut Ennius pos-
tulat; sed a significando quod volt eloqui nusquam digre-
diatur.

26 Censorinus, *Die nat.* 19.1–3

annus vertens est natura, dum sol percurrens XII signa
eodem, unde profectus est, redit. [2] hoc tempus quot
dierum esset, ad certum nondum astrologi reperire potue-
runt. Philolaus annum naturalem dies habere prodidit
CCCLXIIII et dimidiatum, . . . , at noster Ennius
CCCLXVI. [3] plerique praeterea incomprehensibile qui-
dem nec enuntiabile esse existimarunt, sed pro vero, quod
proximum putabant, amplexi sunt: dies scilicet CCCLXV.

27 Censorinus, *Die nat.* 24.4

post supremam sequitur vespera, ante ortum scilicet eius
stellae, quam Plautus [*Amph.* 275] vesperuginem, Ennius
vesperum, Vergilius [*Ecl.* 8.30, 10.77] hesperon appellat.

25 Fronto, *Correspondence*

And I do not criticize this, that you have advanced rather boldly in the metaphorical transfer of a word, since I judge by Ennius' statement that an orator must be bold. An orator may well be bold, as Ennius demands, but he should on no occasion depart from indicating what he wishes to say.

26 Censorinus, *The Birthday*

The year turns in its natural course when the sun, moving through the twelve signs ‹of the zodiac›, returns to the same place from whence it started. [2] How many days this period requires, astronomers have not yet been able to determine for certain. Philolaus[1] reported that the natural year has 364 and a half days . . . but our Ennius 366 days.[2] [3] Moreover, most have judged this to be something incomprehensible and inexpressible, but have embraced in place of the truth what they believed to be closest, namely 365 days.

[1] A Pythagorean of the 5th century BC.   [2] Presumably the poet Ennius, who evokes natural phenomena in many of his works.

27 Censorinus, *The Birthday*

Evening follows after the end of day, that is, of course, before the rise of that star Plautus [*Amph.* 275] calls Vesperugo, Ennius Vesper, Virgil [*Ecl.* 8.30, 10.77] Hesperos.

28 Porph. ad Hor. *Sat.* 1.1.61

"at bona pars hominum": bona nunc pro magna dictum, ut saepe Ennius et alii veteres.

29 Diom., *GL* I, pp. 344.28–45.2

iterativa sive frequentativa est verborum qualitas quae assiduam in agendo vim habet, unde et appellationcm subit, quoniam frequenter agendi iteret effectum, velut . . . item adeo adis: hoc iteramus adito aditas dictitantes, ut Ennius:

   ad eum aditavere

30 Diom., *GL* I, p. 400.15–28

plura enim verba quae vulgo passivo more declinamus apud veteres diversa reperiuntur enuntiata declinatione. . . . ; moro, quod crebro moror dicimus; . . . haec et alia apud veteres reperimus contra morem doctorum posita. . . . moro . . . Ennius:

   † an aliquid quod dono illi morare sed accipite †

   † an . . . accipite † *Jocelyn*: an . . . accipite *codd.*

28 Porphyrio, *Commentary on Horace*

"but a good part of men": "good" [*bona*] is here said in place of "large" [*magna*], as Ennius and other ancients often did.[1]

[1] Because *bona* in this sense is always combined with *pars* in early and classical Latin, Ennius is likely to have used a version of the phrase *bona pars*, perhaps in the *Annals*, since Porphyrio otherwise quotes only from that work.

29 Diomedes

Iterative or frequentative is a quality of verbs that has a regular force in the action, whence it takes on that appellation, since it repeats the effect of the action frequently, just as . . . likewise *adeo* ["I go to"], *adis* ["you go to"]: we repeat this when we say *adito* ["I go frequently"], *aditas* ["you go frequently"], as Ennius:

they frequently went up to him

30 Diomedes

Very many verbs that we normally conjugate in the passive voice can be found among the ancients expressed with a different conjugation. . . . *moro* ["I delay"; active form], which we often say as *moror* [deponent form] . . . these and others we find among the ancients, put against the practice of the learned. . . . *moro* ["I delay"] . . . Ennius:

(?) . . . (?)[1]

[1] The text of this line cannot be restored with certainty: it seems to be a question, it involves a gift, and there appears to be hesitation to accept it.

31 Non., p. 90.5–11 M. = 128 L.

CONCIERE: cum perturbatione conmovere. Accius Medea [Acc. *Trag.* 399 R.$^{2-3}$] . . . . Afranius Deposito [*Tog.* 45–46 R.$^{2-3}$] . . . . Ennius ‹. . . Pacuvius› Duloreste [Pac. *Trag.* 140–41 R.$^{2-3}$]: . . .

Ennius ‹. . . Pacuvius› *Mueller*: Ennius *codd.*: Pacuvius *Scaliger*

32 Non., p. 192.9–14 M. = 282 L.

ARANEAE et feminini sunt generis. . . . Ennius:

buxus araneae

33 Non., p. 194.18–24 M. = 286 L.

BUXUM generis neutri. . . . feminini, Ennius:

buxus vincta, taxus tonsa

34 Non., p. 448.10–14 M. = 719 L.

EDOLARE fabrorum est verum verbum cum materiarum conplanatur asperitas. usi sunt eo laudandi scriptores vetustatis etiam ad alias fabricas rerum. Varro Bimarco [*Sat. Men.* 59 B.]: "cum Quintipor Clodius tot comoedias sine ulla fecerit musa, ego unum libellum non 'edolem,' ut ait Ennius?"

31 Nonius

conciere ["to rouse up"]: "to bring in motion with complete disturbance." Accius in *Medea* [Acc. *Trag.* 399 R.$^{2-3}$] . . . Afranius in *Depositus* [*Tog.* 45–46 R.$^{2-3}$] . . . Ennius ⟨ . . . Pacuvius⟩[1] in *Dulorestes* [Pac. *Trag.* 140–41 R.$^{2-3}$]: . . .

[1] Assuming no error on Nonius' part, a line of Ennius has been lost, since the transmitted text attributes to him a line from *Dulorestes*, a play known to be by Pacuvius. Ennius presumably used a form of *conciere*, probably also in a play.

32 Nonius

araneae ["spiders"] are also of feminine gender [i.e., there is also a feminine form]. . . . Ennius:

a box tree, spiders

33 Nonius

buxum ["box tree"] is of neuter gender. . . . Feminine in Ennius:

a box tree bound, a yew tree pruned

34 Nonius

edolare ["to hew out"] is a word appropriate to craftsmen when the roughness of timber is smoothed out. Praiseworthy writers of antiquity also used it for the skillful production of other things. Varro in *Bimarcus* [*Sat. Men.* 59 B.]:[1] "when Quintipor Clodius[2] has made so many comedies without a single Muse, may I not 'hew out' one little book, as Ennius says?"

[1] One of Varro's *Menippean Satires.*   [2] Apparently a writer of comedies, probably of the late Republic.

35 (cf. *Inc*. F 13) Donat. ad Ter. *An*. 505.3

"nihil iam mutire": Ennius:

> nec dico nec facio ‹mu›

unde et mutos dicimus,—quod Graeci φθέγγεσθαι.

‹mu› *add. Columna*

36 Serv. Dan. ad Verg. *Ecl*. 9.23

"inter agendum": dum agis. et honesta locutio est, si dicamus, inter cenandum hoc sum locutus. [*add. Serv. Dan.*] Afranius [*Tog*. 422 R.²⁻³]: "inter loquendum"; Ennius:

> inter ponendum

37 Serv. ad Verg. *Ecl*. 10.10

"indigno": vel meretricio vel magno: nam et Ennius ait:

> indignas turres

id est magnas.

38 Serv. ad Verg. *Aen*. 1.26

"alta mente repostum": secreta, recondita. repostum autem syncope est; unam enim de medio syllabam tulit. sed cum omnes sermones aut integri sint aut pathos habeant, hi qui pathos habent ita ut lecti sunt debent poni: quod etiam Maro fecit, nam "repostos" [*Aen*. 6.655] et "porgite" [*Aen*. 8.274] de Ennio transtulit: integris autem et ipsis utimur et eorum exemplo aliis.

35 (cf. *Inc.* F 13) Donatus, *Commentary on Terence*

"now ‹I dare› not say a word [*mutire*]": Ennius:

> neither do I speak nor make ‹a *mu*›

whence we also call the mute [*muti*],—which thing [*muttire*] the Greeks call "to make a sound."

36 Servius Danielis, *Commentary on Virgil*

"while doing": "when you do." And this is a respectable expression, if we were to say, "I said this while eating." Afranius [*Tog.* 422 R.$^{2-3}$] says, "while speaking"; Ennius:

> while putting

37 Servius, *Commentary on Virgil*

indigno ["beyond what is appropriate"]: either [in a negative sense] "relating to prostitutes" or [in a positive sense] "great": for Ennius too says:

> towers beyond what is appropriate

that is, great.

38 Servius, *Commentary on Virgil*

"stored deep in the mind": "secret," "hidden." Moreover, "stored" [*repostum*] is a syncope, for he took one syllable away from the middle [*repositum*]. But since all utterances are either unaltered or have some modification, those that have a modification must be rendered in the shape in which they were collected, which Maro [Virgil] certainly did. For "stored" [*Aen.* 6.655] and "stretch out" [*Aen.* 8.274] he took over from Ennius: moreover, we use both these unaltered and others on the model of these.

39 Serv. Dan. ad Verg. *Aen.* 1.190

"tum vulgus": bene "vulgus" ductoribus interemptis. [*add. Serv. Dan.*] Ennius "avium vulgus" et alibi "hastarum," id est multitudinem hastarum et avium.

Vahlen, Thilo: ennius avium vulgus et hastarum et avium *cod.*[1]: alibi multitudinem et hastarum et *supra* et avium *scripsit cod.*[2]

40

a Serv. ad Verg. *Aen.* 1.741

sane Atlas Graecum est, sicut et Nilus; nam Ennius dicit Nilum Melonem vocari, Atlantem vero Telamonem.

b Schol. ad Luc. 10.252

"ducit aquas" Ennius hoc de Nilo ait, quod per aestatem sol ab inferioribus aquam supra revocet et hinc eo tempore Nilus increscat.

Cf. Serv. ad Verg. *G.* 4.291; *Aen.* 4.246; Paul. *Fest.*, pp. 7.8–9, 16.28–30, 111.24 L.

41 Serv. ad Verg. *Aen.* 2.651

"nos contra": praepositiones vel adverbia in a exeuntia modo producunt ultimam litteram, excepto puta et ita, apud Ennium et Pacuvium brevia sunt [i.e., contră].

39 Servius Danielis, *Commentary on Virgil*

"then the masses" [*vulgus*]: appropriately "the masses" after the leaders have been killed. Ennius says "masses of birds" and elsewhere "of lances," i.e., a large number of lances and birds.

40

a Servius, *Commentary on Virgil*

Certainly Atlas is a Greek term, as is also Nile, for Ennius says that the Nile is called Melo and Atlas Telamon.

b Scholia to Lucan

"it attracts water": Ennius says this about the Nile, since throughout the summer the sun brings the water from below up to the surface and hence at this time the Nile increases.

41 Servius, *Commentary on Virgil*

"we on the other hand": prepositions or adverbs ending in *a* [here, *contra*] now lengthen the last letter, except *puta* ["suppose"] and *ita* ["so"]. In Ennius and Pacuvius they are short.[1]

[1] The standard scansion in early Latin, as in Inc. *Ann.* F 42, 111, and regularly in Plautus.

42 Serv. Dan. ad Verg. *Aen.* 3.241

"foedare": cruentare. Ennius:

> ferro foedati iacent

43 Serv. ad Verg. *Aen.* 4.9

"insomnia terrent": et "terret" legitur et "terrent." sed si "terret" legerimus, "insomnia" erit vigilia: hoc enim maiores inter vigilias et ea quae videmus in somnis interesse voluerunt, ut "insomnia" generis feminini numeri singularis vigiliam significaret, "insomnia" vero generis neutri numeri pluralis ea quae per somnum videmus, ut [Verg. *Aen.* 6.896] "sed falsa ad caelum mittunt insomnia manes." sciendum igitur, quia, si "terret" dixerimus, antiqua erit elocutio; "insomnia" enim, licet et Pacuvius et Ennius frequenter dixerit, Plinius tamen exclusit et de usu removit. sed ambiguitatem lectionis haec res fecit, quod non ex aperto vigilasse se dixit, sed habuisse quietem inplacidam, id est somniis interruptum, ut intellegamus eam et insomniis territam, et propter terrorem somniorum vigilias quoque perpessam.

Cf. Serv. ad Verg. *Aen.* 5.840; Donat. ad Ter. *Eun.* 219.3; *Excerpta ex cod. Cass.* 402, *CGL* V, p. 553.1–2.

42 Servius Danielis, *Commentary on Virgil*

foedare ["to pollute"]: "to stain with blood." Ennius:

stained with blood by the sword, they lie[1]

[1] The phrase is generally attributed to a tragedy, most frequently to *Hectoris lytra.*

43 Servius, *Commentary on Virgil*

"insomnia terrify": both "terrifies" [sg.] and "terrify" [pl.] are read, but if we read "terrifies," *insomnia* [fem. sg.] will be "wakefulness": for our ancestors wished there to be the following difference between wakefulness and what we see in sleep, namely that *insomnia*, of feminine gender and singular number, denotes wakefulness, but *insomnia*, of neuter gender and plural number, what we see in sleep, like [Verg. *Aen.* 6.896] "but the shades send false dreams to the world above." Hence one must know that, if we said "terrifies" [sg.], it will be an archaic expression; for, even if Pacuvius and Ennius frequently said *insomnia* [fem. sg.], Pliny nevertheless excluded it and removed it from usage.[1] But this fact has created an ambiguity in the reading, since she said that she [Dido] had not been openly awake, but had had a restless quiet, i.e., interrupted by dreams, so that we understand that she was both terrified by dreams and, because of the fear caused by the dreams, also suffered wakefulness.

[1] Presumably in *Dubii sermonis libri VIII* (see Kaster 1988, 193–94).

335

44 Serv. ad Verg. *Aen.* 9.255

"integer aevi": "integri aevi," figurate: id est adulescens cui aetas integra superest, unde Ennius deos aevi integros dicit quibus multum aevi superest.

45 Serv. Dan. ad Verg. *Aen.* 9.744

"intorquet": versat, librat, iactat. et est Ennianum:

versat mucronem

46 Serv. Dan. ad Verg. *Aen.* 10.10

ordo autem "quis metus suasit aut hos arma sequi fer- rumque lacessere"; non est enim "hos suasit," ne fiat σολοικοειδές: quamvis inveniatur huius modi figura; ut "Iuturnam misero, fateor, succurrere fratri / suasi" [Verg. *Aen.* 12.813–14; cf. Macrob. *Sat.* 6.6.11] et Ennius:

quis te persuasit?

47 Serv. ad Verg. *Aen.* 12.298

"torrem": autem erit nominativus "hic torris," et ita nunc dicimus: nam illud Ennii et Pacuvii penitus de usu reces- sit, ut "hic torrus, huius torri" dicamus.

44 Servius, *Commentary on Virgil*

"untouched with regard to age": figuratively, "of untouched age": i.e., a young man for whom age remains untouched, whence Ennius calls the gods untouched with regard to age, for whom a long lifetime remains.

45 Servius Danielis, *Commentary on Virgil*

intorquet: "he turns," "he poises," "he tosses." And there is the Ennian phrase:

> he tosses the sword.

46 Servius Danielis, *Commentary on Virgil*

Moreover, the order is "what terror has suggested that they pursue arms and provoke the sword"; for it is not "it has prompted these men" [(*per*)*suadere* + acc.], so that it becomes solecistic:[1] even though an expression of this type is found, as in "I have advised Juturna, I admit, to help her poor brother" [Verg. *Aen.* 12.813–14] and Ennius:

> who has persuaded you?

[1] In recasting Virgil's sentence, Servius omits an initial *aut hos* and changes the word order to make clear that *suasit* governs an infinitive clause and not, as he understands Ennius, an accusative object.

47 Servius, *Commentary on Virgil*

torrem ["firebrand"; acc.]: the nominative will be *hic torris* ["this brand"], and so we say now, for that expression of Ennius and Pacuvius has faded far from usage, that we say *hic torrus, huius torri* ["this brand, of this brand"]: following the second declension].

48 Serv. Dan. ad Verg. *Aen.* 12.605

"flavos Lavinia crines": antiqua lectio "floros" habuit, id est florulentos, pulchros, et est sermo Ennianus. [*add. Serv. Dan.*]: Probus sic adnotavit: neotericum erat "flavos"; ergo bene "floros": nam sequitur "et roseas laniata genas" [Verg. *Aen.* 12.606]. Accius in Bacchis [*Trag.* 255 R.²⁻³]: "nam flori crines, video, ei propessi iacent"; in iisdem [*Trag.* 246 R.²⁻³] "et lanugo flora nunc demum inrigat"; Pacuvius Antiopa [*Trag.* 18–19 R.²⁻³]: "cervicum / floros dispergite crines."

49 Charis., *GL* I, p. 98.12–13 = p. 125 B.

"erumnam" Ennius ait per e solum scribi posse, quod mentem eruat, et per a et e, quod maerorem nutriat.

50

a Hieron. *Apol. adv. Rufinum* 2.11, *PL* 434C

in primo libro Περὶ Ἀρχῶν, ubi Origines lingua sacrilega blasphemavit quod Filius Patrem non videat, tu etiam causas reddis, quasi ex persona eius qui scripsit, et Didymi interpretaris σχόλιον in quo ille casso labore conatur alienum errorem defendere, quod Origines quidem bene

---

[1] An early Christian writer (ca. AD 185–254).   [2] Rufinus of Aquileia (ca. AD 345–411/12), who translated Origen's work while changing passages that might be heretical.   [3] Didymus the Blind, a theologian who produced commentaries on large parts of the Bible (ca. AD 313–398).

48 Servius Danielis, *Commentary on Virgil*

"Lavinia, her golden [*flavos*] hair": an old reading had *floros* ["fair"], that is "flowery," "beautiful," and this is Ennian language. Probus[1] commented thus: *flavos* was Neoteric; hence *floros* works well, for "having also torn her rosy cheeks" [Verg. *Aen.* 12.606] follows. Accius in *Bacchae* [*Trag.* 255 R.$^{2-3}$]: "for his flowery [*flori*] hair, I see, lies spread out"; in the same play [*Trag.* 246 R.$^{2-3}$]: "and only now the flowery [*flora*] down is flooding"; Pacuvius in *Antiopa* [*Trag.* 18–19 R.$^{2-3}$]: "spread out the flowery [*floros*] hair at your neck."

[1] Marcus Valerius Probus, Roman grammarian of the first century AD.

49 Charisius

Ennius says that (*a*)*erumna* ["distress"] could be spelled with *e* alone because it uproots [*eruat*] the mind, and with *a* and *e* because it fosters sorrow [*maeror*].[1]

[1] Work and context are impossible to determine: *aerumnas* is attested at 1 *Ann.* F 36. This comment too might perhaps be attributed to the grammarian Ennius (T 69, 114).

50

a Jerome, *Apology against Rufinus*

In the first book of *On first principles*, where Origen[1] blasphemed in sacrilegious language, saying that the Son does not see the Father, you[2] even offer reasons, as if in the role of the person who wrote it, and you translate the comment of Didymus[3] in which he tries with fruitless labor to defend another person's error, that Origin at least

dixerit, sed nos, simplices homines et cicures enniam,[1] nec illius sapientiam nec tuam, qui interpretatus es, intellegere possimus.[2]

[1] cincturae senniani *codd. aliqui*: idiotae *unus cod.*
[2] possumus *codd. aliqui, edd.*

b Tert. *Adv. Valent.* 37.1

accipe alia ingenia circulatoria[1] insignioris apud eos magistri, qui ex pontificali sua auctoritate in hunc modum censuit: . . .

[1] circulatoria *Oehler*: Cicuria Enniana *Pamelius*: Currucae Enniani *Priorius*: *alii alia*: circurianiana *vel* circur iamana *vel* circur inaniana *codd.*

51 August. *De dial.* 6

nam sunt qui verbum a vero quidem dictum putant, sed prima syllaba satis animadversa secundam neglegi non oportere. verbum enim cum dicimus, inquiunt, prima eius syllaba verum significat, secunda sonum. hoc enim volunt esse bum, unde Ennius sonum pedum "bombum pedum" dixit, et βοῆσαι Graeci clamare et Vergilius [*G.* 3.223] "reboant silvae." ergo verbum dictum est quasi a verum boando hoc est verum sonando.

Cf. *Gloss. vet. ad Prudentii Apotheos.* 845 (*PL* 59 Migne, col. 988): BOMBUM, sonitum cornu vel tibiae; et Ennius sonitum pedum appellat "bombum."

has said this well, but we, simple men and Ennius' "gentle ones,"[4] can understand the wisdom neither of him [Origen] nor of you, who have translated him.

[4] Jerome identifies *cicures* as an Ennian term suggesting simple people. The word more commonly means "tame" or "domesticated" when describing animals, "mild" or "gentle" on the rarer occasions it describes humans. Jerome's other quotations of Ennius derive from Cicero, who may well be the source of this one, too.

b Tertullian, *Against the Valentinians*

Learn of other clever contrivances characteristic of itinerant performers [or: of simple Ennian people], by a master, rather distinguished among them, who, on the basis of his pontifical authority, decreed in this way: . . .[1]

[1] The text is corrupt, though sometimes emended to yield the same phrase as the passage in Jerome, but with a different case and gender.

51 Augustine, *On Dialectic*

For there are some who believe *verbum* ["word"] to be derived from *verum* ["true"], but, even if sufficient attention is paid to the first syllable, the second one must not be neglected. When we say *verbum*, they claim, its first syllable means "true," its second "sound," for this is what they want *bum* to express; whence Ennius called the sound of feet "the booming [*bombum*] of feet," and the Greeks use "to shout" [Gk. *boao*] for "to utter a loud noise," and Virgil [G. 3.223] says "the woods resound [*reboant*]." Thus *verbum* has been derived from "bellowing forth the truth [*verum boando*]" as it were, that is "sounding forth the truth."

52 Macrob. *Sat.* 3.12.8

Antonius Gnipho [F 2 *GRF*], vir doctus cuius scholam Cicero post laborem fori frequentabat, Salios Herculi datos probat in eo volumine quo disputat quid sit festra, quod est ostium minusculum in sacrario, quo verbo etiam Ennius usus est.

Cf. Paul. *Fest.*, p. 80.27 L.

53 Gramm. inc., *GL* V, p. 584.26

NIX generis feminini, ut Ennius:

hae nives

54 *Fragm. Bob.*, *GL* VII, p. 542.9–10

hoc locum

lectum est aput Ennium, sed nemo dicit hodie.

55 Prisc., *GL* II, p. 383.6–8

Ennius:

adsectari se omnes cupiunt

"adsectari" passive: ἀκολουθεῖσθαι.

52 Macrobius, *Saturnalia*

Antonius Gnipho[1] [F 2 *GRF*], a learned man, whose school Cicero used to visit after the work of the forum, demonstrates that Salii[2] were given to Hercules [cf. Verg. *Aen.* 8.285–304] in that volume in which he discusses what *festra* ["window"; unusual form of *fenestra*] is, which is a rather small opening in a shrine, a word that Ennius too used.

[1] A teacher of grammar and rhetoric at Rome in the first half of the first century BC (cf. T 71, 111).   [2] A particular type of priest.

53 Anonymous grammarian

nix ["snow"] of feminine gender, as Ennius:

> these snows[1]

[1] From a list *De dubiis nominibus*, clarifying the gender of a number of words.

54 Grammatical fragment from Bobbio

> this place [*locus* as neuter]

is read in Ennius, but nobody says so today.

55 Priscian

Ennius:

> they all desire to be followed

adsectari ["to be followed"] passively [in form and meaning, as the Greek verb]: "to be followed."

56 Isid. *Orig.* 11.1.109

denique conplicatum gigni formarique hominem, ita ut genua sursum sint, quibus oculi formantur, ut cavi ac reconditi fiant. Ennius:

atque genua conprimit arta gena

inde est quod homines dum ad genua se prosternunt, statim lacrimantur. voluit enim eos natura uterum maternum rememorare, ubi quasi in tenebris consedebant antequam venirent ad lucem.

Cf. Isid. *Diff.* 2.17.71(135).

57 Paul. *Fest.*, p. 54.22 L.

CONSIPTUM apud Ennium pro conseptum invenitur [cf. *Trag.* F 107].

58 Paul. *Fest.*, p. 54.24–25 L.

CORPULENTIS Ennius pro magnis dixit; nos corpulentum dicimus corporis obesi hominem.

56 Isidore, *Origins*

Finally, a human being is said to be born and formed folded up, so that the knees are upward, whereby the eyes [i.e., eye sockets] are formed to become hollow and recessed. Ennius:

and the cheek tightly compresses the knees[1]

Hence it is that humans, when they stretch out to their knees, immediately cry, for nature wanted them to remember the maternal womb, where they sat as if in darkness before they came to the light.

[1] Meter and work uncertain. Blänsdorf (*FPL*[4]) arranges the words to form the end and the beginning of a trochaic septenarius.

57 Paul the Deacon, *Epitome of Festus*

consiptum is found in Ennius in place of *conseptum* ["enclosure," cf. *Trag.* F 107].

58 Paul the Deacon, *Epitome of Festus*

corpulentis[1] ["large"] Ennius said in place of "big"; we call "large" [*corpulentum*] a man with an obese body.

[1] Cited not in the nominative but in the dative or ablative plural and thus the likely form used by Ennius.

59 Paul. *Fest.*, p. 59.26–29 L.

DAEDALAM a varietate rerum artificiorumque dictam esse apud Lucretium terram [1.7; 1.228: *daedala tellus*], apud Ennium Minervam, apud Virgilium Circen [*Aen.* 7.282; cf. Serv. ad Verg. *G.* 4.179], facile est intellegere, cum Graeci δαιδάλλειν significent variare.

59 Paul the Deacon, *Epitome of Festus*

That *daedalus* ["skillful"], from the variety of things and
works of art, is said of the earth in Lucretius [1.7; 1.228:
daedala tellus], of Minerva in Ennius, of Circe in Virgil
[*Aen.* 7.282; cf. Serv. ad Verg. *G.* 4.179] is easy to under-
stand, since the Greeks have *daidallein* ["to embellish
skillfully"] meaning "to give variety to."

QUOTATIONS DERIVED FROM
UNKNOWN SOURCES

EXCERPTA E FONTIBUS
INCERTIS SUMPTA (F 1–31)

In their search for the remains of early Latin poetry, medieval and Renaissance scholars cast a wide net—and brought in a very mixed catch. Though a few fragments of uncertain pedigree found their way into the Ennian corpus (e.g., 9 Ann. F 8), a combination of questionable sources, problematic linguistic and metrical structures, and suspiciously close similarity to clearly genuine verses by Ennius or some other ancient author have kept most of these just outside its margins.

A large number of these dubious fragments come from the edition of Paulus Merula (Paul van Merle, 1558–1607), who in 1595 edited the fragments of the Annals *attested in antiquity and provided additional verses in an accompanying commentary. These latter do not appear to be genuine, but whether they are outright forgeries by Merula or were extracted by him from sources, now unidentifiable, that he trusted remains unknown (see Blok 1900; Goldschmidt 2012). A second group consists of lines found in the* Cornucopiae *(first ed., 1489) by Nicolaus Perottus*

QUOTATIONS DERIVED FROM
UNKNOWN SOURCES (F 1–31)

(Niccolò Perotti, 1429–1480), which included among many genuine fragments preserved in ancient texts some that are not recorded elsewhere. This lack of provenance has cast doubt on their authenticity, though some scholars have argued that Perotti may have drawn on ancient sources no longer extant (see Oliver 1947; Timpanaro 1947).

Many of these fragments are included in the editions of Vahlen and Skutsch, and some in that of Warmington. They are distinguished in various ways from clearly authentic material. Vahlen relegates Merula's "versus falsi" to a section of their own (pp. 240–42), while Skutsch presents a wider set of "spuria" (pp. 138–41). Warmington's Varia includes a subsection labeled "Spuria?" (pp. 446–65). Other editors ignore them entirely. A collection of these problematic fragments follows. Those explicitly judged spurious by Skutsch, who meticulously reviews the arguments of his predecessors, are marked with an asterisk (*).

Bibl.: Suerbaum 2002, 142.

*1 Lucius Caecilius Minutianus Apuleius, *De orthographia* F 15 (p. 7 Osann 1826)

Olympius sive Olympus appellatus Iuppiter. Ennius . . . :

> decessit Olympius antro

Virgilius [*Aen.* 10.1]: "panditur interea domus omnipotentis Olympi." Domitius Marsus in Melaene [cf. *Mart.* 7.29.8] . . . Aristophanes inter cognomina Iovis ponit Olympius [e.g., *Nub.* 817, 818]. Naevius [Laevius *Osann*]: "panditur interea domus altitonantis Olympi."

> antro *Rhodiginus*: nano *cod.*

Cf. Lodovicus Caelius Rhodiginus (Ludovico Ricchieri, 1469–1525), *Lectionum antiquarum libri* (1516), lib. XI, cap. XIII, pp. 561–62: Et qa de Olympo facta mentio est, Scribit Cæcilius Minutianus Apuleius Olympum etiam dici Iouem, unde Næuius, "Panditur interea Domus altitonantis Olympi." Ex quo Virgilius Omnipotentis Olympi, Quod si est, falluntur, Qui legendum arbitrant, Omnipatentis Olympi. Nam & Ennius ait, "Decessit Olympius antro." Illud vero in Græcorum cõmentariis extritum, & in Hesiodi Aspide ab Interprete relatum.

*2 Osbernus (1123–1200), *Panormia* (A. Mai, *Classicorum auctorum e vaticanis codicibus editorum.* Tomus VIII. *Thesaurus novus Latinitatis, sive Lexicon vetus e membranis nunc primum erutum*, Roma 1836, p. 332)

Item a moveo hoc momentum, ti, eo quod cito etiam transitu moveatur; unde hoc momentillum, li, diminut. et momentaneus, a, um. Inveni quoque hoc momen, nis, pro momento; unde Ennius:

> vestro sine momine venti

*1 Lucius Caecilius Minutianus Apuleius, *On Orthography*

Olympius or *Olympus* ["Olympian": the proper adjective and a wrongly derived one] is Jupiter called. Ennius . . . :

the Olympian went away from the cave

Virgil [*Aen.* 10.1]: "meanwhile the palace of omnipotent Olympus is opened up." Domitius Marsus in *Melaene* [cf. *Mart.* 7.29.8] . . . Aristophanes places *Olympius* ["Olympian"] among the epithets of Jupiter [e.g., *Nub.* 817, 818]. Naevius: "meanwhile the palace of high-sounding Olympus is opened up."[1]

---

[1] Apuleius' quotations are also cited, with the source acknowledged, by Ludovico Ricchieri.

*2 Osbernus, *Panormia*

Equally from *moveo* ["I move"] is derived *momentum*, *momenti* ["movement, moment"], for the reason that there is also movement in quick transit; thence *momentillum*, *momentilli* ["brief moment"], a diminutive, and *momentaneus, -a, -um* ["of the movement, moment"]. I have also found *momen, mominis* ["movement, moment": rare word], instead of *momentum* [usual word]; thence Ennius:

without your movement the winds

Cf. Paul. *Fest.*, p. 123.17–18 L.: momen momentum Lucretius [3.188]: "momine si parvo possint inpulsa moveri"; Prisc., *GL* II, p. 126.7–10: "nuo numen" ("numen" enim est dei nutus. unde Virgilius: "meo sine numine, venti," id est sine meo nutu).

*3 *Gloss. cod. Admuntensis* 472, saec. XII, fol. 13^b (cf. Joh. Huemer, "Zu Isidorus *Etym.* I, 3, 8," *WS* 2, 1880, 305–6)

ALBUS est tabula, ubi scribebantur nomina illorum, qui ad militiam recipiebantur, et si contigisset ut aliquis eorum fuisset interemptus, apponebatur super nomen illius theta littera, quae mortem significat. habet enim haec quoddam iaculum [iugulum *cod.*: *corr. Lindsay*]. Unde Ennius versificator optimus

> o multum ante alias infelix littera theta

Cf. Isid. *Orig.* 1.3.8; *Commentum Cornuti* ad Pers. 4.13.3–4.

4 Niccolò Perotti (1429–1480), *Cornucopiæ, siue linguæ latinæ cõmentarij* (1489)

CONGENERO: qd est associo, adiungo. Accius [*Trag.* 580 R.^2–3]: "hunc enim tibi congenerat affinitas"; & Ennius:

> quem mihi congenerat affinitas

Cf. Non., p. 84.29–30 M. = 120 L.

5 Niccolò Perotti (1429–1480), *Cornucopiæ, siue linguæ latinæ cõmentarij* (1489)

à TROIA tros derivatur. . . . & Troianus . . . & troicus . . . item Troiugena. Ennius:

> troiugenas bello claros

Cf. Lucr. 1.465; Catull. 64.355; Liv. 25.12.5.

*3 A Glossary

albus[1] is a board on which were written the names of those who were accepted for military service, and if it had happened that any of them had been killed, above their name the letter theta [Θ] was added, which denotes death. For this has a kind of javelin, whence Ennius, the best writer of verses, says:

> oh far beyond all others, unhappy letter Theta

[1] So often the glossographers: *album* is the more common classical form.

4 Niccolò Perotti

congenero ["I bind by ties of kinship"]: this is "I associate," "I attach." Accius [*Trag.* 580 R.[2-3]]: "for a relationship by ties of kinship binds him to you"; and Ennius:[1]

> whom [*masc.*] a relationship by ties of kinship binds
> to me

[1] The quotation from Accius appears more fully and more accurately in Nonius Marcellus (under a comparable lemma); the piece from Ennius is attested only here.

5 Niccolò Perotti

From *Troia* ["Troy"] is derived *Tros.* . . . and *Troianus* . . . and *Troicus* [different forms of "Trojan"] . . . equally *Troiugena* ["descendant of Troy"]. Ennius:

> descendants of Troy famous in war [*acc.*]

6 Niccolò Perotti (1429–1480), *Cornucopiæ, siue linguæ latinæ cõmentarij* (1489)

HOMOEOPTOTON, qd à nostris dicitur similiter cadens, cum diuersæ dictiones in similes exeunt casus. Ennius: "Mœrentes, flentes, lachrymantes, & miserantes" [cf. Inc. *Ann.* F 46]. Idem:

> <–> neq; currentem, neq; se cognoscit euntẽ
> tollentemq; manus, saxumq; immane mouentem

Cf. *Rhet. Her.* 4.18; Donat., *GL* IV, p. 398.22–23; Diom., *GL* I, p. 447.16–19; Charis., *GL* I, p. 282.12–13 = p. 371 B.

7 Niccolò Perotti (1429–1480), *Cornucopiæ, siue linguæ latinæ cõmentarij* (1489)

POETIFICUS, quo usus est Ennius, qui Cabalinũ fontem

> poetificum

nominauit.

Cf. Pers. Prol. 1–3: nec fonte labra prolui caballino / nec in bicipiti somniasse Parnaso / memini.

8 Niccolò Perotti (1429–1480), *Cornucopiæ, siue linguæ latinæ cõmentarij* (1489)

à PULCHER fit pulchre aduerbium . . . & pulchritudo. & perpulcher, ac perpulchre. & pulchralis pro pulchro. Enni:

> pulchralibus ludis

Cf. Fest., p. 280.26 L.; Paul. *Fest.*, p. 281.12 L.

6 Niccolò Perotti

homoeoptoton, which is called by our people "ending similarly," occurs when different words conclude with similar endings. Ennius: "grieving, crying, shedding tears and voicing sorrow" [four participles ending in *-tes*] [cf. Inc. *Ann.* F 46]. The same poet:

> he does not realize that he runs and walks and raises his hands and moves an immense rock [four participles ending in *-tem*]

7 Niccolò Perotti, *Cornucopiæ*

poetificus ["poet-making"], which Ennius used, who called the horse's spring

> poet-making [*acc.*][1]

[1] *poetificus* is otherwise unattested. Perotti's term for the Hippocrene (*fons caballinus*) echoes Persius' periphrasis ("the horse's spring") in his prologue. For Ennius and the Hippocrene, see T 50.

8 Niccolò Perotti, *Cornucopiæ*

From *pulcher* ["beautiful"] comes the adverb *pulchre* ["beautifully"] . . . and *pulchritudo* ["beauty"]. And *perpulcher* ["very beautiful"] and *perpulchre* ["very beautifully"]. And *pulchralis* ["beautiful": different word] instead of *pulcher.* A phrase of Ennius:

> at (or: for) beautiful games

*9 Achilles Statius (1524–1581), *Catullus cum commentario* (1566), ad 63.40 (p. 226):

"lustravit aethera album": sic Albae luces a Martiali dicuntur in X [Mart. 10.62.6]: "Albae leone flammeo calent luces." Et Ennius de Sole [1 *Ann.* F 43]: "Interea sol albus recessit in infera noctis." Et in VI

> ut primum tenebris abiectis inalbabat
> dies

Cf. Apul. *Met.* 7.1: ut primum tenebris abiectis dies inalbebat et candidum solis curriculum cuncta conlustrabat, . . .

*10 Achilles Statius (1524–1581), *Catullus cum commentario* (1566), ad 1.9 (p. 16)

Patronam enim Mineruam dicit, cuius in clientela, tutelaq. sint ingenia. Eam uero ut hic Patronam, Ennius & Dominam, & Heram dixit [cf. *Inc.* F 59].

*11 Columna (1590), pp. 35, 83 (= pp. 35–36 Hesselius):

> . . . quem super ingens
> porta tonat caeli . . .

QVEM SVPER INGENS PORTA TONAT CAELEI] In Seneca sic habetur hic locus, *Felicē deinde se putabat, q inuenerit, vnde visum sit Virgilio dicere—quem super ingens Porta tonat caeli,—Ennium, hoc, ait, Homero surripuisse, Ennio Virgilium. Esse etiā apud Ciceronem in ipsis de Repub. hoc Epigramma, "Si fas est plagas Caelestum*

*9 Achilles Statius, *Commentary on Catullus*

"he [Sol] spread light over the white ether": Similarly, white lights are mentioned by Martial in Book 10 [10.62.6]: "white lights [i.e., bright days] glow beneath the flaming Lion." And Ennius about the Sun [1 *Ann.* F 43]: "meanwhile the sun had set into the depths of night." And in Book 6:

> as soon as the day became white, after the shadows had been cast away

*10 Achilles Statius, *Commentary on Catullus*

For he [Catullus] calls Minerva a patron, under whose guardianship and tutelage are the writers. And as he called her a patron, thus did Ennius call her both a mistress and a lady [cf. *Inc.* F 59].

*11 Columna

> . . . above whom
> thunders the immense door of heaven . . .

"Above whom thunders the immense door of heaven": In Seneca the following passage is found: "He [a certain scholar] regarded himself as lucky, since he had found out for what reason it seemed good for Virgil to say 'above whom thunders the immense door of heaven.' Ennius, he said, had taken this from Homer, and Virgil from Ennius." There was also in Cicero in the very same books about the Republic the following epigram: "if it is allowed for anyone to ascend to the realms of the heaven dwellers: for me

359

scandere cuiquam: / Mî soli caeli maxima porta patet."
Hoc modo legitur in vetusto exemplari manuscripto; cùm
in passim vulgatis habeatur, *Esse enim apud Ciceronem*, &
caet. Quòd si postremae lectioni fides haberetur, eum
locum,—*quem super ingens Porta tonat caeli*—Virgilius
haud esset totum ex Ennio mutuatus, cùm tamen illud
appareat in bibliotheca Carbonaria, ex vetusto fragmento
in membranis Anonymi cuiusdam Grammatici; qui agens
de verbis neutris impersonalibus, expressè ex Ennio citat
verba illa,—*quem super ingens Porta tonat caeli.* Quae de
signis Romuli apotheosim praecedentibus intelligenda
sunt.

Cf. Sen. *Ep.* 108.34: felicem deinde se putat quod invenerit unde
visum sit Vergilio [*G.* 3.260–61] dicere "quem super ingens / porta
tonat caeli." Ennium hoc ait Homero [*Il.* 5.749 = 8.393] {se} su-
bripuisse, Ennio Vergilium. esse enim apud Ciceronem in his
ipsis de re publica hoc epigramma Enni [*Epigr.* F 3]: "si fas endo
plagas caelestum ascendere cuiquam est, / mi soli caeli maxima
porta patet."

*12 Columna (1590), pp. 201–2 (= p. 121 Hesselius)

Non explicat Parrhasius, vnde hunc versum transcripserit;
sed ei, vtpotè antiquorum Auctorum maximè studioso,
fides adhibenda est. Ità igitur ille in epistola quadam ad
Antonium Tilesium: Aether, & Dies, eorumq. fratres, &
sorores ex Erebo, & Nocte procreati. Cicero in III. de
Natura Deorum [Cic. *Nat. D.* 3.44]. Quos omnes Erebo,
& nocte natos ferunt. Ennius:

> quos omnes[1] Erebo perhibent, & nocte creatos

[1] omneis *in text. (p. 198)*

alone the gate of heaven is open as wide as possible." It is read in this form in an old handwritten copy, while in the generally available copies it reads, "for there was in Cicero" etc. But if one had confidence in the last reading, Virgil would not have borrowed this passage, "above whom thunders the immense door of heaven," entirely from Ennius, although this seems to be the case ⟨to judge⟩ from an old fragment in the parchment of some anonymous grammarian in the library [of the monastery of St. John de] Carbonaria [in Naples]; while he is talking about neutral impersonal verbs, he explicitly quotes from Ennius those words, "above whom thunders the immense door of heaven." These must be understood concerning the signs preceding Romulus' apotheosis.

*12 Columna

Parrhasius [Aulus Janus Parrhasius, 1470–1522] does not explain whence he has transcribed this verse; but one should put trust in him, as he is a most eager student of the ancient authors. Hence he says this in a certain letter to Antonius Tilesius [Antonio Tilesio, 1482–1534]: "Heaven and Day and their brothers and sisters have been brought forth by Erebus and Night. Cicero in the third book of *On the Nature of the Gods* [3.44]: 'All of whom they say to be born of Erebus and Night.' Ennius:

all of whom [*masc.*] they hold to be brought forth by Erebus and Night

Solvit enim Cicero Ennij carmen, eiusq. numerum ad solutae orationis numeros transfert. Potest etiam hic versus ad Furias referri. Quare cum antecedēntibus quodammodo congruere visus est. Nec refert quòd masculino genere dixerit. *Quos omnes Erebo, & caet.* Nam Virgilius de Alecto inquit [*Aen.* 7.498], *"Nec dextrae erranti Deus abfuit—"*

*13 Columna (1590), p. 209 (= p. 147 Hesselius): e "Ser. 10 *Aen.*":

Saturno sancte create

Cf. Furius Bibaculus, F 11 *FPL*[4] (Macrob. *Sat.* 6.1.32): quod genus hoc hominum, Saturno sancte create.

14 Columna (1590), p. 498 (= p. 329 Hesselius): ex "Antiq. Gloss.":

regredi gressum

*15 Paulus Merula (1558–1607), *Enni Comm.* (1595), p. 41

Pater cultioris & elegantioris apud Latinos Musae, Q. Ennius hoc versu indicat, quid scripturus. Citatur autem a L. Calpurnio Pisone (cuius in Praefatione Lectorem praemonui) lib. I. de continentia veterum Poetarum; quo

---

[1] In the preface Merula explains that he found a work with the following full title, *L. Calpurnii L. F. Pisonis V. C. de continentia veterum poetarum ad Traianum principem,* in a library in

For Cicero removes the meter of Ennius' poem, and he transfers its rhythm to the rhythm of prose." This verse too can be referred to the Furies. Therefore it seemed to agree somehow with the preceding ones. And it does not make any difference that he said this in masculine gender. "All of whom . . . by Erebus, etc." For Virgil says about Allecto [*Aen.* 7.498]: "And the god [i.e., goddess] did not fail his faltering hand—"

*13 Columna

you, holy one, born from Saturn [i.e., Jupiter][1]

[1] Columna (followed by Merula) mistakenly quotes Servius as the source of this phrase.

14 Columna

From "an old glossary":

to retrace the step[1]

[1] Cf. *Trag.* F 5: *gradum regredere*. Columna's source cannot be identified.

*15 Paulus Merula, *Commentary on Ennius*

Ennius, the father of a more cultured and elegant Muse among the Latins, indicates by this verse [quoted below] what he is going to write. And it is cited by Lucius Calpurnius Piso (about whom I advised the reader in my Preface)[1] in Book One of *About the Subject Matter of the Old*

Paris and excerpted from this source (as from a few others) fragments not found in earlier collections. On the truth of this claim, see Goldschmidt 2012, 14–16.

loco de artificiosis illorum Exordijs: . . . *Promittit omnia ad suam usque aetatem Heroice Ennius*:

horrida Romulei certamina pango duellum

textus in comm.: *textus in editione (p. I)*: Horrida Romoleûm certamina pango duellûm

16 Paulus Merula (1558–1607), *Enni Comm.* (1595), p. 165

In Latino sic erat: *Armipotens ὁπλοκράτωρ*. Ennius:

armis conditur Alba potens

Supprimit Glossographus librum. Petitum indubie fragmentum ex Annalium primo.

17 Paulus Merula (1558–1607), *Enni Comm.* (1595), p. 199

apud Calpurnium libro I. de Continentia veterum Poetarum: *Apostrophe*, inquit, ʽ*εὐκτικὴ* (vel *Euctica*, sic lego pro *Entica*) *est, quotiens, aversa jam ad quaevis oratione, miscentur vota vel bona vel mala. Ennius in primo Vrbem condendam compellat, & compellatae omnia, quae magnitudinem ejus testatura, precatur his verbis*:

Poets; there he says about the artful beginnings of those poets: . . . Ennius promises to describe everything up to his own time in heroic verse:

> I compose horrendous contests, the wars of Romulus' descendants

16 Paulus Merula, *Commentary on Ennius*

In Latin it was like this: *armipotens* ["strong in war"], *hoplokratōr* [Greek]. Ennius:

> Alba, strong in war, is founded

The glossographer[1] does not mention the book. The fragment has doubtless been taken from the first book of the *Annals.*

[1] The reference is to the glossary of Gulielmus Fornerus (Guillaume Fournier), author of, e.g., *In titulo de verborum significatione commentarii* (Aurelia 1584).

17 Paulus Merula, *Commentary on Ennius*

In Calpurnius' first book *About the Subject Matter of the Old Poets*: "An apostrophe," he says, "is *euktike* (or *euctica*, this I read instead of *entica*) [i.e., expressing a wish, prayer, or vow], whenever, with the speech directed away to anything, good or bad wishes are mixed in. In the first book Ennius addresses the city [i.e., Rome] as to be founded, and for the benefit of the addressee he asks for everything that will demonstrate her greatness, with these words:

nascere quae populos terraque marique lacesses
belli turbine praepropero, concussa tremiscent
cuncta acres a te vires . . .

& *quae postea: concludens in conventa Romae genetrice:*

. . . in Roma Troja revixsti

hactenus Calpurnius.

*18 Paulus Merula (1558–1607), *Enni Comm.* (1595),
p. 226

In eo [i.e., Glossario Gul. Forneri] enim: *Dispertio*, δια-
νέμω. Ennius:

praedam dispertit

*19 Paulus Merula (1558–1607), *Enni Comm.* (1595),
p. 288

Non uno loco locupletatum prodit Enni nostri Annales
Calpurnius Piso in libris de Continentia Veterum Poeta-
rum. Nam priores hic versus laudantur ab Servio; tertium
duobus addit Calpurnius. . . . Meus autem ille: *Morti
proximum, quum* (emendo *quin*) *mortuum, vivis coloribus
depingit Ennius, libro secundo Annalium, ubi sic scribit*
[Inc. *Ann.* F 36]:

oscitat in campis caput a cervice repulsum
semianimesque micant oculi lucemque requirunt
nequiquam, reliquae carni nihil est animai

emerge, you who will challenge nations by land and
    by sea
with a most precipitate whirl of war; everything,
    shaken by you,
will tremble at your harsh forces . . .

and what follows: concluding with the mother of Rome by
convention:

. . . in Rome you, Troy, have come to life again

So far Calpurnius [cf. F 15].

*18 Paulus Merula, *Commentary on Ennius*

For in this [the glossary of Fornerus, cf. F 16] is: *dispertio*
["I distribute"], *"dianemō* [Greek]. Ennius:

he distributes the booty

*19 Paulus Merula, *Commentary on Ennius*

Not just in a single place does Calpurnius Piso [cf. F 15]
in the books *About the Subject Matter of the Old Poets* put
forward *Annals* of our Ennius for enrichment, for the first
verses here are quoted by Servius; to these two Calpurnius
adds a third. . . . But my author: someone very close to
death, whom (I emend "even") dead, Ennius depicts with
vivid colors, in the second book of *Annals*, where he writes
as follows [Inc. *Ann.* F 36]:

the head, torn from the neck, gapes on the plain
and half-alive, the eyes twitch and seek the light
in vain, nothing of life remains in the body

Haereo, utrum *repolsum*, an vero *revolsum* rei, qua de agitur convenientius. Injuriam autem, credo, faceret Ennio, qui hos versus a praecedentibus revulsos, conaretur alijs collocare.

*20 Paulus Merula (1558–1607), *Enni Comm.* (1595), p. 308

Exstat hoc fragmentum apud Calpurnium Pisonē lib. II. quo loco agit de Vocum Sectione: . . . *Scripsit Ennius, licentia quaedam toleranda, lib. VI:*

> telo
> transfigit corpus, saxo cere comminuit brum

*21 Paulus Merula (1558–1607), *Enni Comm.* (1595), pp. 310–11

Caput his membris adfixi ex Glossis Forneri, ubi: *Tyrannus*, βασιλεὺς. Ennius Annalibus:

> tostumque tyranni
> Tarquini corpus

emendo *postumque.*

I hesitate to say whether *repolsum* ["removed," lit. "driven back"] or indeed *revolsum* ["torn off"] is more appropriate to the matter being treated. But he who tries to place these verses, torn off from the preceding ones, elsewhere does an injustice, I believe, to Ennius.

*20 Paulus Merula, *Commentary on Ennius*

This fragment exists in Calpurnius Piso [cf. F 15] in Book 2, in the passage in which he talks about the division of words: . . . Ennius wrote, with a certain tolerable license, in Book 6:[1]

with a lance,
he pierced the body, he scattered the cran with a rock
ium

[1] A version of the line *saxo . . . brum* appears without attribution in Serv. ad Verg. *Aen.* 1.412; Donat., *GL* IV, p. 401.16; *Explan. in Donat.*, *GL* IV, p. 565; Pomp., *GL* V, p. 310.4–6. For the striking tmesis, see Zetzel 1974.

*21 Paulus Merula, *Commentary on Ennius*

I have added a head to these limbs [i.e., "made the text comprehensible"] from the Glosses of Fornerus [cf. F 16], where: *tyrannus* ["tyrant"], *basileus* [Greek]. Ennius in the *Annals*:

and the roasted body of the tyrant Tarquinius

I emend to "placed" [i.e., *postum*, for *positum*, instead of *tostum* "roasted"].[1]

[1] For the syncopated form *postum* for *positum*, cf. *Inc.* F 38.

22 Paulus Merula (1558–1607), *Enni Comm.* (1595), p. 324

Glossae Forneri: παλαμναῖον *Dirum, quod Deorum iram habet conjunctam. Ennius in tertio:*

dirius supplicium sceleris violentia possit

Lego, *Poscit*, poscente sententia.

*23 Paulus Merula (1558–1607), *Enni Comm.* (1595), p. 327

Ego ex quarto Annalium esse didici ex Glossar. Forneri: Ἀπολειφθείς, *Delictus. Ennius libro tertio* (proculdubio *Annaliū*):

corde suo trepidat, delicto poplite

Lego: *Delicto Coclite.* Retinet tamen hic V. N. Iosephus Scaliger Vulgatam, *poplite.* Emendationi meae lux & fulcrum.

*24 Paulus Merula (1558–1607), *Enni Comm.* (1595), p. 354

Glossar. Forneri: *Divido* διασπείρω. *Ennius in quinto:*

disperge hosteis, distrahe, diduc, divide, differ

FROM UNKNOWN SOURCES

22 Paulus Merula, *Commentary on Ennius*

Glosses of Fornerus [cf. F 16]: *palamnaion* ["abomina-
ble," Greek], *dirum* [Latin], since it has the anger of gods
connected with it [i.e., *dirus* suggesting *deus*]. Ennius in
the third book:

> violence could an even more abominable punishment
> of crime

I read *poscit* ["requires," for *possit* "could"], as the sense
requires.

*23 Paulus Merula, *Commentary on Ennius*

I have learned from the Glossary of Fornerus [cf. F 16]
that this is from the fourth book of the *Annals*: *apoleiph-
theis* ["left," Greek], *delictus* [Latin]. Ennius in the third
book (without doubt in the *Annals*):

> he shakes in his heart, his knee having failed

I read: "Cocles[1] having failed." Still, this honorable gentle-
man Joseph Scaliger [the Dutch scholar, 1540–1609] re-
tains the vulgate "knee" [*poplite*]. For my emendation
there is light and support.

[1] Horatius Cocles, the Roman hero (cf. Liv. 2.10).

*24 Paulus Merula, *Commentary on Ennius*

Glossary of Fornerus [cf. F 16]: *divido* ["I divide"],
diaspeirō [Greek]. Ennius in the fifth book:

> scatter the enemies, draw apart, lead away, divide,
> disperse

*25 Paulus Merula (1558–1607), *Enni Comm.* (1595), pp. 369–70

Glossarium Forneri: Πυργοφόρος, *Torridus. Ennius in V:*

> apta dato signo loca torridis elefantis
> explorant numeri

Nemo non videt legendum haec, & numerum restituendum: πυργοφόρος, *Torritus. Ennius in VI:*

> apta, dato signo, loca torritis elefantis
> explorant Numidae

& connectendum eadem cum ijs, quae apud Macrobium lib. VI. cap. I [*Sat.* 6.1.22]. ubi hoc Virgilij [*Aen.* 8.596]; *Quadrupedante putrem sonitu quatit ungula campũ*, committit cum Enni versu [7 *Ann.* F 25]: *Explorant Numidae, totam quatit ungula terram.* Sunt ecce quaedam Enni & Macrobio & Glossographo communia: nisi quod *Numeri*, lapsu facili, in Glossario; qui recte Macrobio *Numidae*. Ambigo tamen de fido connexu. *Portentum*, inquit V. N. Iosephus Scaliger in suis ad me litteris, *adtribui ungulam Elefanto.* Vere. Non enim ungulae sunt Elefantis, verum *digiti informes numero quidem quinque, sed indivisi ac leviter discreti, ungulisque non unguibus similes, & pedes majores priores*, inquit Plinius libro XI. cap. XLV [Plin.

*25 Paulus Merula, *Commentary on Ennius*

Glossary of Fornerus [cf. F 16]: *pyrgophoros* [lit., "bearing a tower," Greek], *torrĭdus* ["parched," Latin]. Ennius in Book 5:

> once the signal was given, numbers of men with
>   parched elephants
> search for suitable places

Everybody sees that this is to be read and the meter restored: [Greek] "bearing a tower," "turreted" [Latin: *turrītus*]. Ennius in Book 6:

> once the signal was given, the Numidians with
>   turreted elephants
> search for suitable places

and also to be connected with this is what is in Macrobius, Book 6, Chapter 1 [*Sat.* 6.1.22], where he compares this line of Virgil [*Aen.* 8.596], "with galloping sound the horse's hoof shakes the crumbling plain," with Ennius' verse [7 *Ann.* F 25], "the Numidians investigates, the hoof everywhere shakes the ground." Look, there is something shared between Ennius and Macrobius and the glossographer except for "numbers," by an easy lapse in the glossary; they are rightly "Numidians" in Macrobius. Yet I am uncertain about the reliability of the collocation. "As an abnormal phenomenon," says the honorable gentleman Joseph Scaliger [cf. F 23] in his letters to me, "I attribute a hoof to an elephant." Indeed. For elephants do not have hooves, but "unformed toes, though five in number, yet undivided and slightly separated, and similar to hooves, not nails, and the forefeet larger," says Pliny, Book 11,

HN 11.248]. Et ne *Numidae* apud Glossographum (apud Macrobium enim proculdubio tolerandi) nimis adrideant; scio etiam quid in re militari sint *Numeri*. Potest item ut *ungula* hoc loco non Elefantis adtribuatur, sed alijs, quarum in bellis usus, belluis, quarum descriptio in proximis huic fragmento versibus sequebatur.

*26 (cf. 9 *Ann.* F 7) Paulus Merula (1558–1607), *Enni Comm.* (1595), pp. 416–17

Calpurnius ille lib. I ubi de Dissolutionibus . . . Et paullo post: *Quanta autem, audita suorum clade, formidine contramiserint* (lego, quod probat & in suis ad me litteris V. N. Ioseph. Scaliger, *contremuerint*) *Afri, quam repente imo* (ego cum Scaligero *repentino*) *motu illorum animi conciderint, Ennius libro septimo, dissolutiore, id est meliore, describit arte quam Naevius; quod potuit, qui hoc posterior fuit:*

Africa terribili tremit horrida terra tumultu
undique; multimodis consumitur anxia curis;
omnibus inde locis ingens apparet imago
tristitias; oculosque manusque ad sydera lassas
protendunt, exsecrando ducis facta reprendunt
Poeni, pervertentes omnia, circumcursant.

Chapter 45 [Plin. *HN* 11.248]. And so that the "Numidians" in the glossographer do not please too much (for in Macrobius they are without doubt tolerable), I also know what "numbers" are in military matters. It can equally be the case that "hoof" in this passage is not attributed to elephants, but to other animals of which use is made in wars, whose description followed in lines very close to this fragment.

*26 (cf. 9 *Ann.* F 7) Paulus Merula, *Commentary on Ennius*

This Calpurnius [cf. F 15] in Book 1, where he talks about lack of verbal connection [i.e., asyndeton] . . . And a little later: "But with what fear, when they had heard of the defeat of their men, the Africans sent against" (I read 'were shaking,' which the honorable gentleman Joseph Scaliger [cf. F 23] too in his letters to me regards as right), "with what suddenly low (I read, with Scaliger, 'sudden') movement their minds were failing in spirit, Ennius describes in the seventh book more loosely [i.e., without connectors], that is with better art, than Naevius, which he, who was later than him, could do:

> The rough African land trembles with a terrible
> tumult
> everywhere; in many ways it is consumed, anxious
> with cares;
> then in all places appears an enormous specter,
> of sadness; they stretch out eyes and weak hands to
> the stars,
> by cursing they censure the deeds of the leader,
> the Carthaginians run about, destroying everything.

*27 Paulus Merula (1558–1607), *Enni Comm.* (1595), pp. 433–34

Priora exstant in Glossario CL. V. Gulielmi Forneri: φόνευσις, *Funus*, *Caedes. Ennius:*

> . . . multiplicant Romani funera late
> quam pullus furtim noctu . . .

Posteriora apud Macrobium leguntur libro I. Sat. cap. IV [*Sat.* 1.4.17]: *Reliqua autem verba*, inquit, *quae Avieno nostro nova visa sunt, veterum nobis sunt testimonijs adserenda. Ennius enim, nisi cui videtur inter nostrae aetatis politiores mundicias respuendus, noctu concubia dixit his verbis* [7 *Ann.* F 14]: *qua Galli furtim noctu summa arcis adorti / moenia concubia, vigilesque repente cruentant. quo in loco animadvertendum est non solum, quod noctu concubia, sed etiam quod qua noctu dixerit. et hoc posuit in Annalium septimo, &c.* Hic, quam ibi, obscurius & corruptius. Ibi pro *quam* legendum *qua*, docente Macrobio: Hic vero pro *Galli* reponendum inde *Pullus*, & pro *adorti* scribendum *adortus*; hoc modo:

> . . . moltiplicant Romanei funera late,
> Qua Pollus furtim noctu summa arcis adortus
> Moinia, concubia, vigilesque repente cruentant.

Pullus cognomen est familiae *Iuniae*: ut haec proculdubio pertineant ad annum DIV. quo Fasti Capitolini & Siculi

---

1 One of the interlocutors in Macrobius' *Saturnalia*.

2 Macrobius takes *qua* with *noctu*, an interpretation doubted by modern scholars.

*27 Paulus Merula, *Commentary on Ennius*

The former is extant in the Glossary of the most respected gentleman Gulielmius Fornerus [cf. F 16]: *phoneusis* ["murder," Greek], *funus, caedes* ["death," "slaughter," Latin]. Ennius:

> . . . the Romans multiply death widely
> how the young animal secretly at night . . .

The latter is read in Macrobius in Book 1 of *Saturnalia*, Chapter 4 [*Sat.* 1.4.17]: "But the other words," he says, "that seemed novel to our Avienus,[1] have to be defended by us from the testimony of the ancients. For Ennius, unless he seems to anyone in the more polished elegance of our age worthy of rejection, described 'deep at night' with these words: 'when at the time for bedding down at night the Gauls slipped stealthily over the citadel's highest walls and suddenly bloodied the guard.' In this passage one has to note not only that he said *noctu concubia*, but also *qua noctu*.[2] And he has put this in the seventh book of the *Annals*, and so on." Here it is more obscure and corrupt than there. There, instead of *quam* one has to read *qua*, as Macrobius shows; but here, instead of *Galli*, *Pullus* has to be restored, and instead of *adorti* one has to write *adortus*; in this way:

> . . . the Romans multiply death widely
> at bedtime when, deep at night, Pollus secretly attacked
> the citadel's highest walls, and they suddenly bloody the guards

"Pullus" is the cognomen of the Iunius family, so that this refers without doubt to the year 504, for which the Fasti

coss. edunt P. Claudium Ap. F. C. N. Pulcrum, L. Iunium
C. F. L. N. Pullum. Fastos sequitur Censorinus. Sensus
est: Romanos milites funera & caedes multiplicasse, latā
stragem edidisse, vigilesque & praesidiarios milites
cruētasse, inque eos ferro desaevijsse noctu concubia &
intempesta, qua L. Iunius Pullus Consul summa moenia
arcis (sic *Eryx* poetae vocatur, Siciliae urbs, quod nimirum
in sublimi tumulo arcis instar esset sita: videndus Polybius
lib. I) adgressus, victoriae jam contra Poenos faciebat ini-
tium. Hoc lucis illudque medicinae a me his Enni tene-
bris, istique illius vulneri: aliud alij promant.

*28 Paulus Merula (1558–1607), *Enni Comm.* (1595),
p. 551

Glossae Forneri: ἀποκτείνω, *Sterno.* Ennius:

Fulvius nobilis obstravit certamine cerebro
et illos . . .

Elegantissimum fragmētum, sed corruptissimum. In eam-
dem fere emendationem concurrimus ego & V. N. Iose-
phus Scaliger; quod ipse etiam testabitur, quum suas mihi
in scriptis conjecturas ad Enni fragmenta, ex Forneri

Capitolini and Siculi indicate Publius Claudius Pulcher, son of Appius, grandson of Gaius, and Lucius Iunius Pullus, son of Gaius, grandson of Lucius, were consuls [249 BC]. Censorinus[3] follows the Fasti. The meaning is: Roman soldiers multiplied funerals and deaths, created widespread carnage, brought bloodshed to the guards and soldiers of the garrison and vented their rage against them with the sword at bedtime and deep at night, when the consul Lucius Iunius Pullus attacked the wall tops of the citadel (thus called "Eryx" by the poet, a city in Sicily, since, of course, it is located on a high mound similar to a citadel; one should compare Polybius, Book 1) and already made the beginning of victory against the Carthaginians. This light and that medicine is offered by me to these shadows of Ennius and to this injury to him: others may make other suggestions.

[3] Presumably the Roman grammarian and writer of the 3rd century AD.

*28 Paulus Merula, *Commentary on Ennius*

Glosses of Fornerus [F 16]: *apokteinō* ["I kill," Greek], *sterno* [Latin]. Ennius:

> noble Fulvius killed them, too, with battle
> and with brain . . .

A very elegant fragment, but very corrupt. Myself and the honorable gentleman Joseph Scaliger [cf. F 23] agree on almost the same emendation; he himself will confirm this, since he passed on to me in writing his conjectures on Ennius' fragments, extracted from the glossary of Fornerus

Glossario excerpta, tradenti meas etiam de eisdem evestigio monstrarem. Medicina nostra talis:

Folviu' Nobilior stravit certamine crebro
Aitolos . . .

nisi quod vir magnus priores tres voces, quae in scripto exemplari, retineret; . . . : postea tamē facile ductus in meam sententiam. Planus est sensus.

*29 Paulus Merula (1558–1607), *Enni Comm.* (1595), pp. 563–64

Calpurnius libro I: *Vehementissime apud Ennium tonat Clodius Pulcer in M. Aebutium Trib. plebis, quum prohiberet triumphum, quem ob res in Graecia praeclare gestas, decreverat magno consensu Senatus, accusans etiam Manilium. Inter alia*

vim tua noluntas facit imperiosa vetando,
quem consul meruit, quum res bene gesta, triumphū

Ex affectu haec Ennius scripsit in gratiam sui Fulvi, non ex veritate. Lego: Veh. ap. Enn. tonat Clod. Pulc. in M. Aburium (Videndus omnino Livius libro XXXIX. *Abutiorum* tamen, *Aburniorum & Ebutiorum* Familiae etiam Romae fuerunt) *quum proh. triumphum, &c. accusans etiam M. Aimilium.* Designat enim Aimilium, qui Legatos Ambracienses contra Fulvium subornarat; quem item M. Aburius dicit proficiscentem in provinciam sibi mandasse,

[cf. F 16], and I immediately showed him mine as well on the same passages. Our remedy is as follows:

> Fulvius Nobilior killed in thick battle
> the Aetolians . . .

except that the great man retained the three preceding words, which are in the written copy . . . : yet later he was easily brought over to my opinion. The sense is obvious.

*29 Paulus Merula, *Commentary on Ennius*

Calpurnius [cf. F 15] in Book 1: "In Ennius, Clodius Pulcher thunders with very great force against Marcus Aebutius, tribune of the people, when he was preventing the triumph that the senate had decreed with great unanimity for his magnificent achievements in Greece; he also accused Manilius. Among other things:

> your powerful opposition creates force by vetoing,
> the triumph that the consul has earned, since the
>   deed was done well

Out of affection has Ennius written this in gratitude toward his [patron] Fulvius, not out of truth." I read: "In Ennius, Clodius Pulcher thunders with very great force against Marcus Aburius" (in general, Livy is to be compared, in Book 39; not only the family of the Abutii, but also those of the Aburnii and Ebutii existed at Rome) "when he prevented the triumph etc.; he also accused Marcus Aimilius." For he denotes Aimilius, who had briefed the envoys from Ambracia against Fulvius; equally Marcus Aburius says that he [i.e., Aimilius], setting off into

ut disceptatio, an triumphus Fulvio esset decernendus nec
ne, integra in adventum suum servaretur.

*30 Caspar von Barth (1587–1658), *Ad Papinii Statii
Achilleidos libros II animadversiones, ad Stat. Achill.*
1.558 (Stat. [1664] vol. IV, p. 1693)

CARBASUS.] Navis, a velo. Ut Ennius:

> carbasus alta volat pandam ductura carinam

Hæc vetus Scholiastes, auctis Ennii reliqviis. Cui suæ de-
bentur Gratiæ.

Cf. Verg. *G.* 2.445: pandas ratibus posuere carinas.

*31 Caspar von Barth (1587–1658), *Adversariorum com-
mentariorum* liber XXXVIII, cap. 15, col. 1751

Bonus & liberalis in eo diversi sunt, quod bonus est qui
per naturam suam non nocet, liberalis qui libenter pro-
dest. Terentius Adelphis [*Ad.* 463–64]. *Neq; boni officium
functus es, neq; liberalis viri.* Ennius in eo:

> quod bonus & liber populus

hoc est liberalis. Emaculandum dicas. Ennius in primo.

Cf. Donat. *Comm. Ter. Ad.* 464 "neque liberalis functus est offi-
cium viri": quaerendum, inter bonum et liberalem quid intersit:
an bonus est qui non nocet, liberalis qui etiam prodest? an bonus
est qui non peccat in facto, liberalis qui nec in verbo quidem?

his province, gave instructions to him that the argument over whether or not a triumph should be awarded to Fulvius would remain unresolved until his return.[1]

[1] The controversy over Fulvius' triumph probably figured in *Annals* 15. See the Introduction to that book.

*30 Caspar von Barth, *Commentary on Statius*

carbasus ["canvas"]: "ship," from "sail." As Ennius says:

the canvas flies high,[1] about to lead on the curved keel

Thus an old scholiast, whereby the remains of Ennius have been increased. To him due gratitude is owed.

[1] Despite the explanation, *carbasus* makes perfect sense as "sail."

*31 Caspar von Barth, *Notes to Self*

The good man and the generous man are different in this way, because the good man is one who by his very nature does no harm, the generous man is someone who willingly is useful.[1] Terence in *Adelphoe* [*Ad.* 463–64]: "You have done the job of neither a good nor a generous man." Ennius in this phrase:

that a good and free people

This means "generous." You might say that it must be cleaned up. Ennius in the first book.

[1] This observation restates Donatus' gloss on the line of Terence that immediately follows.

CONCORDANCES

TRAGEDIES

CONCORDANCE 1
FRL—Vahlen[2]—Warmington

FRL	Vahlen[2]	Warmington
Achilles (Aristarchi)		
1	15	18
2	10–11	16–17
3	16	19
4	4	4–5
5	13–14	14–15
6	6	6
7	5	13
8	7–9	10–12
Aiax		
9	19	21
10	20	23
11	17	20
Alcmeo		
12	22–26	25–29
13	34, 27–33	37, 30–36
14	21	24

FRL	Vahlen[2]	Warmington
Alexander		
15	47–48	50–51
16	53	56
17	78	82
18	50	52
19	51	54
20	49	53
21	72–75	76–79
22	76–77	80–81
Andromacha (Aechmalotis)		
23	100–101, 85–99	91–92, 94–100, 101–8
24	107–10	113–16
25	105	109
26	111	111
27	103	110
28	102	90
29	80–81	83–84
30	83–84	88–89
31	106	112
32	104	86–87
33	79	85
Andromeda		
34	112–13	117–18
35	120	126
36	115	120
37	117	119
38	114	121
39	116	122

FRL	Vahlen[2]	Warmington
40	118–19	123–24
41	122	125
Athamas		
42	123–27	128–32
Cresphontes		
43	134	138
44	129	136
45	133	137
46	130	139
47	128	133
48	131–32	134–35
Erectheus		
49	137–38	142–43
50	139	144
51	140	145–46
Eumenides		
52	147	149
53	149	155
54	145–46	147–48
55	148	154
Hectoris lytra		
56	178	192
57	184	189
58	160	166
59	177	187–88
60	193	190
61	158–59	164–65
62	188–89	200–201

FRL	Vahlen[2]	Warmington
63	190–92	184–86
64	185	197
65	179	191
66	186	198
67	156	162
68	157	163
69	181	196
70	180	193
71	182–83	194–95
Hecuba		
72	196	203
73	199–201	206–8
74	206	213
75	209	219
76	211–12	217–18
77	195	202
78	202	209
79	207	214
80	197–98	204–5
81	203–4	210–11
Iphigenia		
82	242–44	249–51
83	215–18	222–25
84	234–41	241–48
85	245	252
86	213–14	220–21
87	224	231
88	233	240

TRAGEDIES 1

FRL	Vahlen[2]	Warmington
Medea (exul)		
89	246–54	253–61
90	259–61, 273	266–68, 271
91	257–58	264–65
92	278	286
93	262–63	269–70
94	287–88	294–95
95	284–86	291–93
96	255–56	262–63
97	282–83	289–90
98	280	287
99	279	281
100	281	288
Melanippa		
101	294	302
102	293	303
103	295	299–300
104	291	298
105	289–90	296–97
106	292	301
Nemea		
107	297	305
108	296	304
Phoenix		
109	300–303	308–11
110	306	316
111	298	306
112	304–5	312–13

FRL	Vahlen[2]	Warmington
113	308	314
114	307	315
115	309	317
116	310	318
Telamo		
117	318, 319–23, 316–17	330, 332–36, 328–29
118	324	327
119	329	p. 562
120	325–26	325–26
121	328	338
122	311	323
123	327	337
124	315	324
Telephus		
125	331	340
126	330, 339	339, 341
127	334–35	347–48
128	337–38	345–46
129	333	342
130	332	343
131	336	344
Thyestes		
132	362–65	367–70
133	348	355
134	345	351
135	353	362
136	361	353

FRL	Vahlen[2]	Warmington
137	344	373
138	341	354
139	346–47	350
140	360	352
141	340	349
Incerta		
142	380	386
143	342–43	371–72
144	173	167
145	398–400	412–14
146	141–44	150–53
147	376–77	400
148	412–13	405–6
149	381	387
150	404–5	402–3
151	54–71	57–72, 73–75
152	299	307
153	161–72	169–81
154	176	183
155	205	212
156	392–93	408–9
157	354–56	363–65
158	395	407
159	401	388
160	394	331
161	219–21	226–28
162	18	22
163	402	410
164	409	416

FRL	Vahlen[2]	Warmington
165	403	389
166	210	216
167	388–89	424–25
168	411	421
169	187	199
170	420	433
171	121	127
172	150	156
173	*Ann.* 9	*Inc.* 6
174	396	394
175	232	239
176	397	415
177	417–18	399
178	421	429
179	82	93
180	408	417
181	378	404
182	379	401
183	407	411
184	423	428
185	175	182
186	406	390–91
187	430	422
188	416	420
189	415	426
190	390–91	392–93
191	383	397
192	386–87	418
193	382	398

FRL	Vahlen[2]	Warmington
194	228–29	235–36
195	384–85	423
196	426	436
197	410	419
198	135–36	140–41
199	427	435
200	194	p. 290
201	52	55

CONCORDANCE 2
Vahlen[2]—*FRL*—Warmington

Vahlen[2]	*FRL*	Warmington
Achilles (Aristarchi)		
1–3	t 1	1–3
4	4	4–5
5	7	13
6	6	6
7–9	8	10–12
10–11	2	16–17
12	*Inc.* F 17	7–9
13–14	5	14–15
15	1	18
16	3	19
Aiax		
17	11	20
18	162	22
19	9	21
20	10	23
Alcmeo		
21	14	24
22–26	12	25–29
27–33	13	30–36
34	13	37
Alexander		
35–46	*Adesp.* 76 *TrRF*	38–49
47–48	15	50–51
49	20	53

Vahlen[2]	*FRL*	Warmington
50	18	52
51	19	54
52	201	55
53	16	56
54–71	151	57–72, 73–75
72–75	21	76–79
76–77	22	80–81
78	17	82

Andromacha (*Aechmalotis*)

79	33	85
80–81	29	83–84
82	179	93
83–84	30	88–89
85–99	23	94–100, 101–8
100–101	23	91–92
102	28	90
103	27	110
104	32	86–87
105	25	109
106	31	112
107–10	24	113–16
111	26	111

Andromeda

112–13	34	117–18
114	38	121
115	36	120
116	39	122
117	37	119
118–19	40	123–24

Vahlen[2]	*FRL*	Warmington
120	35	126
121	171	127
122	41	125

Athamas

123–27	42	128–32

Cresphontes

128	47	133
129	444	136
130	46	139
131–32	48	134–35
133	45	137
134	43	138

Erectheus

135–36	198	140–41
137–38	49	142–43
139	50	144
140	51	145–46

Eumenides

141–44	146	150–53
145–46	54	147–48
147	52	149
148	55	154
149	53	155
150	172	156
151–55	Adesp. 52 *TrRF*	157–61

Hectoris lytra

156–57	67, 68	162–63
158–59	61	164–65

Vahlen[2]	*FRL*	Warmington
160	58	166
161–72	153	169–81
173	144	167
174	*Inc.* F 42	168
175	185	182
176	154	183
177	59	187–88
178	56	192
179	65	191
180	70	193
181	69	196
182–83	71	194–95
184	57	189
185	64	197
186	66	198
187	169	199
188–89	62	200–201
190–92	63	184–86
193	60	190
Hecuba		
194	200	p. 290
195	77	202
196	72	203
197–98	80	204–5
199–201	73	206–8
202	78	209
203–4	81	210–11
205	155	212
206	74	213
207	79	214

Vahlen[2]	*FRL*	Warmington
208	*Adesp.* 38 *TrRF*	215
209	75	219
210	166	216
211–12	76	217–18
Iphigenia		
213–14	86	220–21
215–18	83	222–25
219–21	161	226–28
222–23	*Adesp.* 63 *TrRF*	229–30
224	87	231
225–27	*Adesp.* 124 *TrRF*	232–34
228–29	194	235–36
230–31	*Adesp.* 68 *TrRF*	237–38
232	175	239
233	88	240
234–41	84	241–48
242–44	82	249–51
245	85	252
Medea (*exul*)		
246–54	89	253–61
255–56	96	262–63
257–58	91	264–65
259–61	90	266–68
262–63	93	269–70
264–65	*Adesp.* 34 *TrRF*	272–73
266–68	*Adesp.* 71 *TrRF*	274–76
269–72	*Adesp.* 72, 73 *TrRF*	277–80
273	90	271

Vahlen[2]	FRL	Warmington
274–75	*Adesp.* 135 *TrRF*	282–83
276–77	*Adesp.* 25 *TrRF*	284–85
278	92	286
279	99	281
280	98	287
281	100	288
282–83	97	289–90
284–86	95	291–93
287–88	94	294–95
Melanippa		
289–90	105	296–97
291	104	298
292	106	301
293	102	303
294	101	302
295	103	299–300
Nemea		
296	108	304
297	107	305
Phoenix		
298	111	306
299	152	307
300–303	109	308–11
304–5	112	312–13
306	110	316
307	114	315
308	113	314
309	115	317
310	116	318

CONCORDANCE

Vahlen[2]	*FRL*	Warmington
Telamo		
311	122	323
312–14	*Adesp.* 58 *TrRF*	319–22
315	124	324
316–17	117	328–29
318	117	330
319–23	117	332–36
324	118	327
325–26	120	325–26
327	123	337
328	121	338
329	119	p. 562
Telephus		
330	126	339
331	125	340
332	130	343
333	129	342
334–35	127	347–48
336	131	344
337–38	128	345–46
339	126	341
Thyestes		
340	141	349
341	138	354
342–43	143	371–72
344	137	373
345	134	351
346–47	139	350

Vahlen[2]	*FRL*	Warmington
348	133	355
349–52	*Adesp.* 56, 22 *TrRF*	358–60, 361
353	135	362
354–56	157	363–65
357–59	*Adesp.* 55 *TrRF*	356–57
360	140	352
361	136	353
362–65	132	366–70
Scenica fab. inc.		
376–77	147	400
378	181	404
379	182	401
380	142	386
381	149	387
382	193	398
383	191	397
384–85	195	423
386–87	192	418
388–89	167	424–25
390–91	190	392–93
392–93	156	408–9
394	160	331
395	158	407
396	174	394
397	176	415
398–400	145	412–14
401	159	388
402	163	410

CONCORDANCE

Vahlen[2]	FRL	Warmington
403	165	389
404–5	150	402–3
406	186	390–91
407	183	411
408	180	417
409	164	416
410	197	419
411	168	421
412–13	148	405–6
414	*Inc.* F 44	385
415	189	426
416	188	420
417–18	177	399
419	*Inc.* F 12	431
420	170	433
421	178	429
422	*Inc.* F 1	432
423	184	428
424	*Inc.* F 30	430
425	*Inc.* F 29	434
426	196	436
427	199	435
428	*Inc.* F 24	437
429	*Inc.* F 7	427
430	187	422

Varia et incerta

Ann. 9	173	*Inc.* 6

CONCORDANCE 3
Warmington—*FRL*—Vahlen[2]

Warmington	*FRL*	Vahlen[2]
Achilles (Aristarchi)		
1–3	t 1	1–3
4–5	4	4
6	6	6
7–9	*Inc.* F 17	12
10–12	8	7–9
13	7	5
14–15	5	13–14
16–17	2	10–11
18	1	15
19	3	16
Aiax		
20	11	17
21	9	19
22	162	18
23	10	20
Alcmeo		
24	14	21
25–29	12	22–26
30–36	13	27–33
37	13	34
Alexander		
38–49	*Adesp.* 76 *TrRF*	35–46
50–51	15	47–48

Warmington	*FRL*	Vahlen[2]
52	18	50
53	20	49
54	19	51
55	201	52
56	16	53
57–72	151	54–68
73–75	151	69–71
76–79	21	72–75
80–81	22	76–77
82	17	78

Andromacha (Aechmalotis)

83–84	29	80–81
85	33	79
86–87	32	104
88–89	30	83–84
90	28	102
91–92	23	100–101
93	179	82
94–100	23	85–91
101–8	23	92–99
109	25	105
110	27	103
111	26	111
112	31	106
113–16	24	107–10

Andromeda

117–18	34	112–13
119	37	117
120	36	115

Warmington	*FRL*	Vahlen[2]
121	38	114
122	40	118–19
125	41	122
126	35	120
127	171	121

Athamas
128–32	42	123–27

Cresphontes
133	47	128
134–35	48	131–32
136	44	129
137	45	133
138	43	134
139	56	130

Erectheus
140–41	198	135–36
142–43	49	137–38
144	50	139
145–46	61	140

Eumenides
147–48	54	145–46
149	52	147
150–53	146	141–44
154	55	148
155	53	149
156	172	150
157–61	*Adesp.* 52 *TrRF*	151–55

CONCORDANCE

Warmington	*FRL*	Vahlen[2]
Hectoris lytra		
162	67	156
163	68	157
164–65	61	158–59
166	58	160
167	144	173
168	*Inc.* F 42	174
169–81	153	161–72
182	185	175
183	154	176
184–86	63	190–92
187–88	59	177
189	57	184
190	60	193
191	65	179
192	56	178
193	70	180
194–95	71	182–83
196	69	181
197	64	185
198	66	186
199	169	187
200–201	62	188–89
Hecuba		
202	77	195
203	72	196
204–5	80	197–98
206–8	73	199–201

Warmington	*FRL*	Vahlen[2]
209	78	202
210–11	81	203–4
212	155	205
213	74	206
214	79	207
215	*Adesp.* 37–39 *TrRF*	208
216	166	210
217–18	76	211–12
219	75	209
Iphigenia		
220–21	86	213–14
222–25	83	215–18
226–28	161	219–21
229–30	*Adesp.* 63 *TrRF*	222–23
231	87	224
232–34	*Adesp.* 124 *TrRF*	225–27
235–36	194	228–29
237–38	*Adesp.* 68 *TrRF*	230–31
239	175	232
240	88	233
241–48	84	234–41
249–51	82	242–44
252	85	245
Medea (*exul*)		
253–61	89	246–54
262–63	96	255–56

Warmington	*FRL*	Vahlen[2]
264–65	91	257–58
266–68	90	259–61
269–70	93	262–63
271	90	273
272–73	*Adesp.* 34 *TrRF*	264–65
274–80	*Adesp.* 71, 72, 73 *TrRF*	266–72
281	99	279
282–83	*Adesp.* 135 *TrRF*	274–75
284–85	*Adesp.* 25 *TrRF*	276–77
286	92	278
287	98	280
288	100	281
289–90	97	282–83
291–93	95	284–86
294–95	94	287–88
Melanippa		
296–97	106	289–90
298	104	291
299–300	103	295
301	106	292
302	101	294
303	102	293
Nemea		
304	108	296
305	107	297
Phoenix		
306	111	298
307	152	299

Warmington	*FRL*	Vahlen[2]
308–11	109	300–303
312–13	112	304–5
314	113	308
315	114	307
316	110	306
317	115	309
318	116	310
Telamo		
319–22	*Adesp.* 58 *TrRF*	312–14
323	122	311
324	124	315
325–26	120	325–26
327	118	324
328–29	117	316–17
330	117	318
331	160	394
332–36	117	319–23
337	123	327
338	121	328
p. 562	119	329
Telephus		
339	126	330
340	125	331
341	126	339
342	129	333
343	130	332
344	131	336
345–46	128	337–38
347–48	127	334–35

Warmington	*FRL*	Vahlen[2]
Thyestes		
349	141	340
350	139	346–47
351	134	345
352	140	360
353	136	361
354	138	341
355	133	348
356–60	*Adesp.* 55, 56 *TrRF*	357–58, 349–51
361	*Adesp.* 22 *TrRF*	352
362	135	353
363–65	157	354–56
366–70	132	362–65
371–72	143	342–43
373	137	344
Ex fabulis incertis		
385	*Inc.* F 44	414
386	142	380
387	149	381
388	159	401
389	165	403
390–91	186	406
392–93	190	390–91
394	174	396
395–96	—	*Ann.* 526
397	191	383
398	193	382

Warmington	*FRL*	Vahlen[2]
399	177	417–18
400	147	376
401	182	379
402–3	150	404–5
404	181	378
405–6	148	412–13
407	158	395
408–9	156	392–93
410	163	402
411	183	407
412–14	145	398–400
415	176	397
416	164	409
417	180	408
418	192	386–87
419	197	410
420	188	416
421	168	411
422	187	430
423	195	384–85
424–25	167	388–89
426	189	415
427	*Inc.* F 7	429
428	184	423
429	178	421
430	*Inc.* F 30	424
431	*Inc.* F 12	419
432	*Inc.* F 1	422

CONCORDANCE

Warmington	*FRL*	Vahlen[2]
433	170	420
434	*Inc.* F 29	425
435	199	427
436	196	426
437	*Inc.* F 24	428

Varia et incerta

Inc. 6	173	*Ann.* 9

PRAETEXTAE

FRL—Ribbeck$^{2-3}$—Vahlen^{2}—Warmington

FRL	Ribbeck$^{2-3}$	Vahlen^{2}	Warm.
Ambracia			
1	*Praet.* 1	*Scen.* 366	*Fab.* 376
2	*Praet.* 4	*Scen.* 367	*Fab.* 374
3	*Praet.* 2	*Scen.* 368	*Fab.* 377–78
4	*Praet.* 3	*Scen.* 369	*Fab.* 375
Sabinae			
5	*Praet.* 5–6	*Scen.* 370–71	*Fab.* 379–80

COMEDIES

FRL—Ribbeck[2-3]—Vahlen[2]—Warmington

FRL	Ribbeck[2-3]	Vahlen[2]	Warm.
Caupuncula			
1	*Com.* 1	*Scen.* 372	*Fab.* 381
Pancratiastes			
2	*Com.* 4	*Scen.* 373	*Fab.* 382
3	*Com.* 2	*Scen.* 374	*Fab.* 383
4	*Com.* 3	*Scen.* 375	*Fab.* 384
Incertum			
5	Naev. *Com.* 75–79	—	Naev. *Com.* 74–79
Dubium			
6	—	—	—

MINOR WORKS

Epicharmus
FRL—Vahlen[2]—Warmington

FRL	Vahlen[2]	Warmington
1	*Var.* 45	*Epi.* 1
2	*Var.* 52, 53, 46	*Epi.* 8–9, 2
3	*Var.* 59	p. 415 n. a
4	*Var.* 47	*Epi.* 3
5	*Var.* 51	*Epi.* 7

Epigrams
FRL—Vahlen[2]—Warmington

FRL	Vahlen[2]	Warmington
1	*Var.* 19–20	*Epigr.* 5–6
2	*Var.* 15–16, 17–18	*Epigr.* 7–10
3	*Var.* 21–24	*Epigr.* 1–2, 3–4

Euhemerus
FRL—Vahlen[2]—Warmington

FRL	Vahlen[2]	Warmington
1	*Var.* 146	p. 562
2	*Var.* 107–8	*Euh.* 78–80
3	*Var.* 109–12	*Euh.* 81–87
4	*Var.* 132–41	*Euh.* 119–33
5	*Var.* 99–106, 62–63, 98	*Euh.* 66–77, 64–65, 5–6
6	*Var.* 113–15	*Euh.* 88–92
7	*Var.* 60–61	*Euh.* 1–4
8	*Var.* 64–82, 83–86	*Euh.* 8–45
9	*Var.* 87–97	*Euh.* 46–63
10	*Var.* 142–45	*Euh.* 134–38
11	*Var.* 116–31	*Euh.* 93–118

Hedyphagetica
FRL—Vahlen[2]—Warmington

FRL	Vahlen[2]	Warmington
1	*Var.* 34–44	*Hed.* 1–11

Praecepta
FRL—Vahlen[2]—Warmington

FRL	Vahlen[2]	Warmington
1	*Var.* 31–33	*Praec.* 1–3

Protrepticus
FRL—Vahlen[2]—Warmington

FRL	Vahlen[2]	Warmington
1	*Var.* 30	pp. 406–7 n. a

Satires
FRL—Vahlen[2]—Warmington

FRL	Vahlen[2]	Warmington
1	1	1
2	2	2
3	3–4	3–4
4	5	5
5	6–7	6–7
6	10–11	10–11
7	8–9	8–9
8	12–13	12–13
9	14–19	14–19
10	57–58	p. 388
11	59–62	28–31
12	63	22
13	64	21

FRL	Vahlen[2]	Warmington
14	65	20
15	66	24
16	67–68	25–26
17	69	23
18	70	27
19	*Ann.* 16	*Ann.* 14

Scipio
FRL—Vahlen[2]—Warmington

FRL	Vahlen[2]	Warmington
1	6, 7	12–14
2	6–8	13–14
3	3	7
4	13	5
5	9–12	1–4
6	14	6
7	1–2	10–11
8 *Ann.* F 3	4	8–9

Sota
FRL—Vahlen[2]—Warmington

FRL	Vahlen[2]	Warmington
1	*Var.* 25	*Sot.* 2
2	*Var.* 27	*Sot.* 3
3	*Var.* 28	*Sot.* 4
4	*Var.* 26	*Sot.* 1
5	*Var.* 29	*Sot.* 5

UNIDENTIFIED WORKS

FRL	Vahlen[2]	Warmington
1	*Scen.* 422	*Fab.* 432
2	*Inc.* 19	p. 562
3	*Inc.* 20	p. 562
4	*Inc.* 18	*Varia* 32
5	*Inc.* 16	*Varia* 24
6	*Inc.* 53	*Varia* 11
7	*Scen.* 429	*Fab.* 427
8	*Inc.* 17	p. 564
9	*Var.* 48–50, 54–58	*Epich.* 4–6, 10–14
10	*Inc.* 48	p. 564
11	*Inc.* 39	*Varia* 35
12	*Scen.* 419	*Fab.* 431
13	*Inc.* 10	*Varia* 17
14	*Inc.* 7	*Varia* 14
15	*Inc.* 26	p. 563
16	ad *Ann.* 376	p. 434
17	*Scen.* 12	*Fab.* 7–9
18	Ann. 628	*Varia* 15
19	*Inc.* 5	*Varia* 5
20	*Inc.* 42	p. 562
21	*Inc.* 37	p. 563
22	*Inc.* 40	*Varia* 30

FRL	Vahlen[2]	Warmington
23	*Inc.* 38	p. 563
24	*Scen.* 428	*Fab.* 437
25	*Inc.* 21	*Varia* 34
26	*Inc.* 32	p. 438
27	*Inc.* 31	p. 563
28	*Inc.* 22	p. 563
29	*Scen.* 425	*Fab.* 434
30	*Scen.* 424	*Fab.* 430
31	*Inc.* 45	—
32	*Inc.* 12	*Varia* 28
33	*Inc.* 13	*Varia* 29
34	*Inc.* 44	p. 436
35	*Inc.* 9	*Varia* 16
36	*Inc.* 2	p. 563
37	*Inc.* 6	*Varia* 23
38	*Inc.* 23	p. 563
39	*Inc.* 15	*Varia* 27
40	*Inc.* 43	p. 444
41	*Inc.* 30	—
42	*Scen.* 174	*Fab.* 168
43	*Inc.* 25	p. 563
44	*Scen.* 414	*Fab.* 385
45	*Inc.* 3	*Varia* 2
46	*Inc.* 4	*Varia* 33
47	*Inc.* 27	p. 563
48	*Inc.* 24	p. 434
49	*Inc.* 49	p. 564
50	*Inc.* 41	p. 563
51	*Inc.* 50	p. 564
52	*Inc.* 29	p. 563

UNIDENTIFIED WORKS

FRL	Vahlen[2]	Warmington
53	*Inc.* 11	*Varia* 25
54	*Inc.* 51	p. 563
55	*Inc.* 8	*Varia* 31
56	*Inc.* 14	*Varia* 36
57	*Inc.* 33	p. 331n b
58	*Inc.* 34	p. 563
59	*Inc.* 46	p. 562

INDEX

What follows is an index of proper nouns and derived adjectives as they appear in the fragments of Ennius. References are to pages in volumes (I) and (II). For names and places mentioned in testimonia and source passages, consult the introductory essays and headnotes. The highly dubious *Quotations Derived from Unknown Sources* (II, pp. 349–83) are not included.

INDEX

427